FIVE-MINUTE

BEAUTIFUL

NAILS

FIVE-MINUTE

BEAUTIFUL

NAILS

TANYA BODEN

Conceived and produced by Breslich & Foss, London

Photography by Nigel Bradley
Illustrations by Marilyn Leader
Text written in collaboration with Laura Wilson
Designed by Clare Finlaison
Original design by Lisa Tai

Published by Crown Publishers, Inc., 201 East 50th Street
New York, New York 10022.
A member of the Crown Publishing Group.
Random House, Inc. New York,
Toronto, London, Sydney, Auckland.

CROWN is a trademark of Crown Publishers, Inc.

Manufactured in Hong Kong

Library of Congress Cataloging-in-Publication Data

Boden, Tanya.
Five minute beautiful nails/Tanya Boden.
p.   cm.
Includes index.
1. Nails (Anatomy)—Care and hygiene.   2. Manicuring.
3. Beauty.
Personal.   I. Title.
RL94.B83   1993
646.7'27—dc20   92–34328
CIP

ISBN 0-517-59264-9

10 9 8 7 6 5 4 3 2 1

First Edition

CONTENTS

THE FIVE-MINUTE APPROACH

LOOKING AFTER YOUR HANDS

We all aspire to elegant, perfectly manicured hands, usually with long, polished nails. Unfortunately, long nails are not always practical. Even though the advertisements tell us that we should possess perfect nails that never crack, chip or break, such routine activities as opening drawers and dialing telephones can be devastating to them. Of course, the models in the nail advertisements do nothing more arduous than caressing polish bottles – their nails are not constantly endangered by doing the laundry or washing their hair. Even if you are fortunate enough to possess good, healthy nails, the struggle to maintain a uniform set of ten is a tough one. Although there is no magic formula for beautiful nails, there are a lot of things you can do to help maintain them, and none of them will add more than five minutes to your beauty routine.

Manicuring may seem like a mysterious art, only to be practiced by professionals with vast trays of special equipment. It is actually quite simple, once you understand how nails actually "work". The part of the nail that we can see (the nail plate) is made up of layers of dead protein, attached to the nail bed beneath it (see diagram). These protein layers do contain some oil and moisture, but they need to be kept flexible and supple in order to prevent them from breaking. Nails start growing from the matrix, which is underneath the base of the nail, and sometimes a patch of this live nail can be seen. It is called the lanula, or "half-moon". The cuticle, which protects the base of the nail and seals the matrix off from any bacteria which might otherwise work their way beneath the skin, extends around the base and sides of the nail plate.

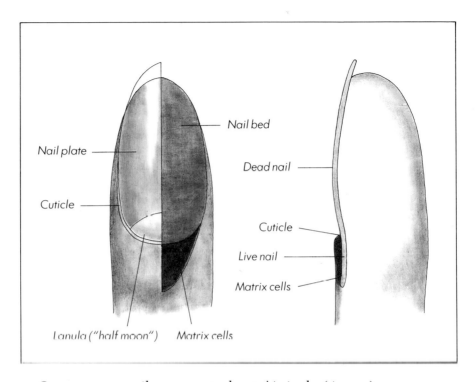

On average, nails grow at about ⅛ inch (4 mm) per month. Of course growth varies from person to person, and, generally speaking, young people's nails grow faster than old people's. Nail growth is stimulated during pregnancy, and in the spring and summer months.

Illness or emotional stress may slow down or even stop nail growth. Signs of ill-health and internal disorders can manifest themselves in nails in the form of splitting, flaking, white specks and ridges or furrows. Cases of anemia, for example, can be diagnosed from a characteristic colorlessness, or an overly curved "spoon" shape to the nails. A well-balanced diet with plenty of vitamins and minerals is just as important for nails as it is for any other part of your body.

PRACTICAL TIPS

- Over frequent applications of polish and the consequent use of polish remover can make your nails brittle or fragile. Most nail polish remover contains acetone, which makes nails very dry. If you can track down a remover which does not contain it, so much the better.

- Detergent is another culprit, so always wear rubber gloves when washing dishes. In fact, it is a good idea to wear them for most household chores, because the chemicals contained in cleaning materials won't do your nails any good, either.

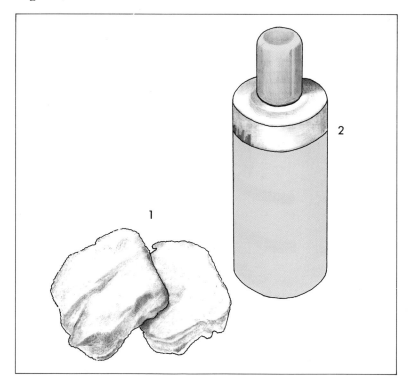

1 *Cotton pads*
2 *Nail polish remover*

- If you work in the garden, make sure you have a pair of gloves for outdoor work. For gardening jobs where gloves are not practical, apply a layer of hand cream, and work some soap under your fingernails before you start. This will save you from having to poke out particles of ingrained soil later.

- If your hands are covered in oil and grease, apply a special heavy-duty hand cleanser designed for this purpose before washing them. This is far better than painfully scrubbing away with a harsh, bristled brush and a bar of soap.

- The best way to apply hand cream is to smooth it on over each finger, as if you were sliding on a ring. For the palm and back of your hand, work the cream into the skin with circular massaging movements of your thumb and fingers. If your nails are very dry and flaky, apply a little moisturizer to them whenever you are using it on your face or body, and keep a pot of hand cream by the sink for use after washing your hands.

- There are several exfoliants available that help to get rid of any dry skin from your hands. If you have a few extra minutes, this is a good way to start your basic manicure. An exfoliant also comes in handy for use on feet and elbows. Remember to moisturize afterwards.

- If your fingers are discolored or stained with nicotine, rub the skin with the cut half of a lemon. Lemon juice contains a useful natural bleaching agent which can also be helpful in removing freckles. If you should find yourself acquiring "age" or "liver" spots on the backs of your hands, you can soak them in lemon juice mixed with oil once a week. This will not remove them entirely, but you will find that it helps to minimize them.

1 *Massage oil*
2 *Hand towel*

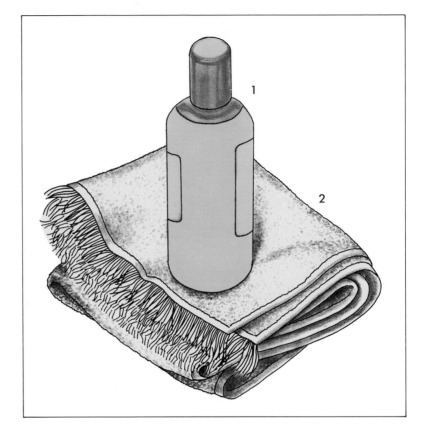

- What color polish will you choose? Slim, elegant fingers look good with any shade. However, if your hands are not your most attractive feature, avoid using bright colors that will draw attention to them; stick to the more natural-looking colors.

- Nails can become stained by the pigment in a dark-colored polish. Usually, the application of a base coat under the color will prevent this pigment from marking your nail. However, should this happen, it is probably best left to go away of its own accord. There are bleaches, but they contain hydrogen peroxide, which has a very drying effect on nails.

- To remove nail polish effectively, moisten a cotton ball with remover, and wrap it around your nail, pressing it firmly for a few seconds to help dissolve the polish before wiping it clean. Use a fresh cotton ball for each nail and, to avoid smearing your fingers with polish, work through your nails methodically, from your thumb to your little finger, finishing one hand before you begin the other. If you are using an acetone remover, massage in a little cuticle oil before applying new polish.

- Finally, remember that however much you manicure and moisturize, the best maintained set of nails will quickly disintegrate if you abuse them. Don't use them as tools. They are not a kit for scraping off labels and prising off lids, so contain your impatience until you find something designed for the job you want to do – it will be worth it in the end!

LOOKING AFTER YOUR FEET

Ever since Cinderella's ugly sisters chopped off their toes to fit the glass slipper, generations of women have endured discomfort in shoes. Fashionable, attractive footwear always seems to have some drawback – toes too pointed, heels too high, not enough support for the foot, or, in the case of mules, the sheer effort of keeping them on one's feet. The majority of problems women have with their feet are caused by ill-fitting shoes, so footwear should be chosen carefully. High heels are fine – but you don't have to wear them everyday. Vary your shoes and, most important, your heel height from day to day. When you are selecting a pair of shoes from your closet, consider what you might be doing during the day. If it's a lot of walking, very high heels are obviously not appropriate, and will make your feet painful and tired. You should never buy a pair of shoes which feel as if they are going to need a lot of 'breaking in'; a good pair of new shoes should be flexible and comfortable.

Practical tips

- It is a good idea to kick your shoes off whenever you get the chance. Wiggle your toes, rotate your ankles and give your feet a shake. Another useful exercise is placing a ball under your foot and moving it around (see pages 72 and 74 for further foot and ankle exercises).

- Relax and literally 'put your feet up' if you have been standing for long periods of time, as this will help to prevent varicose veins. Unfortunately, these tend to run in families – however, anything that restricts the blood flow to the legs or increases the pressure on them should be avoided. Exercise is beneficial, as is a diet containing plenty of fiber.

- It is wonderful to be able to kick your shoes off and walk barefoot, but stick to grass and mud. Don't go barefoot on hard surfaces like asphalt for long distances.

- Your feet, like every other part of your body, need regular moisturizing. Dry cracked skin on the feet can be painful, and a regular application of moisturizer or body lotion will make all the difference. If any area is especially dry, a heavy-duty lanolin-based cream can be obtained at most drugstores. If deep fissures have formed in your heels, you should make an appointment with a chiropodist. In order to prevent these forming, tackle hard skin regularly – but not too roughly – with a pumice stone or a rough skin remover.

- Chilblains on both hands and feet are encouraged by changes of temperature, so don't expose them to the cold and then go straight indoors and cuddle a radiator. Make sure your footwear is dry, and try to keep your feet warm in winter – but don't roast them in front of the fire as this may cause chapped skin.

PRODUCTS AND EQUIPMENT

Artificial Nails: These are very useful as emergency measures when a nail is broken. A full set of artificial nails can look wonderful, but it needs a great deal of maintenance. Acrylic nails are also available, but they are very difficult to apply and should be done by a trained manicurist.

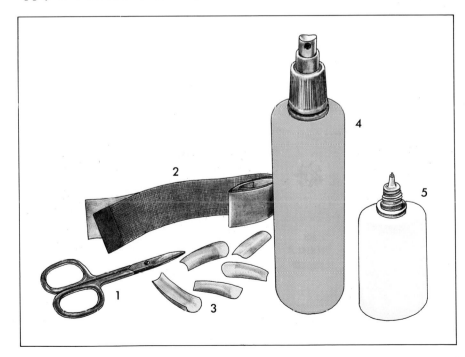

1 *Nail scissors*
2 *Nail wrap*
3 *Artificial nails*
4 *Activator spray*
5 *Glue*

1 *Nail buffer*
2 *Orange stick*
3 *Hoof stick*
4 *Cuticle clippers*
5 *Nail treatment oil*
6 *Nail polish*
7 *Base coat*
8 *Top coat*
9 *Cuticle cream*
10 *Quick-dry spray*
11 *Nail bath*
12 *Emery boards*
13 *Nail scissors*

Base coat: A coat of this applied under your polish is useful because it not only protects your nail, it also helps to prevent the polish from chipping by acting as an added adhesive between it and your nail plate.

Buffer: These come in all shapes and sizes. The most practical is a three-way buffer, which combines three different buffing surfaces, so that you can really build up a shine. There are also the larger, more old-fashioned buffers, which are traditionally used in conjunction with a dab of paste polish. These usually have a polishing cloth which may be taken off and washed, so they tend to be longer lasting.

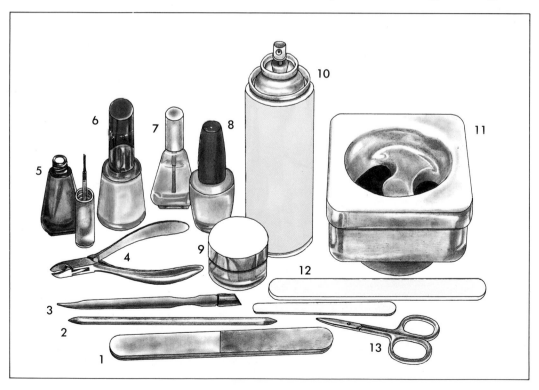

Cuticle cream: This cream, for softening and nourishing cuticles, can be used on both fingernails and toenails. Most brands contain lanolin and petroleum jelly. Cuticle oils, for keeping the skin around the nail soft, are also available.

Cuticle clippers: Similar to nail clippers, these are useful for cutting back cuticles and dealing with hangnails.

Foot bath: Although these can be bought, a plastic bowl of warm soapy water (moisturizing liquid soap) will be just as relaxing.

Glue (resin) and activator spray (fixative): A tube of glue is a handy item in any manicure kit. It is best to get a little set of spray, glue with a detachable nozzle, and a glue remover. The activator spray, or fixative, should be used in conjunction with the glue when fitting fiberglass nail wraps (below). Hold it at least 6 inches (15.5 cms) away from your hand when spraying and be careful not to get any in your eyes.

Hand mask: Essentially the same as a face mask, applied to the hands.

Nail clippers: Both fingernail and toenail clippers are available from most drugstores. For toenails, clippers are preferable to scissors.

Nail file: Emery boards are the best type of nail file, and they come in various weights. Very coarse emery boards and steel files are best avoided. Larger, heavy variants are available for the feet, to smooth down calluses and rough skin. (The alternative, rubbing heels with a pumice stone in the bath, is equally effective.)

Nail Polish (or Enamel): Polish will certainly help to protect your nails, but claims that it will actually nourish them are dubious. It is used to best advantage in conjunction with

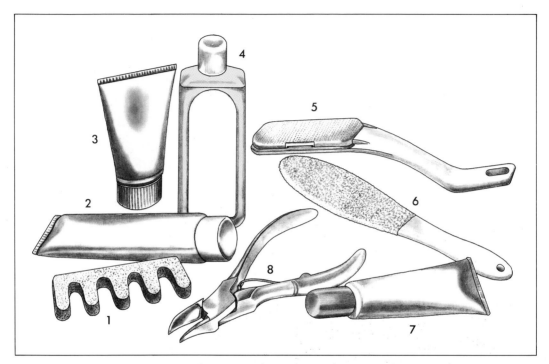

1 Toenail separators
2 Exfoliant
3 Sunscreen
4 Body lotion
5 Metal foot file
6 Plastic foot file
7 Handmask
8 Toenail clippers

a base coat and top coat. You should always allow sufficient time for two coats of polish to dry. Both liquid and aerosol 'quick-dry' products for nails are available, but they are of limited use and tend to make the polish lose its sheen.

Nail Polish Remover: These contain organic solvents such as acetone for dissolving old polish.

Nail Strengthener: Used to help prevent fragile nails from splitting or tearing, strengtheners can be applied to the nail before the base coat.

Nail Wraps: Made from silk, linen or fiberglass, these are a comparatively new addition to the manicure kit, and are available in sheets which can be cut to size.

Orange sticks and hoof sticks: Both are useful for pushing back cuticles, although a hoof stick with a rubber-tipped end is best. If you are using an orange stick, wrap a little cotton around the end to soften it.

Ridge filler: If your nails have a slightly grooved surface, this can be applied under a base coat to smooth them.

Top coat: This should be applied over dry nail polish. Like the base coat, it protects the polish by acting as a sealant.

SOME PROBLEMS

Athlete's Foot: This is a fungal infection, most commonly found between the toes. It can be treated with surgical spirit to dry out the skin, and anti-fungal creams. To prevent it, dry thoroughly between the toes after washing.

Bunions: An enlarging of the toe joint, usually on the big toe. Often very painful, the most common cause of bunions is ill-fitting, tight shoes. Once bunions have developed, there is little that can be done apart from wearing comfortable shoes and padding them to ease the pressure on the bunion. Surgery, a last resort, is often unsatisfactory.

Corns: These develop as a result of pressure or friction, usually on the toes. Medicated corn pads and removers are available at drugstores, but if corns persist, they should be treated by a chiropodist.

Foot odour: If this is a problem, you can help to prevent it by wearing natural fibers next to your skin. After bathing, apply surgical spirit foot spray or talcum powder.

Hangnails: Pieces of skin torn away from, but still attached to, the base or side of a fingernail. These are caused by the cuticle splitting around the nail, often as a result of incorrect cuticle removal. They can usually be taken care of with a cuticle clipper, but if you are concerned about them go to a professional manicurist.

Ingrown Toenails: Incorrect trimming and filing, or an injury to the toe, can cause the edge of the nail to grow into the skin. These can be very painful and should be treated by a doctor.

Leuconychia (white spots): These are either caused by general wear and tear, or by blows to the matrix of the nail. They have also been linked to a zinc deficiency, so try to ensure that you have enough in your diet (seafood is a rich source). They will grow out naturally, with the nail.

Nail Biting: There are a number of ways to kick this habit – try painting them with one of the special foul-tasting solutions from the drugstore, or with neat bitter aloes which is even more unpleasant. If all else fails, you could try applying artificial nails, as even the most hardened nail biter will have difficulty chewing through them.

Paraonychia: Inflammation of the skin surrounding the nail, often caused by a bacterial infection. Wearing rubber gloves for any wet job can go a long way to prevent this, but if it occurs you should see a doctor.

Verruca: A highly contagious viral wart-like infection found on the sole of the foot. It is usually easy to get rid of, either by seeking advice from your doctor or chiropodist, or using home remedies from the drugstore.

Warts: These are often found on the hands, but they can occur on any part of the body. Usually dark in color with a rough, horny surface, many, if left untreated, will eventually disappear of their own accord. If you feel that they are unsightly, see your doctor about having them removed.

1
MANICURES

Cuticle care

What you need
Cuticle cream
Hoof stick or orange
  stick
Bowl of warm soapy
  water
Cuticle clippers
Towel

Cuticles are important because they protect the base of all the vital matrix cells (see page 7). So, although it may seem like a time-saver, resist the temptation to poke your cuticles back with the nearest sharp object, or you may end up with sore, red-rimmed nails. You may also damage the lanula or 'half-moon' at the base of the nail and so affect the new nail growth. To keep your cuticles neat, and help prevent hangnails, push them back gently with the towel when you dry your hands. For manicuring, use either a rubber-ended hoof stick or an orange stick with its tip wrapped in cotton.

Cuticle cream is used to soften the cuticle. A cuticle oil, usually containing almond oil, can also be used, or, if your drugstore does not stock it, try baby oil. Massage it well into your cuticles and the skin surrounding them with the ball of your thumb. This helps to stimulate your circulation, giving your nails an attractive pink glow.

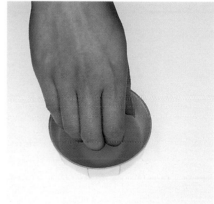

1 *Apply a small amount of cuticle cream to each cuticle with a hoof stick. Massage it in with circular motions of the thumb.*

2 *Soak fingertips in a bowl of warm soapy water for at least one minute. Dry thoroughly afterwards.*

3 *Push back cuticles very gently with a hoof stick.*

4 *Trim any hangnails carefully with cuticle clippers.*

TRIMMING YOUR NAILS

What you need
Nail scissors
Nail file

Although long fingernails look very glamorous, short nails can look fabulous, too, if they are clean and well-kept. There may be times when it is more appropriate to keep your nails trimmed – if, for example, you are a keen gardener or do a lot of cooking – and less healthy nails will certainly look better if they are kept short. Cutting your nails is not the ideal way of shortening them, but if you want to take off a length of nail, it is much quicker than filing.

Choose scissors in preference to clippers, as these can cause cracks.

Always remove polish before cutting your nails. As with filing (see page 26), you can make one single cut straight across the top of your nail if you prefer a squared-off finish to a rounded one. Otherwise, nails should be cut on each side, going from the edge to the center. When you are cutting your nails, concentrate on the length you want, rather than the shape. This can be achieved afterwards, with a file.

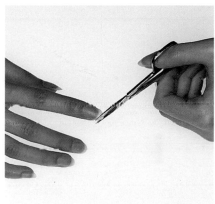

1 *Cut from the side to the middle of the nail, to the desired length.*

2 *Repeat on the other side. Don't worry about the final shape at this point.*

3 *File each side of your nail from the sides to the center, holding the file at an angle of 45° (see page 26).*

4 *Holding the file vertically, file the tip of the nail using a downward motion.*

FILING YOUR NAILS

What you need
Nail file

Generally speaking, it is better to file your nails than to cut them. Steel files may last a long time, but, because they are harsh and inflexible, they can tear or split your nails. Buy a packet of fine emery boards instead.

Before you start, decide which shape will suit your nails best. Square nails, unless they are very long, give your hands a practical look, which may not always be flattering if your fingers are short. Although easier to break, rounded nails tend to look more elegant.

For rounded nails, always file from the edge to the middle, trying to achieve a nice smooth curve. Never file back and forth, as this can cause the nail layers to split, and be careful not to file right down into the corners, as this can cause ingrown nails.

Most importantly, your nails should all be the same length – it is not worth hanging onto that one long nail in the hope that the others will eventually catch up with it.

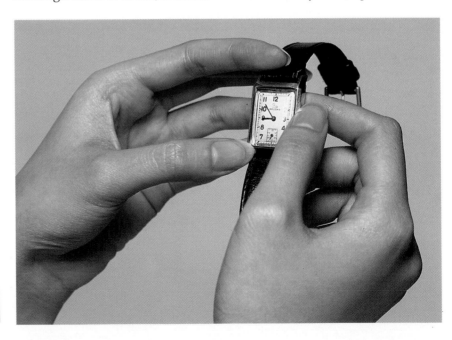

Round 1 *File each side of your nail from the side to the center, holding the emery board at an angle of 45°.*

2 *Holding the file vertically, file the tip of the nail using a downward motion.*

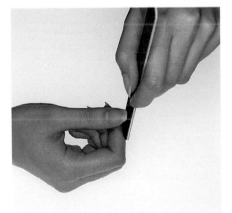

Square 1 *Having removed any old polish, file straight across the top of the nail in one direction only.*

2 *Holding the file vertically, file the tip of the nail using a downward motion.*

INSTANT NAIL REPAIRS

What you need
Glue
Nail file
Nail strengthener

A single tear in a perfect set of nails can be heartbreaking, especially if you have worked hard to get them in good condition. However, if you act quickly, it may be possible to repair the nail with glue. Assess the tear to see if it is worth saving, but don't fiddle with it. Remove any polish from the nail beforehand, since polish that has been stuck down with glue is impossible to get rid of with an ordinary polish remover, and has to be whittled away with a file.

Nail glue is available from most drugstores – it is a useful thing to have in your nail kit at all times. If possible, buy a brand of glue which comes with a nozzle, as it is very easy to overdo it – and very frustrating when your fingers get stuck together. Once the glue is safely on your nail, make sure that it is hardened before you buff. Once you have completed the buffing and applied a couple of coats of nail strengthener, the tear should hardly be visible.

1 *Apply glue sparingly along the line of the break.*

2 *Hold the edges of the nail together while the glue sets.*

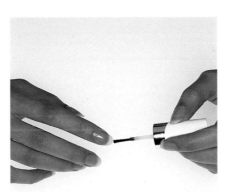

3 *Buff the repaired area, and paint whole nail with strengthener.*

Buff up and clear polish

What you need
Nail buffer
Cuticle oil
Nail polish remover
Cotton ball
Clear polish

Healthy, shining nails are the best finishing touch for a natural looking make-up. Practical and versatile, they will go with every outfit in your closet, from a sweat suit to a cocktail dress.

Buffing won't dry out your nails at all and is an excellent way of stimulating the circulation and smoothing the nail surface. If your nails are in a poor condition, it is far better to treat them to a good buffing than to try and disguise them by slapping on coats of polish.

We have used a liquid polish here, but if you prefer it, paste polish may be used instead. Apply a small amount of the paste to each nail with an orange stick, and buff with firm downward strokes from the base of the nail to the edge, lifting the buffer after each stroke.

Here, we show a three-way buffer, which is much handier than the large, old-fashioned type. You should work through all three sections, from the roughest to the very smoothest.

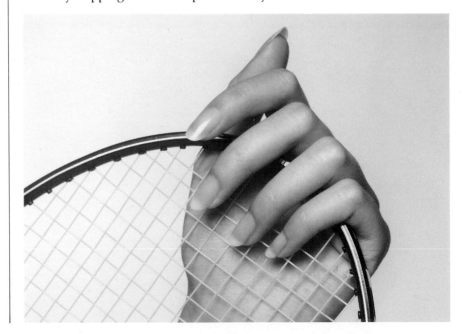

1 *Buff your nails, using all the sections of a three-way buffer.*

2 *Apply oil around cuticle to remove any dust created by buffing. Massage it in with the ball of your thumb.*

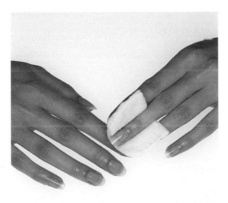

3 *Remove oil with a touch of nail polish remover and wipe dry with cotton ball.*

4 *Apply clear liquid polish. If you are using paste polish, buff your nails after applying.*

PAINTING YOUR NAILS

What you need
Base coat
Colored nail polish

Beautifully colored nails give any outfit a chic, finished look, and this deep red will go equally well with a tailored suit or a cocktail dress.

For a strong color, you should apply two coats of polish, always over a transparent base coat. Apply the first coat sparingly, but don't worry about allowing the polish to dry between coats: the first nail will be dry enough for a re-application by the time you get back to it. Try to leave a hair space between the polish and your cuticles, so that it doesn't spill over onto your fingers.

Paint each nail with three strokes only: the first straight down the middle, followed by one stroke on either side. If the polish smudges, dip an orange stick in some remover and carefully wipe it away.

Ideally, you should allow your nails about half an hour to be completely dry. There's a world of difference between 'touch-dry' and hard, and there are few things more irritating then a smudge on an otherwise perfect set of nails.

1 *Paint your nail with a base coat so the polish is less likely to chip.*

2 *Paint a strip of red down the center of your nail.*

3 *Paint down the sides – a single stroke for each.*

REPAIRING CHIPPED POLISH

What you need
Nail buffer
Nail polish

Nail polish chips for a number of reasons: either the polish has been applied too thickly or without a base coat or top coat, the nail is in a dry and flaky condition, or there is oil or moisture on the nail surface. But the most expertly applied polish will, after a couple of days, become chipped from general wear and tear and need repairing.

It is usually best to try and repair chipped polish, rather than getting out the remover, because you may end up unwittingly removing polish from other nails. However, if the rest of the polish on the chipped nail is flaking away, then it may be best to remove it, and start again.

When you are painting over the chipped area, just "dab" it lightly with the brush. (Always paint your nails in strips from the base to the end of the nail, never from side to side.) If you are in a tearing hurry, you can apply a quick-drying spray or a gentle blast of warm air from your hairdryer, but don't hold it too close to your nails.

1 *Take a close look at the chipped area, to see if it is worth repairing.*

2 *Using a medium weight buffer, smooth over the chipped area.*

3 *Paint over the chipped area with a thin layer of polish.*

4 *Wait until this is 'touch-dry', and then paint over the entire nail.*

French manicure

What you need
Base coat
White nail polish
Pale pink nail polish
Top coat

This chic variation on the natural look has become very popular, and is very useful if you have a number of quick changes to perform and no time for taking off and re-applying colored polish. Until recently, it was necessary to color underneath your nail tip with a white pencil to achieve this look, but now there are complete French manicure kits available, containing a base coat, a white polish to be painted across the nail tips, a natural looking pink polish, and a top coat.

French manicures look especially good if you have a white 'half moon' or lanula showing at the base of your nail, but if you can't see them all, don't try to force your cuticles back as you may damage the living nail underneath.

It is important to wait until the white polish on the nail tips is *thoroughly* dry before applying the pink over it. With a base coat and a top coat, a single application of the pink polish will be sufficient, as it should not be completely opaque.

1 *Apply base coat to protect your nails and help prevent chipping.*

2 *Apply two thin coats of white polish to the nail tips in a single stroke from side to side.*

3 *Once the white polish is completely dry, apply pink polish over entire nail.*

4 *Apply top coat over entire nail, for extra protection.*

NAIL WRAPPING

What you need
Nail buffer
Nail scissors
Nail wrap
Glue
Activator spray

If you are tired of finding your nails breaking just as you have succeeded in growing them to a reasonable length, you could try using nail wraps. "Wrapping" your nails with prepared strips of silk, linen or fiberglass is an excellent method of strengthening them. Like artificial nails, the wraps will "grow" with your real nail, and the gap that is left at the base will need filling periodically with a small strip of fiberglass. This may, in the long run, prove considerably more time-consuming than a regular manicure routine, but the pay-off will be the absence of broken, cracked or torn nails.

Make sure that the wrap is placed in position on your nail before applying any glue to it. The glue will soak through the wrap, making it adhere to your nail. It should be perfectly dry before you begin buffing.

Make sure that you cut the wrap to the exact shape of your nail – if you use the glue carefully, you can trim the end once it is in place.

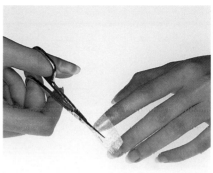

1 *Having buffed your nail with a medium weight buffer, cut a strip of the wrap to the required length with scissors.*

2 *Apply it to your nail and cut to fit the natural shape.*

3 *Attach the wrap to the nail with two coats of glue.*

4 *Spray with activator spray, and then buff, work through all the sections on a three-way buffer, until smooth and shiny.*

REPAIRS WITH WRAPS

What you need
Glue
Activator spray
Nail wrap
Nail buffer

If you find yourself with a split nail and a long wait before you can get to your manicure kit, you may need something stronger than glue to fix the damage. Even quite badly broken nails can be salvaged with the aid of a fiberglass wrap. Glue plus a wrap is preferable to glue on its own, and likely to last far longer. However, it is a fiddly procedure which requires a steady hand and total concentration. Wash your hands and remove any nail polish before you begin.

Apply glue to the broken nail and allow it to dry first, then fix the wrap to the nail. The final buffing should be very thorough, to smooth out any tell-tale ridges. This is important, because polish applied on an uneven surface chips very easily. One disadvantage of wrapping is that a close look at the finished nail reveals a fine mesh, which clear polish does not hide. However, the palest of opaque polishes will easily obscure it if you apply two coats.

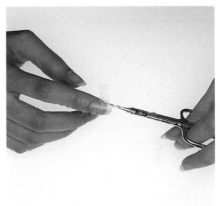

1 *Apply glue to break (see page 28), and buff lightly.*

2 *Once the glue has dried, cut a thin strip of nail wrap and apply to break.*

3 *Apply glue, and spray with activator spray, holding it at least 6" (15.5cms) away from your hand.*

4 *Buff nail with three-way buffer, first using the rough side, and then the lighter side, until the nail is smooth and shiny.*

ARTIFICIAL NAILS

What you need
Artificial nail(s)
Glue
Activator spray
Nail buffer
Nail polish

Artificial nails are very useful if you have broken a single nail and don't want to have to file down the other nine to match it, and a lot of fun if you want a set of long scarlet temptress's talons to carry off a party outfit. Also, if you are a compulsive nail biter it may be that the simplest way to remove temptation is to cover your nails over with false ones. Protected, they will have a chance to grow and, perhaps, when the plastic comes off, pride will prevent you from ever chomping on them again.

Like many cosmetic innovations, artificial nails came from Hollywood, where, in the 1930s, crude plastic replica nails adorned the stars' fingers. Now, they are far more sophisticated, and, if applied carefully and polished, can look just like the real thing.

False nails "grow" with the real nail, leaving a gap at the base after about two weeks, which will need filling. This can be tricky and is usually best left to a manicurist.

1 *After buffing your nail, select a suitably sized artificial nail, apply glue to the underside, and attach to natural nail.*

2 *Blend the artificial nail into your own with a light weight file until the join disappears. File into the desired shape.*

3 *Apply glue over the entire surface and spray with activator spray.*

4 *Buff with a three-way buffer and apply polish.*

DECORATED NAILS

With a set of false nails and a steady hand, the possibilities for decoration are endless – black and white motifs, stars and stripes, Christmas trees, and practically any other festive or personalized variation can be achieved with some perseverence.

Good quality polish is vital; it must be easy to apply, have an even consistency and color, and be very long lasting. Whether or not you intend to decorate your nails with patterns, it is worth shopping around for reliable polish – as with many other cosmetic products, price is usually a good indication of quality.

If you find painting your nails difficult, these effects will take some practice. Try it on one hand only at first.

Painting a stripe straight onto a nail is very difficult, and it is far easier to paint something else and then apply it to the nail afterwards. Here, we have used a metallic strip, and finished with a clear top coat.

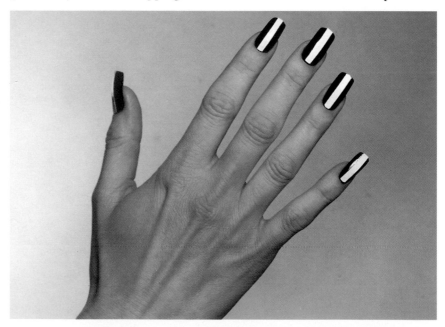

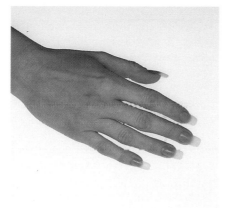

1 *Apply false nail (see page 42), filing it into the desired shape.*

2 *Apply black nail polish with brush (see page 32).*

3 *Paint metallic strip with white polish. Single strokes will give the best finish. Leave until completely dry.*

4 *Attach white strip to nail with glue before applying a clear top coat.*

SUMMER HANDS

What you need
Almond oil
Nail polish remover
Moisturizer
Base coat
Nail polish

As soon as the weather hots up, we apply sunscreen religiously to our faces and bodies – but the backs of our hands, the most exposed areas of all, tend to go unprotected. It is true that hands rarely get sunburnt in the way that shoulders and legs do, but the back of the hand is one of the places where skin cancer may develop, particularly if you live in a very hot climate.

Hands also age faster than any other part of the body, and there is little you can do about it. As well as causing premature ageing, too much sun can make liver spots appear on the backs of hands. These can be minimized by applying lemon juice (see page 9).

It is also thought that the sun may weaken and damage the nails themselves, so if you are not wearing polish to go to the beach, it is a good idea to put some sunscreen on them at the same time as you do your hands. Soaking your fingertips in almond oil will help to keep the cuticles soft and the nails flexible.

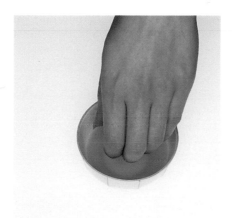

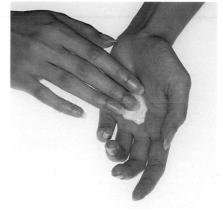

1 *Soak your nails in almond oil, and before painting remove all excess oil.*

2 *Massage hands thoroughly using a moisturizer, preferably with added sunscreen. Make sure that it is rubbed in well.*

3 *Apply base coat to protect your nails and help prevent polish chipping.*

4 *Apply colored polish to suit your mood or the occasion.*

Winter hands

What you need
Exfoliant
Hand mask (or face
  mask)
Moisturizer

In winter, hands can get very dry, rough and sore. Washing them will make them rougher still, so do it gently, and try to avoid scrubbing at your nails with a hard brush. Aggressive scrubbing will certainly weaken your nails, and it may force the nail plate up and away from the nail bed (see diagram on page 7).

To protect your hands from chapping, take extra care to dry them thoroughly after washing. It will also help the skin to stay supple and well-nourished if you keep a heavy-duty moisturizer by the sink for an application after every wash.

Try to avoid exposing your hands to harsh, biting winds, because this can leave them very sore indeed. Invest in several pairs of winter gloves that match your clothes.

Poor circulation can lead to unattractive, mottled, pink and purple fingers, and blue nails. A vigorous massage will help improve the flow of blood to the hands generally and to the nail bed (see page 64), restoring a healthy glow.

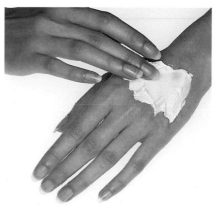

1 *Apply a small amount of exfoliant with circular motions of your finger. Then wash your hands and dry thoroughly.*

2 *Apply a thick layer of hand mask (see page 15).*

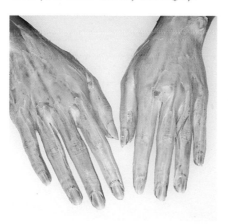

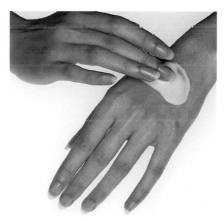

3 *Keep the hand mask on for as long as possible.*

4 *Apply a rich moisturizer. Work into the skin with a circular motion, as before.*

Quick manicure

What you need
Cotton ball
Nail polish remover
Shallow bowl
Orange stick
Base coat

If your nail polish needs changing, or you've had a hard day and want to pamper yourself, why not give your hands a treat by incorporating this simple manicure into your beauty routine?

Try to choose a non-acetone polish remover, and apply it with a cotton ball or pad. Hold the cotton ball down on your nail for a few seconds to dissolve the polish, then rub it off with a stroking movement from the base of your nail to the tip. Use a fresh cotton ball for each nail.

If you don't own a special manicurist's bath, it doesn't matter: a soup bowl will do just as well. Fill it with warm soapy water.

Wrap some cotton around the end of your orange stick before attending to your cuticles – never poke at them with anything sharp.

One layer of base coat should be enough to protect your nails, provided you aren't planning to go coal mining or mountaineering! For the evening, you can apply colored polish straight over it.

1 *Remove any old nail polish using a cotton ball or pad.*

2 *Soak your nails. Allow at least one minute for each hand.*

3 *Push back your cuticles gently with an orange stick. Do not force them.*

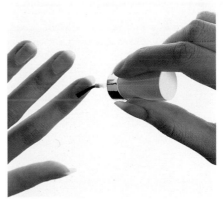

4 *Paint your nails with a base coat before applying a colored polish.*

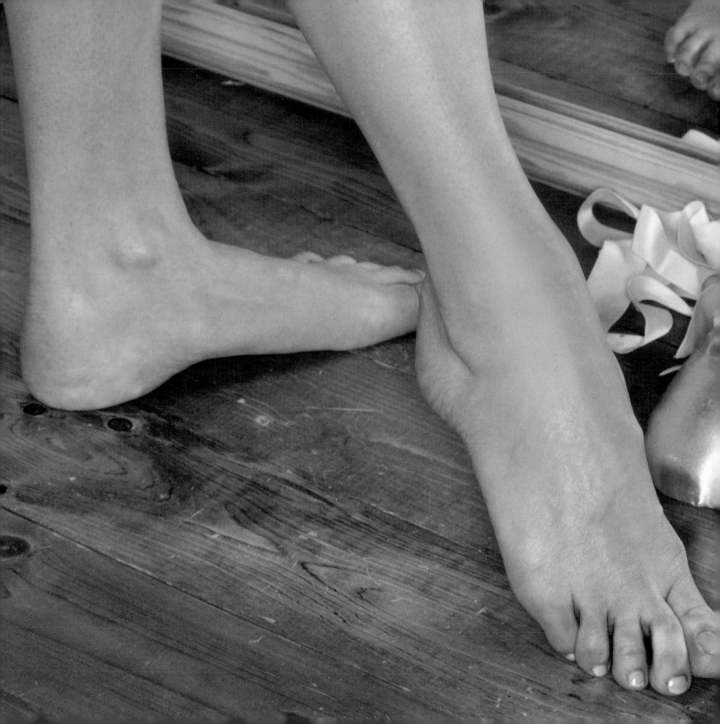

2
PEDICURES

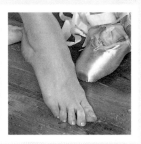

Skin softener

What you need
Bowl of warm soapy
  water
Metal file or pumice
  stone
Medium weight
  (plastic) file
Body lotion

Feet take a lot of punishment from high heels, tight shoes, synthetic fabrics and sidewalk pounding, so it is hardly surprising that they develop areas of rough skin and calluses. Hard skin needs to be tackled regularly with a special file or pumice stone in order to keep it down. If you have a big build-up of hard skin, you should see a chiropodist rather than trying to remove it yourself.

If your feet are aching, try giving them a soothing soak in warm water with added bath salts. When you are drying your feet, take the opportunity to inspect them for any problems such as corns or athlete's foot. Be especially careful about drying thoroughly between your toes, as bacteria can breed far more easily in this area if it is moist.

When you rub in a skin softening cream, massage all the areas of your feet as thoroughly as possible: your sole, heel, and instep, as well as the top of your foot and your ankle (see page 70).

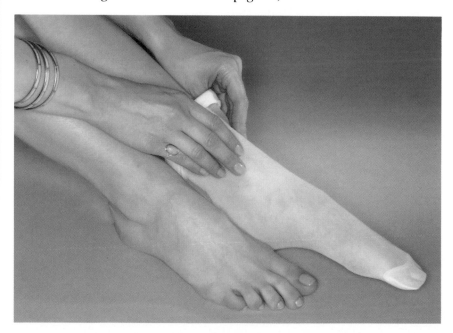

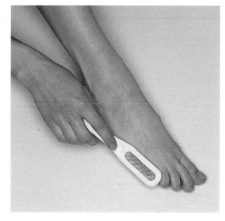

1 *Soak your feet in a bowl of warm soapy water. Dry them thoroughly.*

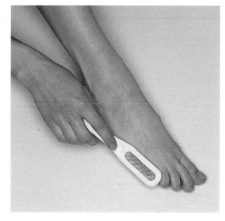

2 *Rub off any dead skin around your heels with a hard skin remover like this metal one, or a pumice stone.*

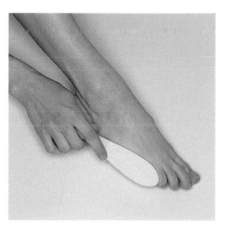

3 *Smooth the area off with a medium weight file, like the plastic one here.*

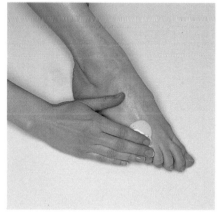

4 *Rub hand cream or body lotion into your feet, especially around the heels.*

TRIMMING TOENAILS

What you need
Toenail clippers
Nail file

Although toenails tend to grow considerably more slowly than fingernails, they are not subjected to the same kinds of wear and tear, so they do need to be trimmed regularly. Over-long toenails, as well as being a menace to tights and stockings, can make shoes very uncomfortable; and constant jabbing against the inside of a shoe can, in time, lead to a bruised and sore toenail.

Be careful not to cut or file your nails right back into the corners, as this can cause ingrowing toenails (see page 18). As they can become quite hard and horny, toenails should be cut with clippers designed for the purpose, not with nail scissors or fingernail clippers. A pair of scissors that isn't up to the job will tear and splinter the nails, so it is worth investing in some decent clippers.

A medium weight nail file is shown here, but if your toenails are really tough, you may need to use something stronger.

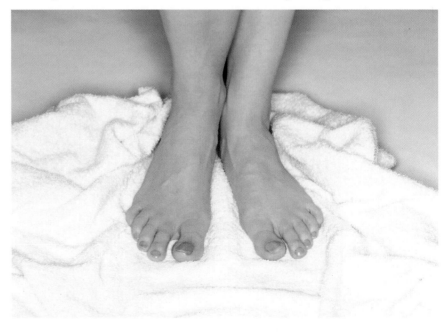

1 *Always use proper toenail clippers, like the ones shown.*

2 *Cut toenails straight across with clippers in a single motion, taking care not to make them too short.*

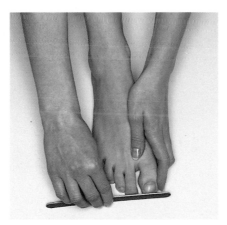

3 *File nails straight across with a medium-weight file.*

QUICK PEDICURE

What you need
Nail file
Toenail clippers
Cuticle cream
Hoof stick or orange
   stick
Exfoliant
Body lotion

Feet tend to be neglected in favor of hands, simply because we don't see our unshod feet as often. Over winter, encased in thick tights and stout shoes for most of the time, our feet often receive no attention at all. However, tired, sore feet should never be ignored, because they can be the harbinger of a whole series of health problems.

   If you want to give your feet a much deserved pick-me-up, this pedicure is an ideal way to do it. The best time is after a bath, when your feet will have had a good soak. The cuticles on your toenails serve the same purpose as those on your hands, and should be treated with equal respect. Use a rubber tipped hoof stick or an orange stick wrapped in cotton to push cuticles back. You can also push gently with the towel, when drying your feet. When you rub in the hand cream, avoid the areas directly between your toes; these should be kept as dry as possible so as not to encourage fungal infections.

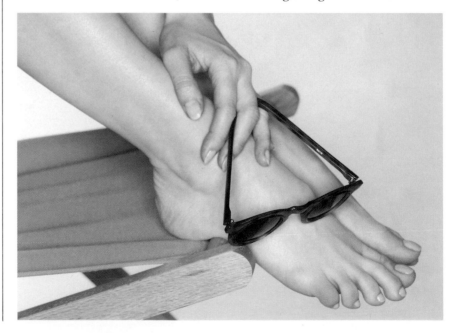

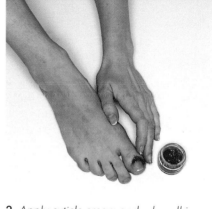

1 Clip your toenails straight across, and file smooth with an emery board (see page 56).

2 Apply cuticle cream and rub well in with the balls of your thumbs.

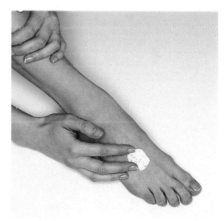

3 Push back your cuticles with a hoof stick or cotton wrapped orange stick.

4 Apply exfoliant with circular motions of your fingers. Rinse your feet and dry thoroughly. Rub in body lotion.

Painting toenails

What you need
Separator or cotton
 balls
Base coat
Nail polish
Top coat

Painted toenails take a notoriously long time to dry. For a really professional effect, paint your nails when you know you won't need to wear shoes for a couple of hours. If you only leave them for ten minutes before stuffing them into shoes, the polish will smudge.

Your toenail polish needs to match your shoes, outfit, and finger nails – scarlet toenails, however beautifully painted, will look unbalanced if they are matched with frosted pink fingernails (although natural or pale toenails will coordinate with any color fingernail). If you have slender, straight toes, then a bright color will enhance them. However, if they are not your best feature, try a clear or pale colored polish.

Before you start, make sure that any old polish has been thoroughly removed. If it is difficult to remove the varnish around the cuticle with an ordinary cotton ball, tease out a portion of the cotton ball and wrap it around an orange stick.

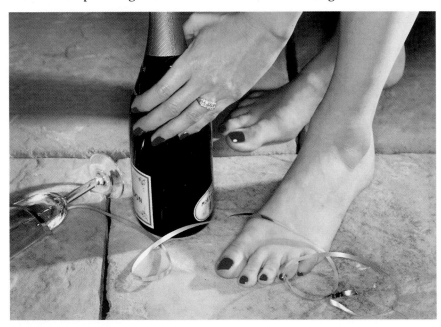

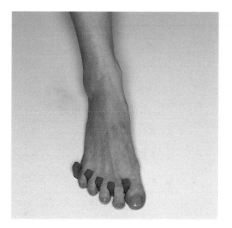

1 *Separate your toes with a foam rubber separator. If you do not have one, cotton balls will do.*

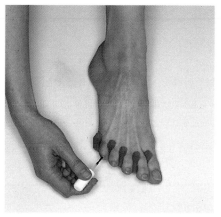

2 *Apply base coat as a first layer, and leave to dry.*

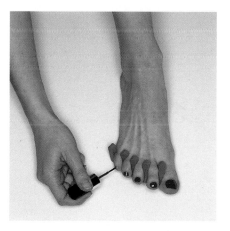

3 *Apply two coats of colored polish and leave to dry.*

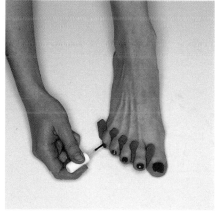

4 *Apply top coat. Leave to dry thoroughly before putting on shoes.*

3
MASSAGES AND
EXERCISES

FINGER MASSAGE

What you need
Massage oil

Massage can help to soothe away aches and pains, relieve tension and make you feel relaxed. Of course, it is nicer when there is someone else to massage you, but hands and fingers, unlike shoulders and backs, can be reached more easily by their owners.

Establish a smooth rhythm, and go lightly over any areas where the bones are near the surface of the skin, such as the backs of the hands. The metacarpals, which are the bones of your hand, are quite near the surface, so take care not to dig into them too hard with your thumb.

There are plenty of rich massage oils available, but if you don't have any, olive oil from the kitchen will do. Apply it liberally – you can always wipe off the excess afterwards with a paper towel.

Don't give yourself a hand or finger massage if you suffer from arthritis, rheumatism or swollen and painful fingers, as you will probably do more harm than good.

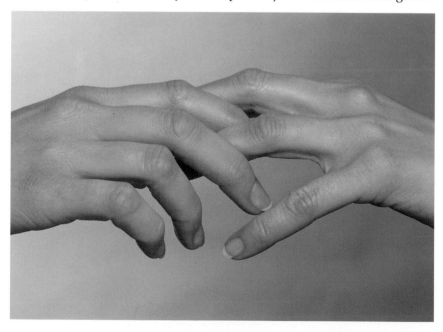

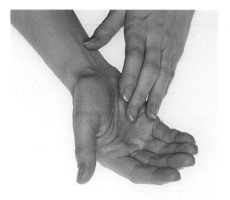

1 *Pour a small amount of massage oil into your palm.*

2 *Massage between metacarpals with the thumb of your other hand, using a circular motion.*

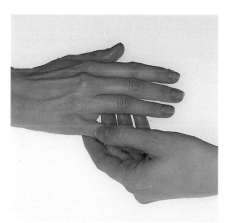

3 *Massage, using the same circular motion of the thumb, down the length of each finger.*

4 *'Scissor' your fingers with the first and second fingers of the other hand, using a firm backwards pulling motion.*

PALM AND ARM MASSAGE

What you need
Massage oil

Regular massaging helps to improve your skin tone and texture by increasing the circulation of the blood directly beneath the skin. When applying pressure on the hand and arm, as in steps 3 and 4 shown here, always move upwards, towards your heart.

There are three different massage strokes. *Effleurage* is a soothing, stroking movement with the fingertips, or, on larger areas, the palm of the hand. *Pettrissage* is a deeper movement for relieving tension. As when kneading bread dough, the tissues are pressed and then relaxed. *Friction* is a circular movement of the thumbs which stimulates the circulation and releases 'knotted' muscles.

If you are concerned about the state of the skin on your hands, try to put in a few minutes of massage every time after drying them, especially in the winter. You will be helping to prevent dryness and chilblains as well as improving your skin tone.

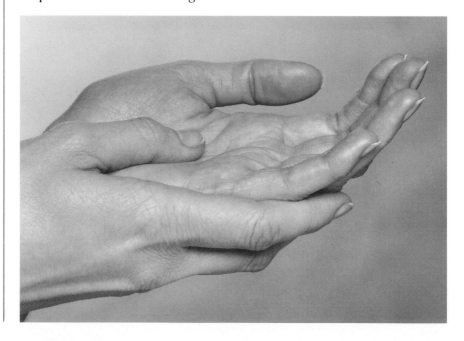

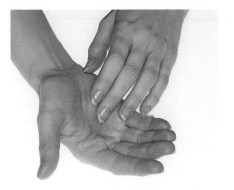

1 *Pour a small amount of massage oil into your palm.*

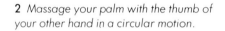

2 *Massage your palm with the thumb of your other hand in a circular motion.*

3 *Stroke your arm towards the elbow, using firm upward movements, lifting your hand away each time.*

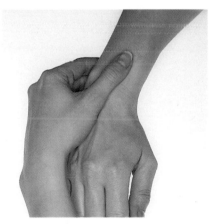

4 *Rub your forearm from wrist to elbow with firm circular movements of the thumb.*

EXERCISES FOR HANDS

What you need
Comfortable chair

If you find yourself with a spare moment, a few simple hand exercises will improve flexibility and circulation. Manipulating joints loosens them up and increases their suppleness.

Hand exercises do not require any special equipment, and they don't work up a sweat, so you can do them anywhere. Here are a couple to add to your exercise routine: rest the tips of your fingers lightly on a firm surface, such as a table, and drum with your fingers, quite quickly, as if you are impatient. Then, removing your hands from the table, clench both your fists tightly, and then open up your hands, stretching out your fingers to their fullest extent. Repeat this ten times.

A good way to start and finish your hand exercises is to stand with your arms hanging loosely by your sides, allowing your hands and wrists to relax and go completely limp. Then give them a good shake until they are tingling.

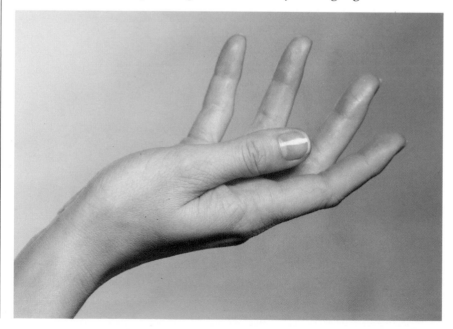

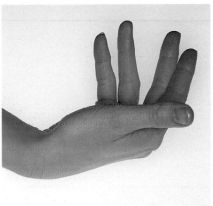

1 *Rotate each finger three times in each direction, manipulating it between the thumb and first finger of your other hand.*

2 *Rotate your wrists gently, first in one direction and then the other.*

3 *Bend wrist backwards by pressing the heel of your other hand against the palm.*

4 *Bend wrist downwards by pressing the palm of your other hand against the back of the hand.*

FOOT AND LOWER LEG MASSAGE

What you need
Massage oil

A massage can work wonders on tired, aching feet, and it is an excellent way to relieve stress. Here's one that you can do yourself. Give your feet a quick wash, dry them thoroughly, and make sure you are sitting in a comfortable position – there's no sense in massaging your feet and straining your back at the same time.

Although a massage can give you a great feeling of well-being, it is not a substitute for exercise, and it cannot reduce fatty deposits in the body. While you are massaging, take a look at your ankles. If they are puffy, it may be due to water retention or bad circulation. There are several things you can do to help this – don't sit with your legs crossed or tucked in underneath your body, as this will cut off the circulation. If you have spent much of the day standing up or pounding the sidewalk, put your feet and ankles in a bowl of hot water for three minutes, followed immediately by cold water.

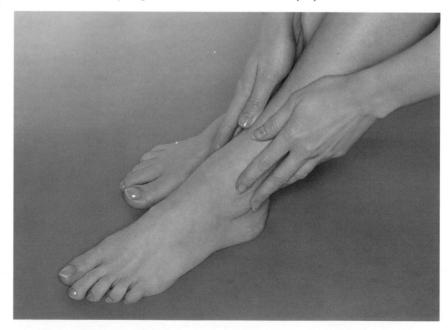

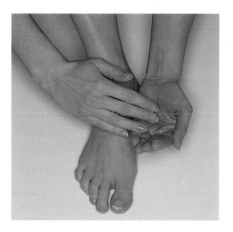

1 *Apply a small amount of oil to palm and spread over both hands.*

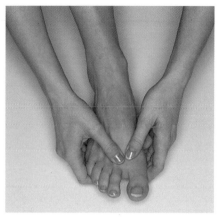

2 *Massage between the metatarsals with both thumbs, using a circular motion.*

3 *Massage the soles of the feet with both hands, using circular movements.*

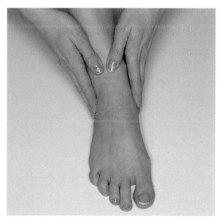

4 *Starting from your ankle, make circular movements with your thumbs, going up towards your knees.*

ANKLE EXERCISES

What you need
Cushion

Ankles vary considerably, and, although exercise cannot turn a thick ankle into a thin one, it is possible to trim off at least some of the fat. Besides looking great, a pair of strong, firm ankles will help to keep your feet in good condition.

Rotating the ankle can be done whenever you're sitting or standing for long periods of time. Anything that relieves the pressure on your ankles is helpful, which is why it is a good idea to finish your exercises by lying down with your feet a little higher than your head. Another exercise which may be helpful is to stand on tiptoe on the edge of a thick book placed on the floor. Keeping your toes in position on the book, and holding onto a chair to prevent you from toppling over, lower your heels to the floor and bring them up again slowly.

Remember that high heels do not necessarily flatter your ankles – heels, especially with an ankle-strap, can have a disastrous effect on thick ankles and calves.

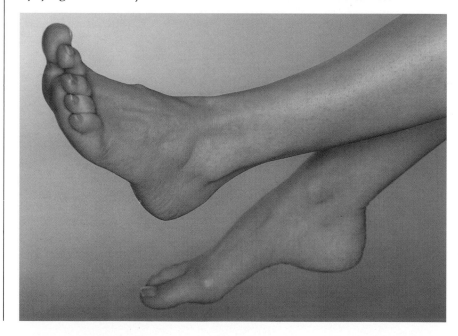

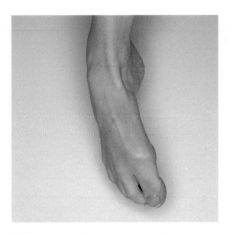

1 *Rotate each ankle ten times in each direction.*

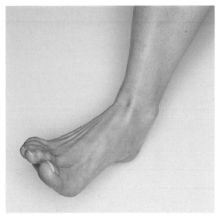

2 *Flex the foot up and back, hold it there for a count of ten, and then relax. Repeat this ten times.*

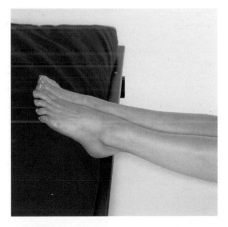

3 *When you have finished exercising, lie flat on the floor with your feet raised.*

LEG EXERCISES

What you need
Hard chair
Object such as
    wastepaper basket

The first of these exercises may be done anywhere there is a chair and a wastepaper basket. If you are using a woven wastepaper basket, like this one, be careful not to snag your stockings on it. Exercises 2 and 3 require a bit more room. Make sure that you have a comfortable floor or blanket to lie on before you start.

If you have goose-pimply legs and lifeless-looking, grey skin, rub your legs vigorously with body lotion every day before you begin your exercises. A massage with a body glove or loofah while you are in the bath or shower will help to prevent this by stimulating the circulation.

Make the most of your legs: everyone has a skirt length which they feel suits them best – mid-calf length skirts are flattering to most legs, but be careful that the hemline does not cut across the widest part of your calves. Similarly, heavy legs do not look their best in pale-colored stockings.

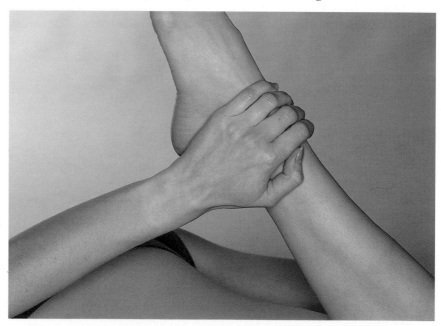

1 Sitting on a chair, hold the basket between your ankles. Lift and hold for a count of twenty. Repeat ten times.

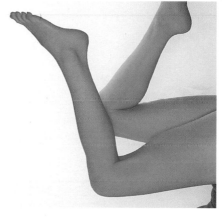

2 Lie on your back, and lift your legs in the air. Supporting your hips, make bicycling movements with your legs.

3 Lie on your stomach and pull your ankle towards your bottom. Count to ten. Repeat twenty times and then change legs.

INDEX

AIRCRAFT CARRIERS

AIRCRAFT CARRIERS

ANTONY PRESTON

BISON GROUP

First published in 1979 by
Bison Books Ltd
Kimbolton House
117A Fulham Road
London SW3 6RL
England

ISBN 0 86124 197 5

Printed in Hong Kong

Reprinted 1991

CONTENTS

1 EARLY STEPS

The aircraft carrier is an anomaly. At once the most vulnerable of warships, she is also the most powerful. Her rise to this position of pre-eminence has been meteoric. As late as 1940 she was regarded by many naval men as ancillary to the battleship, yet only five years later she had relegated the battleship to obsolescence. Thirty years after that, the carrier's own future is under discussion, and many feel that she is a doomed dinosaur.

It is often claimed that the battleship became too expensive, but even during World War II the latest carriers cost as much to build and needed more men to man them. Today the cost of the *Carl Vinson* and *Nimitz* averages out at about $2,000 million *each* and they need over 6000 men apiece. A visitor from another planet might wonder at the human race's talent for self-punishment.

The answer to these riddles is complex, and it lies in the simple fact that the aircraft

carrier, whether in its crudest form or its most advanced form, is a hybrid creation which enables Man to conquer (if he ever does so on anything but a temporary basis) both sea and air simultaneously. The sea forms two-thirds of the Earth's surface, and when Man learned to control the use of that sea, great power passed into the hands of those who achieved the greatest measure of control. Similarly, the conquest of the air promised power to anyone who could exert the most influence. But the sea proved to be intractable, for its distances were too much for the first aircraft to cross. There were other problems too, and even today's hypersonic, long-range aircraft find peculiar problems when operating at any distance from land. The air may be indivisible, but the air over the world's oceans has proved baffling to many land-based air forces, and it will continue to do so.

Below: The *Pennsylvania's* crew prepares the platform for Ely's take-off.

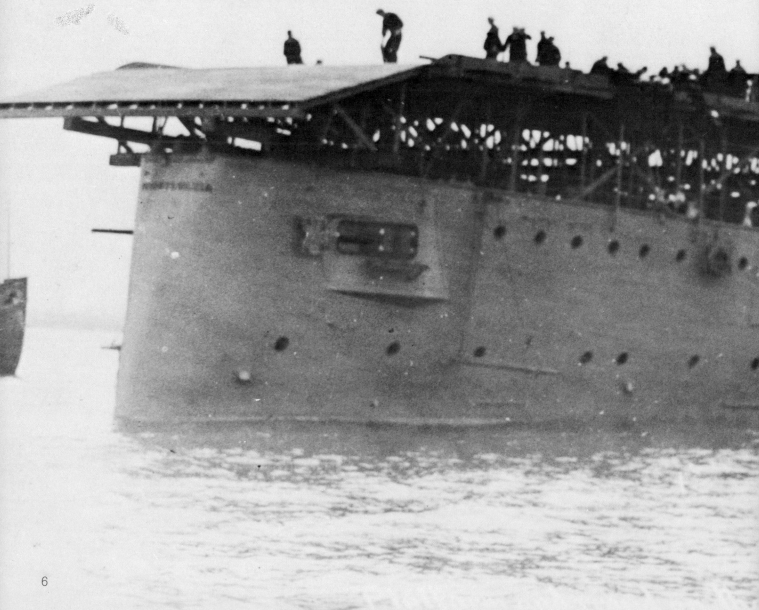

Above: Eugene B Ely readies
his Curtiss Pusher aircraft for
the take-off from the cruiser
Pennsylvania on 18 January
1911.

One of the most remarkable facts about the very first aircraft carriers is not how long they took to be introduced, but how quickly their potential was realized. Even in the last years of the previous century some balloonists talked of using 'captive' balloons from ships. From the moment the Wright brothers made their first flights, therefore, the question of how to use powered aircraft from ships was bound to be pursued. Certainly in 1909, when Clement Ader published his *L'Aviation Militaire*, he talked of the indispensable need for a ship to operate aircraft in terms which make it clear that considerable thought had gone into his book.

Ader's foresight is astonishing, for he predicted not only the take-off and landing of aircraft, but also the need for a wide, flat deck, deck-lifts, island superstructures, hangars, and high speed. The crude aircraft of the day could barely have taken off from a ship let alone land on one, and if they were going to attempt to take off they would definitely want the ship to be either at anchor or moving very slowly, so as not to cause too many wind-eddies.

As with so many prophets, Ader was without honour in his country, and France was to turn her back on shipboard aviation for another ten years. This left the United States and Great Britain to make the running, the Americans because of the great interest in aviation and the British because they had the world's leading navy and needed to keep up-to-date with developments.

The naval aircraft requirement stemmed from one basic need which had been valid since Nelson's day: reconnaissance. There is a practical limit to visibility with the naked eye, and even a lookout at the tallest mast-head, using the most powerful binoculars or telescope could not see more than 40 miles in perfect conditions. To provide the vital information about enemy movements 'scouting' cruisers had to be stationed in patrol lines, near enough to remain in visual contact with one another to be able to pass signals. The invention of radio had helped to reduce the dependence on visual signalling, but there was still the problem that an individual ship could not hope to find anything outside her limit of visibility.

In 1908 it had been proposed to launch an aircraft from one of the US Navy's battleships, but nothing happened for two years as the US Navy did not own any aircraft. The trigger was to be an announcement that a Hamburg-Amerika liner would fly a mail-carrying plane off a platform on her foredeck to speed up mail delivery to New York. Already the first hint of war was in the air, and the immediate suspicion was that the German military authorities were using the mail service as a 'cover' for testing a new technique for attacking the United States. Captain Washington I Chambers, Assistant to the Secretary of the Navy's Aide for Materiel, and recently charged with the responsibility of keeping in touch with aviation matters, profited by the announcement and got immediate permission to fly an aircraft from a warship. On 9 November 1910 the new light cruiser *Birmingham* was earmarked for installation of a platform over her bows.

Chambers had more trouble finding a pilot than a ship, but after trying several people including Wilbur Wright, he met an exhibition pilot working with another great aviation pioneer, Glenn Curtiss. His name was Eugene B Ely and he was delighted to do the

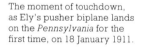

The moment of touchdown, as Ely's pusher biplane lands on the *Pennsylvania* for the first time, on 18 January 1911.

job for the Navy. To add to the air of barn-storming which hung over the scheme, the newspaper *The World* now decided to back the attempt of another Curtiss pilot, J A D McCurdy, to fly from the Hamburg-Amerika liner, *Pennsylvania*, in order to beat the US Navy. McCurdy made his attempt on 12 November, but just as he started his engine, the propeller hit an oil-can and shattered the blade.

Spurred on by the competition, Norfolk Navy Yard spent the next day, a Sunday, finishing off the platform over the forecastle of the *Birmingham*. It was an 83-foot long, 24-foot wide wooden runway which sloped gently down from the cruiser's bridge to her forecastle. Early on 14 November Ely Curtiss's pusher biplane was hoisted aboard; it had been modified with inflated air-bags in case he failed to gain height and had to hit the water.

The *Birmingham* duly steamed out of Hampton Roads into Chesapeake Bay, while four destroyers took up station along the route. In the middle of the afternoon the weather finally cleared enough to allow the trial to begin, and as the cruiser ploughed steadily on at 10 knots Ely raced his 50 horsepower engine and started to roll down the ramp. To the horror of the onlookers the biplane kept going down after it left the ramp, and the wheels, floats and tips of the propeller blades hit the water. But despite some damage to the propeller, it kept turning and the aircraft began to climb. It climbed clear of the ship and vanished into the drizzle. The world's first flight from a ship was a success.

As a matter of interest, Ely was soon lost in the poor visibility, but he landed safely about 2.5 miles from the ship. The effect on the Navy was instantaneous. Chambers proposed that all cruisers should be fitted with similar platforms, and ideas flooded in for launching platforms on the gun-turrets of battleships, and other novel concepts. Fortunately the enthusiasm did not get out of hand, and the main result of the *Birmingham* flight was that in December the US Navy's first pupil pilot, Lieutenant Theodore G Ellyson was chosen to be trained by Glenn Curtiss.

The next step was, however, very ambitious. Chambers got permission for Eugene Ely to *land* on the big cruiser *Pennsylvania*. This was a much harder operation, and the risks were considerable to the ship as well. A platform nearly 120 feet long and 31.5 feet wide was erected over the cruiser's stern, sloping from the mainmast back to a steep overhang right aft. The intention was for Ely to touch down on this deck while the ship was under way, so that the speed of the wind over the deck would give him better control. As his plane had no brakes, a crude 'arresting' gear of 22 wires weighted with sandbags was provided.

On the day, 18 January 1911, the weather in San Francisco Bay was poor. To make matters worse the *Pennsylvania*'s captain felt that his ship had too little room to manoeuvre, and so the ship remained at anchor with the wind behind her. This was the worst possible combination for any pilot, then or now, but perhaps wearing the invincible armour of ignorance, Ely flew out to the ship, making a low approach to her stern. He pulled the plane up just short of the sloping tail of the platform and then cut the engine; his momentum and the tail wind took him right over the

No sooner was he down than Ely had to take off again, to return to Selfridge Field. This was his second take-off from a ship, the first having taken place from the USS *Birmingham* two months earlier.

first 11 cross wires before the hooks on his undercarriage engaged, bringing him to a stop in 30 feet.

Eugene Ely's feat marked the first quickening of naval aviation, but at the same time we can see now that the high hopes it engendered were premature. For one thing, Ely was a well-trained exhibition pilot, a 'stuntman' who was prepared to gamble his life in what was certainly a highly dangerous landing; it would be a long time before the US Navy could hope to have sufficient pilots and aircraft to be sure of repeating his performance every time. For another the aircraft itself was still at a crude stage of development, with no means of communicating with the ground or of conveying anything more lethal than a hand grenade. This helps to explain why the next step was away from the concept of landplanes capable of landing on decks, towards development of the seaplane, floatplane or hydroaeroplane. This was either a specially designed aircraft with floats underneath the wings or a landplane fitted with gasbags around its wheels to permit it to float on water. Having been launched from a ramp as before, the floatplane would land on the water close to its parent ship and then be hoisted back on board by crane. This was done in February 1911 by Glenn Curtiss in San Diego harbour, and the ship was again the *Pennsylvania*.

A month later Congress voted $25,000 to the Navy to allow the aviation experiments to continue. As Captain Chambers pointed out, a series of giant strides had been taken inside a year. It had been proved that photographs could be taken from aircraft, that they could stay aloft for several hours, and that floatplanes could be recovered in a moderately calm sea. With the encouragement of Congress it was possible to capitalize on these achievements, and soon a second naval officer, Lieutenant John Rodgers, was sent to the Wright brothers for training. Two Curtiss A-1 aircraft and one Wright machine were bought, and the first took to the air in July 1911.

There were setbacks too. Towards the end of 1911 Eugene Ely was killed in an accident, only a few months after his triumph. Ironically he received nothing from the US Navy for his services apart from a letter of thanks, and it was left to a private fund to award him $500 for his two flights. Twenty-five years later, however, he was awarded the Distinguished Flying Cross posthumously in belated recognition of his contribution to naval aviation.

By April 1914, when the United States became embroiled in yet another dispute with Mexico, the US Navy had 12 hydro-aeroplanes, and it is measure of the faith shown in the new air arm that six of them were sent to Vera Cruz to provide reconnaissance. They were carried on board the battleship *Mississippi*, and they provided valuable scouting for the landing parties. When one returned with a bullet hole in his tailplane the incident was reported in the press as the 'first aerial combat', although this was stretching it a bit too far.

Meanwhile the Royal Navy was showing as much zeal in developing naval aviation. The Wright brothers had been turned down by the Admiralty in 1907 when they had tried to sell a machine in England, but only two years later the verdict that the aircraft was 'of no practical use to the Naval Service' was partly rescinded. Captain Reginald Bacon, one of the Navy's most talented technical officers, had already been sent to Reims in 1908 to report on an international aviation exhibition, and the following year he was appointed as the naval member of the Government's Advisory Committee for Aeronautics. Early in 1909 the sum of £35,000 was authorized for the building of a rigid airship for the Navy, and then another gifted technician, Captain Murray Sueter, was appointed Inspecting Captain of Airships.

The reason for the British bias towards airships at this stage is not hard to deduce. Across the North Sea was Britain's arch-rival, Germany, building a fleet of dreadnoughts clearly intended to match the Royal Navy's in size. Also in Germany was the world's leading designer of dirigible airships, Count von

On 10 January 1912 Lieutenant Charles Samson RN made the first British takeoff from a warship, in an S.27 biplane. The runway was built over the 12-inch guns and forecastle of the battleship *Africa*, and similar flights were made from the *Hibernia* and *London*.

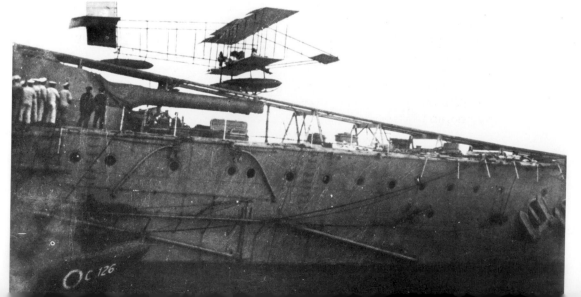

Zeppelin. To keep abreast of Zeppelin's developments seemed a logical aim, although, as we shall see later, the answer lay elsewhere. The British might well have ignored the American phenomenon and continued to persevere with airships had it not been for a series of coincidences.

In May 1911 the *Mayfly* was found to lack sufficient lift to get airborne, and in September 1911, when the faults had been rectified, she was caught by a sudden gust of wind as she left the hangar and broke her back. Sueter and his assistant, Commander Schwann, were abruptly returned to normal duties and the Admiralty's airships section was disbanded. The energy, however, was not dissipated, for the Admiralty gave permission for five officers to undergo training as pilots: Lieutenant Charles Samson, Lieutenant Arthur Longmore, Lieutenant R Gregory, and two Royal Marine Lieutenants, E L Gerrard and G Wildman-Lushington. There were in addition two other naval flyers, Lieutenant Colmore and Commander Schwann, who had learned to fly privately. Schwann went further and used his own money and donations from air-minded brother-officers to buy his own aircraft.

The first British waterborne take-off was made by Schwann on 18 November 1911, but he crashed while trying to land on water. It was left to Arthur Longmore to achieve this two weeks later in a Short S.27 on the River Medway. Charles Samson was keen to emulate Eugene Ely and obtained permission to fly off the forecastle of the battleship HMS *Africa*, which he achieved on 10 January 1912. To cap his achievement he repeated it at a naval review at Weymouth the following May, from the battleship *Hibernia* and again from the *London*.

May 1912 was a turning point in British naval aviation. In that month the influential Committee of Imperial Defence presented its White Paper on aviation to Parliament, calling for the establishment of an aviation service with separate army and naval wings. The service was to be called the Royal Flying Corps, but there was to be no single command for the two services, and within two years the separate status of the naval wing was made even clearer when it was renamed the Royal Naval Air Service. In the meantime the flamboyant Samson was made Commandant of the Naval Wing of the Royal Flying Corps (RFC), an appointment which annoyed many people who disliked his flair for publicity.

At the end of that year the Admiralty took a further step by ordering the old light cruiser *Hermes* to be converted as a 'parent ship' for naval aircraft. This involved fitting her with a platform over her bows for launching floatplanes, and a platform over her quarterdeck for stowing them after landing. One of the first experiments was to try the Short Folder aircraft, with wings designed to fold, a pointer to the future. The brash young First Lord of the Admiralty, Winston Churchill showed particular interest in naval aviation, and even intervened to ban the clumsy term hydro-aeroplanes; he much preferred the simpler seaplanes, and the name has stuck ever since.

The *Hermes* carried out numerous experiments, including some with aircraft bought in France, and took part in the Annual Manoeuvres in 1913. A momentary panic was caused when one of her aircraft got lost and was rescued by a German ship – it was treated as a major security leak. So successful was the old cruiser that plans were approved to buy a mercantile hull on the stocks – a collier – and convert her to a proper seaplane carrier capable of accommodating ten seaplanes.

The new carrier would be a great improvement over all the conversions and experiments so far. She would be able to launch seaplanes by using light jettisonable trolleys, a method already tried on the *Hermes*, and she would have a proper hold, workshops and heavy cranes for hoisting in the aircraft. The name chosen for her had not been used since the battle against the Spanish Armada in 1588, but it was highly appropriate for a ship which would send out flying machines to bring back information – *Ark Royal*.

In other countries there was interest in all these developments. The Germans, as we have seen, preferred to exploit the talents of Count Zeppelin, for his dirigibles offered great range and even the capacity to drop a considerable weight of bombs. The Italians toyed with the idea of launching an aircraft from a ship and had even got as far as embarking an aircraft in the battleship *Dante Alighieri* in 1913, but nothing came of it. The French were much more ambitious, and converted an old torpedo depot ship, the *Foudre*, to operate seaplanes. She started her duties in 1912 and took part in the 1913 Manoeuvres. Being a big ship (6000 tons) the *Foudre* could house as many as eight seaplanes, although when first commissioned she only carried two.

The Japanese, who had scored their victory over the Russians in 1904 because they were up-to-date, did not ignore the developments in Britain and America. The first naval aircraft flown in Japan were two British- and one American-built machines in November 1912. A mercantile vessel was converted at the end of 1913, the *Wakamiya*, to carry two seaplanes and parts for a second pair.

2 THE TEST OF WAR

By 1917 many British cruisers were fitted with platforms to allow them to fly off Sopwith Pups or Camels to counter Zeppelin airships. This is HMAS *Sydney*'s Pup.

When war broke out in 1914 the British Government immediately ordered the dispatch of nearly all the Army's aircraft to France, soon to be followed by a squadron of RNAS seaplanes under Squadron Commander Samson. As the British Isles were now without air defence of any sort it fell to the Navy to take responsibility for this job. Given the lack of any air-to-air weapons, other than rifles, shotguns and even flare pistols, it was just as well that the Germans had no immediate plans for bombing British cities. It did mean that the bulk of the RNAS could continue the painstaking task of finding out how to operate with the Fleet.

The *Ark Royal* was not yet ready, but it was seen as the first requirement to get more seaplanes to sea. The Admiralty requisitioned three cross-Channel steamers, the SS *Empress, Engadine* and *Riviera,* for conversion. They were fast, which met the principal requirement, and with the promenade and boat decks cleared there was room for a large canvas hangar and cranes to handle four seaplanes. Since they were intended only for the Channel route, these vessels lacked endurance, and so in response to a request from the Grand Fleet a larger and faster ship was sought. As it happened the old record-breaking Cunard liner *Campania* had just been sold for scrap, and was lying derelict, ready for the breakers. Here was a ship with sufficient coal to cross the Atlantic and sufficient speed (22 knots) to accompany the battleships of the Grand Fleet.

The old ship was stripped down to the upper deck, and a ramp was built from the forefunnel down to the bow. After trials it was found that the runway was too short and so the forefunnel was taken out and replaced by two thin uptakes set as far apart as possible – the first time that the requirements of aircraft-operating had forced such a radical change in a ship, but the precursor of many more drastic mutilations. Although the aged machinery of the *Campania* was always a worry, she met the basic requirement of being able to keep up with the Fleet, and as such she is entitled to the credit for being the first 'fleet' carrier.

It was some months before the first seaplane carriers finished their conversions, but the naval air squadron sent to France was soon in the thick of the fight. Samson and his men had been sent first to Ostend on the Belgian coast to support a landing by Royal Marines. When the port was abandoned before the advancing Germans the aircraft and all their supporting vehicles fell back to Dunkerque, but not before they had had several brushes with German cavalry. It was typical of Samson that he should organize an armoured car detachment to extend the reconnaissance done by his aircraft. Using borrowed machine guns fitted to the civilian cars which had been requisitioned for the squadron back in England, his officers careered

Capital ships launched their aircraft from platforms on the gun turrets. HMAS *Australia's* Sopwith 1½-Strutter takes off from her starboard wing turret.

about the Belgian countryside, taking pot shots at Uhlan patrols. At the same time the pilots carried out invaluable reconnaissance flights, scouting for the Army and giving news of German troop concentrations.

But the restless mind of Winston Churchill was not content with his naval squadrons playing cowboys and Indians in Belgium, and he prodded the Admiralty into planning a bombing raid on the Zeppelin sheds in Cologne and Düsseldorf. Working on the sound military principle of getting the first blow in, the RNAS planned to send two aircraft to Cologne and two to Düsseldorf, each armed with three 20-1b bombs. The raid was planned for 12 September, but all four aircraft were destroyed in a storm; Samson immediately prepared another four aircraft, and they took off ten days later.

Luck was against them. Three pilots had to turn back when they hit a dense bank of fog, and although the fourth reached the Düsseldorf Zeppelin sheds his attack was unsuccessful. He misjudged his height, with the result that only one of the three tiny bombs exploded. The next raid, however, on 8 October destroyed not only a shed but the Zeppelin inside, for the loss of one aircraft. Flushed by this success the Royal Navy decided on something much more ambitious, an attack across the North Sea on the German base at Cuxhaven. This meant using the three new carriers *Empress, Engadine* and *Riviera*, each with three seaplanes embarked, and a large screening force of light cruisers, destroyers and submarines was provided.

The raid took place as planned on Christmas Day, 1914. Although two of the aircraft failed to take off from the water (the three carriers had no bow ramps), the launch of seven aircraft promised success. Then a German Zeppelin and an aircraft appeared overhead and tried to bomb the carriers, but without scoring any hits. The carriers were only 12 miles North of Heligoland, on the German Navy's doorstep, and could expect an attack by surface ships any time. When three of the seaplanes returned some time later it was decided to embark them as quickly as possible and withdraw, without waiting for any more stragglers.

The remaining four seaplanes had reached Cuxhaven safely, but found low cloud and fog over the target, and could not make out the Zeppelin sheds. Although the pilots did the next best thing and bombed the ships in the harbour their puny little bombs inflicted little damage. They then had to find their parent ships, which had, of course, been withdrawn. Fortunately the first three seaplanes back at the rendezvous saw the submarine *E.11*, which had been told to remain behind in case she was needed. Although the last pair had an unwelcome escort in the form of a Zeppelin, which tried to bomb the submarine, *E.11* calmly took the pilots and observers on board, destroyed the seaplanes and then submerged. The fourth aircraft was forced to land alongside a Dutch trawler, and the crew was interned in Holland.

The failure of the Cuxhaven raid did not discredit the concept of seaplane carriers,

and the Admiralty pressed ahead with the conversion of three longer legged ships, the Isle of Man steamers *Ben-my-Chree, Manxman* and *Vindex*. The *Ark Royal* also joined the Fleet, and she was sent to the Mediterranean to provide support for the Dardanelles operations which began in the spring of 1915.

Despite her slow speed of ten knots the exploits of the *Ark Royal* and her eight seaplanes made her famous. The tasks were humdrum reconnaissance and spotting for the guns of the bombarding battleships, and they tested the frail and clumsy seaplanes to the maximum. Land aircraft with wheeled undercarriages were much lighter than seaplanes and so could gain height faster. To improve the reconnaissance the RNAS sent out a squadron of land aircraft under Samson (now promoted to Wing-Commander). This was the sort of challenge that Samson enjoyed hugely, and No 3 Wing and its Nieuport Scouts made a constant nuisance of themselves by strafing Turkish positions and harassing road transport.

The *Ark Royal* was still very valuable, but her slow speed made her vulnerable to attack from German U-Boats, and so it was decided to replace her with the 24-knot *Ben-my-Chree* in mid-1915. Ideas about weaponry were advancing rapidly, and on board she had two Short S.184 seaplanes, each capable of dropping a 14-inch torpedo (Samson had previously dropped a 500-lb bomb to show what could be done). At last a suitable target presented itself, a 5000-ton Turkish supply ship on the Northern side of the Sea

of Marmora, beyond the Golden Horn. The *Ben-my-Chree* steamed to the Gulf of Xeros, and at first light on 12 August hoisted out the Short S.184.

When Flight-Commander Edmonds sighted the target he manoeuvred into position, cut his engine and glided in at a height of only 15 feet, and released the torpedo. It ran true and hit the ship, causing a big explosion. Unkind fate cast doubt on this exploit, for a British submarine was also stalking the Turkish supply-ship, and claimed to have torpedoed her as well. This may well have been the beginning of a long-standing difference of opinion between submariners and naval aviators about which branch formed the elite of the Navy. There were no submarines about to spoil the aviators' pleasure when, five days later, two Shorts sank a supply ship and a tug just above the Narrows. The sinking of the tug was accomplished after the heavily laden seaplane had been forced down by engine trouble. As it taxied towards the tug the pilot released his torpedo, and the sudden reduction in weight allowed it to take off again.

To support the sterling work done by the *Ben-my-Chree* two German prizes, the steamers *Anne* and *Raven II*, were converted to carry seaplanes. Under the command of Samson, the 'task force' operated in the Eastern Mediterranean and the Red Sea, Turkish lines of communication in Syria, Palestine, Sinai and what is now Saudi Arabia were wide open to attack by aircraft, and the seaplanes were almost unopposed by hostile aircraft. Samson took the *Raven II* right down to

Ceylon on one occasion, on a search for the German surface raider *Wolf.*

In January 1918 the Turkish battlecruiser *Yavuz*, which as the German *Goeben* had played a significant part in 1914 in bringing Turkey into the war, sortied from the Dardanelles, but ran aground after sinking two British ships. Here was a tempting target for air attack, and the *Ark Royal* and *Manxman* were sent to see what they could do. However, despite a total of some 15 tons of bombs, the heaviest sustained attack of the war against any ship, the 65-lb and 112-lb bombs failed to make any impression on the *Yavuz*. It was hoped to launch torpedoes, but as the 14-inch torpedo had no hope of crippling a modern dreadnought it would have been necessary to use the 18-inch torpedo. This weighed over 1000 lbs, and the seaplanes failed repeatedly to get airborne with such a weight slung underneath.

Back in the North Sea, the ubiquitous Zeppelins were proving a great nuisance. Not only were they damaging civilian morale by bombing British cities, but their unfailing reconnaissance flights gave away the position of British forces and prevented the big fleet action that the Grand Fleet was trying to achieve. Civilian morale could be supported in a number of ways, but the frustration of the Grand Fleet was a major strategic setback for the British. Thousands of millions had been spent to build a fleet of dreadnoughts, purely for the purpose of bringing the German High Seas Fleet to battle, and so long as this was not achieved the British were failing to achieve their principal war aim.

The first initiative to combat the 'Zeppelin Menace' came from Commodore Tyrwhitt's Harwich Force, a striking force of light cruisers and destroyers based on the east coast of England. At Tyrwhitt's instigation a number of his cruisers were fitted with a ramp over the forward 6-inch gun to allow a French Deperdussin monoplane fighter to take off. The experiment failed to come to

anything because the aircraft could not gain height fast enough to intercept the Zeppelin, and at the higher altitudes the engine became even less efficient. The means were to hand, for incendiary ammunition had been developed for use against observation balloons in France, but until aircraft of the highest performance could be used from ships there was little hope of downing a Zeppelin.

The first positive step was on 3 November 1915, when a Bristol C-type Scout was flown from the *Vindex*, with flotation bags for a landing alongside. This was the first take-off from the deck of an aircraft carrier, and it was made by Flight Lieutenant H F Towler. This was still not enough, and nothing much was to happen for another two years. On 4 May 1916 the *Vindex* and *Engadine* were used to launch 11 seaplanes against the Tondern Zeppelin sheds, but again a series of accidents ruined the operation, and the solitary aircraft which reached Tondern found the sheds hidden in mist. The only crumb of comfort was that a Zeppelin was shot down by the submarine *E.11*, which had distinguished herself in the Cuxhaven raid in 1914.

Before the month was out a magnificent opportunity went begging, when the Grand Fleet at last met the German High Seas Fleet in the only full-scale fleet action of the war. The Battle of Jutland was brought about when the British battlecruisers met their German opposite numbers and was followed by a general engagement as each main fleet came up in support of its scouting forces. The *Campania* was assigned to the main British fleet, while the slower *Engadine* operated with the battlecruisers. The *Engadine* put to sea with Admiral Beatty's battlecruisers as planned, but when the Grand Fleet left its anchorage on the evening of 30 May the *Campania* did not receive the signal to weigh anchor, and so she remained tucked away in her remote anchorage on the north side of Scapa Flow. When she did at last put to sea next day she was too far behind the Fleet to catch up, and

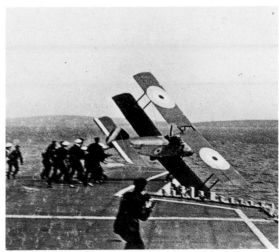

so her seaplanes failed to provide the reconnaissance which was so desperately needed by the British Commander-in-Chief.

The *Engadine* performed her tasks as ordered, and got one of her Short S.184 seaplanes aloft early in the afternoon, to investigate suspicious smoke on the horizon. The pilot, Flight Lieutenant F J Rutland, and his observer became airborne after only half an hour of preparation, and sent three sighting reports back to the ship. Unfortunately the crude radio equipment in the *Engadine* meant that she took considerable time to relay the information back to the flagship, and to make matters worse the low cloud forced Rutland to fly at only 900 feet, and he could see very little. The result was that *Engadine*'s prodigious efforts were not taken very seriously by Beatty's staff, and in any case a broken fuel-line forced Rutland to abort his mission. He had proved that it was possible for aircraft to talk to ships during a fleet action. Had communications been better and had the *Engadine* been faster she might have proved the point even better.

The Battle of Jutland brought many recriminations in its train, and the lack of reliable information was a recurring theme in the avalanche of reports which issued from the various committees. At the end of 1916 an important staff conference held at Longhope in the Orkneys reached the conclusion that more aircraft should be taken to sea. The first step was to set up the Grand Fleet Aircraft Committee under Rear-Admiral Sir Hugh Evan-Thomas to translate this directive into practical terms. The most valuable and also the most controversial recommendation was that a large and fast ship must be requisitioned for conversion to a carrier of fighter aircraft. Admiral Beatty, now Commander-in-Chief of the Grand Fleet, endorsed the committee's findings, saying that the 'provision of anti-Zeppelin machines' and 'ships to carry them' was most urgent.

The committee had its eye on a suitable ship, the so-called 'large light cruiser' *Furious*, which had been laid down in June 1915 and was nearing completion at Newcastle upon Tyne. She was a strange hybrid, a 31-knotter with the armour protection of a light cruiser but two colossal 18-inch guns in single turrets forward and aft. This strange combination was the result of the brief tenure of office of Lord Fisher as First Sea Lord, and she had been intended as a shallow-draught support vessel for his projected amphibious landings in the Baltic. With the passing of Fisher from the scene, sanity had returned and the naval staff had begun to wonder how to employ the *Furious*; her two guns were too unwieldy for accurate shooting and her eggshell plating was vulnerable to shells from a small cruiser.

After some haggling over the details it was agreed at the end of March 1917 that the *Furious* was not to receive her forward 18-inch gun (it had not yet been installed), and the space occupied by the turret, barbette and magazine should be used to provide a hangar for four 2-seater reconnaissance seaplanes and four fighters. A large hangar was to be built, with weatherproof doors and special ventilation, heating and lighting. The shell-rooms below were to be converted to a bomb-store and stowage was to be provided for 1200 gallons of petrol in 2-gallon cans. The flying-off platform was to be provided on the roof of the hangar, with a 228-foot runway down to the bows.

This was not a lengthy conversion, and the ship commissioned on 26 June; in addition to her crew of 796 she also carried 14 officers and 70 ratings of the RNAS under Squadron Commander Ernest Dunning, three Short seaplanes and five Sopwith Pups. Trials of the ship were completed a month later, but trials of the aircraft and the perfection of new techniques were considered more important.

Dunning believed that it would be possible, given a strong wind to improve handling, to develop Eugene Ely's feat of landing

Above left: Squadron Commander Dunning's successful landing on HMS *Furious* on 2 August 1917. The officers on deck are trying to catch the rope toggles on the wings to brake the aircraft's speed.

Above: Dunning's second attempt on 7 August led to his death when the Pup's engine stalled and the aircraft cartwheeled over the side.

Top: After Dunning's death the *Furious* was restricted to operating 'blimp' airships. She is seen here with an anti-submarine SSZ-type airship landing on the flight deck.

Above: Even after her second conversion HMS *Furious* was something of a white elephant. Although she could fly off aircraft from the forecastle the big landing deck aft was too dangerous.

on the *Pennsylvania*. He proposed to fly parallel to the ship, then slip sideways around the funnel and superstructure, and land on the deck. Given the docile handling of the Pup and a good deal of luck it was feasible, and numerous trial flights without actually landing showed that it might work, but the problem remained of how to slow down the aircraft once it was on the deck, for no wheel-brakes were fitted. Despite these doubts Dunning was given permission to try the first landing on a ship under way.

On 2 August conditions for the attempt were ideal, with a steady 21-knot wind, and so, with the ship making 10 knots Dunning brought his Pup in, close to stalling speed. He passed up the port side, slipped in over the hangar top and touched down on the centre of the runway; a handling party rushed forward and grabbed hold of special toggles on the trailing edges of the wings, to stop the Pup taking off again.

Five days later Dunning tried again, this time in more gusty conditions. He made a successful touchdown but damaged an elevator, and so had to effect repairs before making a second attempt. This time he was a bit higher off the deck, and as he had passed over the limit for a safe landing Dunning waved away the handling party, indicating that he would make a second circuit. Then the Pup's engine stuttered and stalled, and the little biplane came down heavily on one wheel and cartwheeled over the starboard side into the water. The gallant Dunning was trapped in the wreckage and drowned before anyone could get to him, a fate which has overtaken many carrier pilots since then.

The tragedy put an end to the experiments, for it was wisely reckoned that only very experienced pilots could manage such a complex manoeuvre, and even then, only in a 'gentleman's aircraft' like the Pup, which was renowned for its docility. On the other

Top: One of the many
landings attempted on
Furious, using a Sopwith Pup
fitted with skids instead of
wheels, and a crude
arresting gear of longitudinal
wires. The ropes are part of
the crash-barrier.

hand, even a moderately accomplished pilot
should be able to land on a full-length deck,
and in September 1917 a committee of enquiry recommended that the 'landing deck'
should be at least 300 feet long and the full
width of the ship.

Such a vessel was already 'in the pipeline'.
She was the *Argus*, which had been laid
down in 1914 as the Italian passenger liner
Conte Rosso. In August 1916 the hull had
been bought by the Admiralty for conversion into a carrier, and she was launched
in December 1917. The initial design had
been for a ship with separate flying-off and
landing decks, divided by a centreline
funnel and superstructure, but the *Furious*'s
problems had been spotted in time, and her
design was altered to a flush flight deck, with
funnel gases and smoke diverted through a
horizontal duct which vented aft, below the
edge of the deck. These modifications took
time, and it was to be September 1918 before

she joined the Fleet.

By now there was mounting impatience in
the Fleet and at the Admiralty to get a proper
carrier to sea, and so in November 1917 the
Furious was sent back to the factory for
modifications, in an attempt to speed up progress. There was not enough time to have a
flush deck fitted, but replacement of the after
18-inch gun and turret by a landing deck was
authorized. This deck was 284 feet long and
70 feet wide, and ran from just aft of the funnel
and superstructure to the stern. It was in
effect a large box, inside which was a new
hangar with workshops and a big lift to carry
aircraft to the flight deck. It was connected to
the forward flying-off deck by gangways to
port and starboard, around the superstructure, to allow aircraft to be wheeled forward.
An important innovation was a primitive
arresting gear, with longitudinal and transverse wires raised slightly above the deck
by wooden pegs. The idea was to use air-

craft with skids instead of wheels, and to fit the skids with hooks to catch the wires; two different systems were proposed, one to catch the longitudinal wires and the other to catch the transverse wires. As a final defence there was a 'crash barrier' of ropes suspended from a folding gantry, so that an aircraft which missed the wires would not continue forward to crash into the superstructure.

The system had been tried on land with some success, but on sea in HMS *Furious* it proved a failure. The combination of gusts of wind and the eddies and cross-draughts, caused by the hot gases from the funnel and wind coming around the funnel and the angular superstructure, was impossible to predict. Landing operations began in April 1918,

but at the end of May it was reported that out of 13 landings attempted only three had been successful; all the others had resulted in damaged aircraft, and in some cases, injured pilots. As with Dunning's experiment it was clear that landing on HMS *Furious* was only for the exceptional pilot, and once again the landing experiments had to be suspended. Although the remedy was to remove the funnel, the ship could not be spared for another period in dockyard hands as the war was moving to its climax, and apart from the small seaplane carriers *Furious* was the only carrier in service.

Throughout the summer and autumn of 1918 the *Furious* continued to serve with the Grand Fleet, flying off aircraft which then

'ditched' alongside, as it was reckoned that aircraft were expendable. Later the ban on landings was modified to allow pilots to attempt a landing if they judged it to be safe, but understandably they always chose to 'ditch'. Her Air Group now comprised a total of 14 Sopwith 1½-Strutters for reconnaissance, while the Pups had been replaced by eight 2F.1 Camels, a 'navalized' version of the famous Sopwith Camel land fighter. The Camels were specially equipped to deal with Zeppelins, having an extra .303-inch Lewis machine gun on the upper wing, mounted so as to be able to fire directly upwards. The 1½-Strutters were used to spot German minefields, while one or two Camels were always kept ready for take-off in case a Zeppelin should be sighted.

In June the *Furious* and her escorting light cruisers and destroyers were attacked by German seaplanes, and although the first pair of Camels failed to deal with the intruders and had to 'ditch', a second attack was met successfully, with the loss of one enemy seaplane. But this sort of action was a waste of the *Furious'* potential, and in the same month permission was given for a final attempt on the Zeppelin sheds at Tondern, in Schleswig-Holstein. The choice of Tondern was dictated by the Camels' lack of range; 1½-Strutters could have gone further afield but were considered too valuable in their reconnaissance role.

Operation F.6 was to be the first attack

Bottom: A busy scene on the flight deck of the *Furious*, with parties of seamen and officers securing the airship *SSZ.59*.

Below: Seven Sopwith Camel 2F.1 fighters on the flying-off deck of the *Furious*, behind a windbreak of palisades. These are probably the seven Camels which carried out the Tondern Raid in July 1918.

HMS *Argus* under way,
showing how the problem of
funnel smoke was dealt with.

ever made by shipboard aircraft on a land objective, and was originally planned for 27 June, but had to be postponed because of bad weather. Redesignated F.7, it went ahead on 17 July, when *Furious* left the Firth of Forth accompanied by five light cruisers. A day later she was in position off the Danish coast, only 80 miles from the target. At 0304 on the morning of 18 July she was steaming at 18.5 knots, with the Camels ready to be launched, but a sudden thunderstorm broke. As all the indications were that the force had not been detected it was decided to postpone the operation for 24 hours, rather than cancel it, and so the *Furious* and her destroyers withdrew. They manoeuvred out of sight of land for the rest of the day, and at nightfall moved in again. This time the weather stayed reasonable, and at 0313 the first Camel rolled forward down the launching ramp. Seven were launched, but one returned soon with engine trouble

The objective, the Tondern base of the German Naval Airship Division, comprised three huge sheds. The largest, code-named *Toska*, was 787 feet long, while *Tobias* and *Toni* were 603 feet long. The two smaller sheds contained only one captive balloon, but in *Toska* were the airships *L.54* and *L.60*, exactly the sort of target the British were hoping to find. The attack came as a complete suprise, with only three minutes' warning from the time the first Camel appeared to the dropping of the first bombs.

The first three Camels appear to have gone into a gliding attack, diving low and then pulling up to clear the target. Their bombs went straight into the *Toska* shed and set fire to the millions of cubic feet of hydrogen gas contained in the envelopes of the two Zeppelins. Fortunately for the Germans the hangar doors were open, and so the colossal fire which ignited did not destroy the structure, although the column of smoke was said to have risen to a height of a thousand feet. The second flight of Camels arrived ten minutes later and put their bombs into the *Tobias* shed and destroyed the balloon, but failed to set alight a wagon-load of hydrogen cylinders nearby.

The six pilots now had to make the long trip back to the ship, always a worry for naval aviators. Three, believing that they were too low on fuel, decided to land in neutral Denmark, but two reached the covering force and 'ditched' close to a destroyer. The sixth was never seen again, and it is believed that he ran out of fuel, 'ditched' safely but died of drowning or exhaustion. The three who landed in Denmark were all released within a day or two, and illegally returned to England. At 0740 *Furious*, her mission over, increased speed to 20 knots and headed for home. She and her air group had succeeded at last.

The Tondern raid was not repeated, despite its success. For one thing the other Zeppelin bases were either too far away or too well defended. For another the death of Peter Strasser, head of the Naval Airship Division, had robbed the Zeppelins of the imaginative leadership they had once enjoyed, and they were growing more and more vulnerable to fighter aircraft. Instead British thoughts turned more to the promising idea of a torpedo raid on the High Seas Fleet in its own harbours, a precursor of the Taranto and Pearl Harbor attacks 20 years later.

The *Argus* had a leading role in these plans, for she was to embark no fewer than 20 Sopwith Cuckoo aircraft, the first landplane designed to operate from ships as a torpedo-carrier. The Cuckoo owed its inspiration to the foresight of Commodore Murray Sueter, who in October 1916 issued a secret memorandum to the Sopwith company, asking them to investigate the possibilities of building an aircraft capable of carrying one or even two torpedoes, but also having four hours' endurance. Sueter also enquired about the possibility of using catapults to launch the aircraft, although the RN had no catapult of any sort under consideration. The prototype flew in June 1917, and was a remarkable aircraft in many ways, with folding wings and a wide, sturdy undercarriage capable of carrying a 1000-lb 18-inch torpedo. The name Cuckoo was a whimsical reference to its ability to 'lay eggs in other people's nests'.

A total of 90 Cuckoos were delivered by the Armistice, and they were earmarked for the operation against the High Seas Fleet. Unfortunately their promise was never fulfilled, as production ceased in November 1918, but the two marks built showed the way to the successful torpedo-bombers of World War II. Significantly the Japanese acquired six Cuckoo Mk IIs in 1922.

Apart from the *Argus* there was also the *Hermes* under construction. She was ordered in April 1917, the first warship in the world designed from the start to operate aircraft, and she was to carry the same number of aircraft as the *Argus*. She also had a full-length flight deck, but instead of the flush deck with all the technical problems of exhausting the smoke through long horizontal ducts, she had a small superstructure on the starboard side, enclosing the funnel – the first 'island' superstructure, an arrangement which was to become standard. Although soon outclassed by bigger carriers, the little *Hermes* showed considerable ingenuity, especially when it is remembered that her design was drawn up with only the experience gleaned from a variety of conversions, such as those made on the *Ark Royal*, the cross-Channel steamers and the *Furious*. She had good speed for her day (25 knots), was weatherly, and carried only medium-calibre guns, as it was (rightly) seen that her main role was to avoid surface action.

The *Hermes* was not laid down until January 1918, and would not be ready for two or three years, so to expedite matters in the autumn of 1917 the Admiralty decided to convert the hull of the Chilean battleship *Almirante Cochrane*. She had been suspended in 1914, but was fairly advanced. Work was restarted, and in February 1918 she was formally purchased and renamed HMS *Eagle*. Features already settled for the *Hermes* were incorporated in her design too, the island superstructure and the light scale of armament for example, but her greater size meant that she could have a much bigger hangar with two lifts. HMS *Eagle* was launched in June 1918, and so she was also too late.

Returning to developments in the United States, mention must be made of the progress in shipboard catapults. The first primitive catapult, if it can be called that, was tried in 1911 by Lieutenant Theodore Ellyson at the Hammondsport, NY works of Glenn Curtiss. It was no more than an 'accelerator', using three inclined wires and a counterweight. The head of naval aviation, Captain Chambers, recognized the weaknesses of the idea, but persevered with his own improvement, a launching device using compressed air, much the same as a torpedo-tube, for pushing an aircraft off the deck of a ship. The device was ready in June 1912 and was installed at the Santee Dock at Annapolis.

The first launching attempt on 31 July 1912 nearly killed Ellyson as the sudden acceleration made the engine of his Curtiss A-1 seaplane stall and he crashed into the sea. The builder of the catapult, Constructor Holden C Richardson, made several improvements, and on 12 November the same year Ellyson was able to make the world's first successful catapult take-off. Further work followed, but it was not until October 1915 that a test-model was installed on the quarterdeck of the armoured cruiser *North Carolina*. She launched a Curtiss AB-3 piloted by Lieutenant-Commander Henry C Mustin on 5 November 1915. Early in 1917 similar catapults were installed in the armoured cruisers *Seattle* and *Huntingdon*, but they were removed soon after the United States' entry into World War I, on the grounds that they would interfere with the ships' ability to convoy shipping.

The British had pushed ahead with the technique of launching fighter and spotter aircraft from small platforms on the gun turrets of battleships and the forecastles of light cruisers, but the American experience with catapults clearly pointed the way to more ambitious operations with heavier aircraft. In 1916 the RN converted a hopper barge, the *Slinger*, into a catapult trials ship. It was, however, very heavy, and as the light aircraft platforms were adequate to meet existing requirements nothing further was done until after the War.

For some years the catapult seemed to be useful only for launching seaplanes, for the wheeled landplanes in vogue, with their light weight and low wing-loading, hardly needed any persuasion to get airborne. The first American carrier, the *Langley*, was given two catapults in 1922, but they were removed in 1928 for that reason. Similarly the giant flywheel catapults fitted in the big carriers *Lexington* and *Saratoga* were removed.

Let us leave naval aviation in all its permutations as it stood in November 1918. Many ideas had been tested, many more were ready to be tried, but the full spate of development was to be checked sharply. While the War lasted no expense was spared in testing new concepts, but a harsh new climate was waiting. Not only would the civilian authorities be unwilling to sanction expenditure on untried ideas but in addition there would be fierce opposition from traditionalists in the services, to say nothing of the vociferous new land-based air power lobby, which saw naval aviation as a rival to its claims for money.

The end of the War inevitably put the brakes on many promising developments in naval aviation, for the victors were only too anxious to beat their swords into ploughshares. But the tranquillity was illusory, for within a year the latent tensions between the Allies became more obvious. For one thing, the United States had a new-found confidence as the moral leader of the world, and coincidentally the major creditor-nation. She saw herself not only as challenging the British position as the premier naval power, with her vast industrial potential, but also taking on the Japanese in the Pacific.

The British were still in a very powerful position, with the largest navy in the world, and also the latest ideas, particularly in naval aviation, but financially exhausted after four years of colossal expenditure of men, money and resources. The Japanese, on the other hand, still basked in the glory of their victory over the Russians in 1904–1905, and had done extremely well out of the recent war, with huge contracts for shipbuilding and armaments from the Allies.

Fired by the example of the Royal Navy, the Japanese went ahead with their own design of aircraft carrier in 1919. She was to be similar in size and speed to the British *Hermes*, but with three diminutive funnels set on the starboard side of the flight deck, which were hinged to allow them to be lowered to a horizontal position when flying was in progress. She too adopted an island superstructure, but had two centreline lifts, and because the scale of armament was lighter could accommodate 26 aircraft. After trials in 1923 the island was removed to provide a clear deck, on the lines of HMS *Argus*. The *Hosho* was rushed into service ahead of the *Hermes*, and so she qualified as the first purpose-built carrier in service.

The US Navy was also influenced by the *Hermes* because, paradoxically, relations with the British had been so harmonious in 1917–18. Late in 1917 Naval Constructor Stanley Goodall was seconded to the Bureau of Construction and Repair's section dealing with preliminary design. Goodall took with him the design of the *Hermes*, and was also able to supply the invaluable details of British war experience. Goodall's ideas are now known to have been very influential on American ideas, for when in June 1918 the Director of Naval Aviation asked the General Board to put forward a requirement for an aircraft carrier, the British designer was asked to comment on the proposals.

Goodall summarized British ideas, and stated, 'Such a type of ship is essential for the British Navy. . . . A fleet should . . . be attended by reconnaissance machines and fighting machines. . . . An armament of four 4-inch guns is insufficient, and a larger number of guns – preferably 6-inch – should be carried, together with one or two anti-aircraft guns. Although such a ship should not by any means be regarded as a fighting ship, it should be sufficiently powerfully armoured to be able to brush aside light vessels of the enemy, so that its machines can be flown off in comparatively advanced conditions. . . . The speed proposed – namely 30 knots – is considered a minimum.'

In July 1920 it was proposed to lay down four carriers over a three-year period and a year later the construction of at least three was demanded as top priority. Without tactical experience the US Navy had to rely heavily on war-gaming, and great attention was paid to the findings of the War College. In 1922 a General Board Hearing was told that the previous year had been devoted to war-games with carriers taking part in various simulated engagements, and all of them showed that aircraft would influence the outcome, even if they could not dominate a naval battle.

But this is going ahead too fast, for the US Navy's ambitious plans were affected by the financial constraints imposed by Congress. The United States was hardly impoverished, but the mood of withdrawal from the world stage which set in after the Peace Conference was convened at Versailles made Congress unwilling to vote large sums of money for armaments. The General Board hoped to get approval for a large carrier capable of carrying 24 planes in the programme for Fiscal Year 1920 (which ran from July 1919 to June 1920). The design proposed had its origins in a study initiated by Goodall in August 1918, for a 22,000-ton ship some 800 feet long. By October 1918 it had been refined to a 35-knot ship displacing 24,000 tons, armed with ten 6-inch guns. In March 1919 the General Board decided to increase the armament to four 8-inch guns, six 6-inch, four torpedo-tubes and four 4-inch anti-aircraft guns. Such a scale of armament meant a bigger ship, and to save time Construction and Repair adapted a design for a 34,800-ton battlecruiser, one of the preliminary versions which led to the 43,000-ton *Lexington* Class.

The design featured *two* islands, one to port and one to starboard, with the 8-inch guns in single positions forward and aft. The 6-inch guns were sited on each broadside and in a twin position aft below the end of the flight deck, while each island was to have a big 'cage' mast, as in battleships. The normal displacement was calculated to be just over 29,000 tons, and to make 35 knots she would need about 140,000 horsepower.

But Congress was adamant, and refused to sanction any carriers in Fiscal Years 1920

Left: The Japanese *Hosho* was completed with an experimental 'island' for trials in 1923, but this was removed soon afterwards.

Left: After trials the *Hosho*'s temporary island was removed and she spent the rest of her career as a flush-decked carrier.

and 1921. The funds for conventional ships planned as far back as 1916 were drying up, and there was no question of embarking on costly novelties. All that was done was to permit the conversion of a big fleet collier, the *Jupiter* (AC.3), into a carrier for experimental work. This ship was one of a pair of 5500-ton, 15-knot colliers built seven years earlier; her sister had been lost in an accident in 1918, and the *Jupiter* was now redundant as the majority of the fleet's newer battleships were either oil-fired or planned to change over from oil. She had been the first sizeable USN ship with turbo-electric drive, and in 1917 had carried the first naval aviators to France.

The General Board was not happy with the collier conversion, and regarded it merely as a stopgap, but better than no carrier. Her name was soon changed to *Langley* in honour of the pioneer Samuel Pierpont Langley, and her designation changed to Aircraft Carrier No 1 or *CV.1*. Despite her lack of length (only 542 feet overall) and slow speed she had certain advantages: The deep holds would provide ample room for aircraft and workshops, and she would need a relatively small crew to operate her. She entered Norfolk Navy Yard in March 1920 for two years' conversion, during which her superstructure and coaling derricks were cut away, the

Right: The British *Hermes*, first carrier built from the keel up, at Chefoo, China in 1931. Although too small to operate an efficient air group she was an inherently sound design, with good seakeeping.

holds were converted and a wooden 534-foot by 64-foot flight deck built over the hull.

The *Langley*'s six holds were all converted, the foremost into a tank for avgas, the next two into a hangar, the fourth into a magazine for ordnance and a storeroom, with a lift-well above, and the last two into a second hangar. A total of 55 aircraft were stored in the two hangars, and were hoisted out by a pair of 3-ton travelling cranes running on a fore-and-aft girder under the flight deck, and then deposited on a lift which took them to the flight deck. The term 'hangar' is misleading, for there was no hangar deck in the conventional sense, merely two pairs of holds into which the aircraft had to be lowered by the crane. There was also a crane for hoisting out seaplanes on either side amidships. The big open space between the flight deck and the tops of the holds was available for working on aircraft.

When first completed the ship had a hinged funnel on the port side, which lowered during flying operations, as in the Japanese *Hosho*; later this was altered to provide a second funnel. The navigating bridge was sited right forward, underneath the overhang of the flight deck, and the two masts were telescopic, leaving the entire deck free for flying. Although not a pretty ship, the 'Covered Wagon' soon endeared

herself to the aviators after she recommissioned in March 1922.

The only other carrier to appear during this period was the British *Eagle*. She, as we have already seen, had been a Chilean battleship until March 1918, and was launched three months later. Like the 1918–19 American designs she was intended to have a double island superstructure, with a funnel in each, as well as a tripod mast. There is also mention of an intriguing proposal for a connecting 'bridge' between the islands, 20 feet above the flight deck and strong enough to carry four 4-inch anti-aircraft guns and a navigating position. Fortunately the *Furious* trials showed that her 'goalpost' arrangement was a failure, and the more practical solution of a single starboard island was substituted. Unlike the little island in the Japanese *Hosho*, the *Eagle* was given a large structure, 130 feet long, with two funnels, proper navigating and fire-control positions and a large crane at the after end.

The choice of the starboard side was made on the recommendation of Captain Nicholson of HMS *Furious* and Wing-Captain Clark Hall of the RNAS. For some reason pilots prefer to turn to port if they make a faulty landing, and a port island causes more landing accidents than a starboard one. Having settled the basic layout of carriers in perpetuity, work

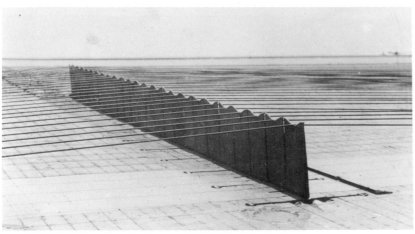

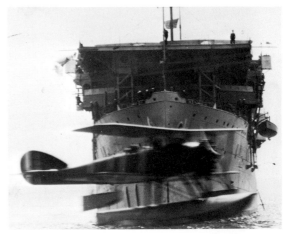

could continue, but in spite of the Admiralty's anxiety to get *Eagle* into service she was not ready until April 1920. Even then she had only one funnel in place, two boilers working and no lifts, but she left the Tyne to go south to Portsmouth to start flying trials.

When the ship arrived at Portsmouth at the end of April 1920 she was only fit for experimental work, with the lift-wells plated over and a wooden hut on the island to act as a navigating position and charthouse. A new longitudinal arresting gear was transferred from the *Argus*, a collection of 190-foot wires (later extended to 320 feet) intended more for keeping the aircraft straight than stopping it. The first aircraft to land in May 1920 were Sopwith Camels, Cuckoos and Parnall Panthers, and her captain was able to report that she was now a 'going concern'. HMS

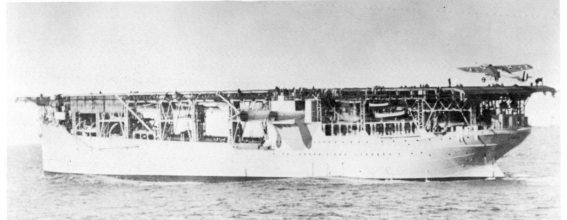

Eagle then paid off for completion, and as some major work still had to be done the work was not finished until September 1923.

Today we take the island superstructure for granted, but it is interesting to note that *Eagle's* captain regarded it as a serious handicap, while the Naval Air Section said that it was a nuisance but helped to provide the pilot with a reference point for his height and alignment if conditions were good. As there were several other arguments in favour of the island configuration the whole matter was handed over to the scientists for wind-tunnel testing. As a result of tests it was decided to change the island in *Hermes* to a much shorter and wider form, and to do away with it completely when *Furious* came up for reconstruction.

In fact *Furious* went into Devonport Dockyard in June 1922 for a massive reconstruction. She had been laid up at the end of 1919, widely regarded as a white elephant in spite of her achievements. While arguments went on about how best to improve her as a carrier she lay stripped, but in April 1921 the broad outlines of her refit were approved by the Admiralty. This time she was to have a 576-foot by 91-foot flush flight deck, a double-storeyed hangar and retractable navigating bridges.

By the summer of 1922, not 20 years after the first powered flight and little over a decade since the first flight from the deck of a ship, there were three converted aircraft carriers in service, the *Furious*, *Argus* and *Langley*, a fourth nearly ready (*Eagle*) and two purpose-built carriers nearing completion, the *Hosho* and *Hermes*.

4 POLITICS AND PERSONALITIES

Although the British held a commanding lead in naval aviation at the end of the war in 1918, they had already made a decision which was to have disastrous consequences. Following two effective daylight raids on London in 1917 the Cabinet had panicked, and had convened a committee to study the problem of air defence and procurement of aircraft.

The committee was under the chairmanship of the brilliant South African General Jan Smuts, a former guerrilla leader of the Boer War whose formidable intellectual powers were regarded as vital to unravel the complexities of the problem. Brilliant Smuts may have been, but it is doubtful whether his two-month rush through the evidence of naval and military strategic aims, industrial problems, aerial tactics, to name only a few, could have produced anything but a glib simplification. In fact his opening preamble embraced the new principle of 'strategic air power', a dazzling view of a future in which 'aerial operations, with their devastation of industrial and populace centres on a vast scale, may become the principal operations of war, to which the older forms of military and naval operations may become secondary and subordinate'. In the words of the Italian General Giulio Douhet, it might even be possible for a future war to be won by bombers without the opposing armies and navies firing a single shot. Ironically the first 'strategic' bombing raids – ie, raids against targets inside Germany rather than against front-line targets – had been carried out by RNAS aircraft in France in 1915, but the exponents of strategic bombing quite overlooked or overestimated the paltry results of such raids.

The solution to the undoubted muddle in supply of aircraft and conflict between the RNAS and RFC for aircraft and pilots was to be solved by unifying both under one umbrella, a new Royal Air Force. Administratively this arrangement had a lot to recommend itself, although the crisis point of the whole war was possibly not the moment to put it into effect, and it was originally envisaged that the RAF would continue to subdivide its resources between supporting the Army and the Navy, as before. But Smuts had gone on to much more contentious matters. Once the present shortage of airframes and engines was overcome, said the report, the surplus could be devoted to the formation of an 'independent' or 'strategic' bombing force to 'carry the war into Germany'.

In fairness to these ardent apostles of strategic bombing, there was an exaggerated fear of the effects of bombing against civilian targets; the outcry in 1917 had frightened the British Cabinet into thinking that civilian morale was about to break down.

Furthermore the slaughter on the Western Front had shown that conventional military solutions were apparently ineffective, and the new idea of raining bombs on German cities and factories seemed so much cheaper in human life – for one's own side at any rate. With these considerations the British Government formed a new Air Ministry in November 1917, followed by the formation of the Royal Air Force on 1 April 1918, the world's first independent air service. Despite his misgivings Brigadier-General Hugh Trenchard became the first Chief of the Air Staff and then Commander-in-Chief; in addition he subsequently took command of an Independent Bombing Force of British, French, Italian and American bombers, just before the Armistice.

The effects of the changes on naval flying hardly had time to be felt before the Armistice, and were confined to administrative details. But the Air Staff was formed mainly of ex-RFC officers, and the naval viewpoint was quickly overshadowed. The pilots were all to be RAF as were the maintenance personnel, and naval personnel were encouraged to transfer in order to make up numbers. The change was beneficial to the RAF, but it meant that the Navy was robbed of its keenest air-minded officers; very few aviators could remain loyal to the Senior Service at the cost of giving up their beloved flying. Thus at a crucial stage in the evolution of naval tactics, there was a weakened voice speaking for aviation, and the traditionally loud voice of the gunnery branch continued to dominate the debate.

To do the Admiralty justice, it did realize the dangers, and in 1924 the Fleet Air Arm was re-established within the RAF as a branch in its own right. Senior RAF officers, particularly Trenchard, became increasingly concerned to safeguard the independence of the Royal Air Force, and in their zeal they fastened on the role of strategic bombing as the main, indeed the only, worthwhile role. The teachings of Giulio Douhet were taken literally, despite the fact that they had scarcely been proved by the events of the recent war. The debate on air power became more and more unreal, with parrot-cries of, 'the bomber will always get through' – from which followed the logical conclusion, that there was no point in building fighter aircraft! At every turn the politicians and press were bombarded with claims that any ship could be blown out of the water by high-level precision bombing.

The claims of the bomber enthusiasts could have been excused on the grounds of exuberance, but the practical effect was to siphon off the limited funds available for building bombers. The Fleet Air Arm was a

Left: HMS *Furious* emerged from her second reconstruction in 1925 a successful carrier at last. She was, however, the last British flush-decked carrier.

Left: A flight of Fairey Seal bombers over the *Furious*. To the Royal Navy she too was affectionately known as the 'Covered Wagon'.

very low priority, and as the design and procurement of naval aircraft remained firmly in RAF hands it would have been impossible even for a very air-minded Admiralty to exert any influence over the performance of its future aircraft. As a result the performance of British carrier-borne aircraft, having been as good as it could be in 1918, dropped steadily behind that of land-based aircraft, and even behind that of Japanese and American naval aircraft.

The US Navy also had its fair share of problems. After the armistice US Army aviator Brigadier-General William Mitchell started to agitate for an independent air force along the lines of the Royal Air Force. Like Trenchard, Mitchell was an Army officer who had taken to flying late, and like all converts he was more zealous than the zealots. But, unlike Trenchard, he chose to wage his war in peacetime, when the overriding need to find a quick solution was absent. Thus both the Army and the Navy were free to concentrate on the case against an independent Air Force, and the struggle was much fiercer as a result.

The first practical bombing tests were, ironically, carried out by the Navy, when in November 1920 the old pre-dreadnought battleship *Indiana* was subjected to a series of tests. She was first loaded with aircraft bombs placed in vital positions on board, and then attacked with dummy bombs. Billy Mitchell had been invited to watch the tests, and he was delighted to see that the old battleship sank, but what he would or could not admit was that the on-board detonations had sunk the ship, whereas the air-dropped bombs had been dummies. What was equally important was that the *Indiana* was a small and obsolete warship, never intended to cope with aerial bombardment.

Notwithstanding Mitchell continued to agitate publicly for a separate 'air department'; both sides dug in, and inevitably the most extreme views prevailed, boiling down to bombers-versus-battleships and nothing in between. As Mitchell intended, the US Navy Department was put under strong pressure from Press and Congress to give the aviators a chance to prove their point. The Navy agreed to stage a series of tests in June-July 1921, using surrendered German warships as the targets.

The tests had a strong element of farce about them. Despite the claims of the bomber-exponents of the Army Air Service they had to borrow radios, compasses and even bomb-sights from the Navy, and had to have ships stationed off the coast to enable them to find the targets, as Army aircrews had never flown as far as 60 miles offshore.

On 21 June 1921 the first test began, with three Navy flying boats attacking a U-Boat, each with three 180-lb bombs. The results were decisive: *U.117* sank 12 minutes after the first hit. Next it was the turn of the old battleship *Iowa*, a contemporary of the *Indiana*; she was attacked by Navy aircraft with dummy bombs. The Navy claimed that Mitchell's bombers were not permitted to attack the *Iowa* as she was 'cheating' by manoeuvring under radio-control, and given the crude navigation of the day it is doubtful if they could even have found her, let alone hit her. The destroyer *G.102* and the light cruiser *Frankfurt* were both sunk by heavy bombing.

The three ships sunk so far had either been very old or small, but the final test was to be against a modern battleship, the 22,800-ton dreadnought *Ostfriesland*. Built in 1911, she had fought at the Battle of Jutland, and had been designed when air attack was unthought of. Still, German battleships were regarded as the best protected in the world, and Mitchell's supporters took good care to spread the idea that the *Ostfriesland* was thought to be 'unsinkable, like the *Titanic*'. In fact she was in poor condition, and had needed repairs to enable her to cross the Atlantic in safety.

On 20 July Navy and Marine Corps aircraft dropped 34 light bombs on the *Ostfriesland*, of which six hit. An inspection should have followed, but without warning six Army bombers arrived on the scene and dropped a number of 600-lb bombs, of which only two hit. This time the inspection was carried out properly and the ship found to have no appreciable damage between decks. Next day eight Army MB-2 bombers each dropped two 1000-lb bombs and scored six hits, but the inspecting team reported that the ship was still seaworthy.

The Army bombers returned in the afternoon, this time armed with 2000-lb bombs, the biggest in the world. One bomb bounced off, two missed and the fourth hit. Even so the *Ostfriesland* took the rest of the day to sink, with no fire-parties or damage-control parties to control the flooding. Nor had the ship put up any sort of resistance, even by manoeuvring to avoid the bombs, for she was an inert hulk. But these points did not matter, for as Mitchell boasted, he had sunk a battleship by air attack, and had 'proved the ability of aircraft to destroy ships of all classes on the surface of the water'.

Further tests followed, and they tended to confirm Mitchell's claim. Two months later another old battleship, the *Alabama* was sunk by Army bombers, and in September 1923 the pre-dreadnoughts *New Jersey* and *Virginia* were sunk. Not until November 1924 was a modern battleship, the unfinished

The Billy Mitchell bombing trials – on 18 July 1921 at 1400 hours an Army 300lb bomb lands alongside the German light cruiser *Frankfurt*.

On 13 July a Martin bomber scores a hit on the German destroyer *G.102*.

On 20 July at 1440 hours an Army bomber scores a near-miss on the German battleship *Ostfriesland*.

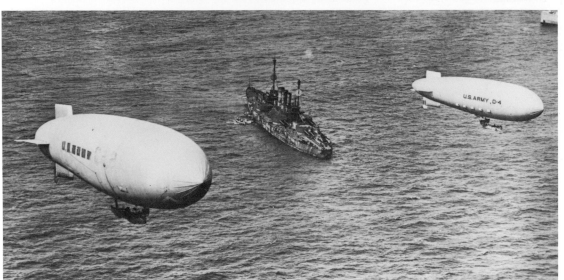

Top: Next day, at 1239 hours the *Ostfriesland* begins to list to starboard.

Above: Framed by two Navy blimps, the *Ostfriesland* is beginning to show signs of flooding.

Below: The *Ostfriesland* finally gives up the struggle and sinks.

Washington, subjected to a series of scientific tests, in which the effects of torpedoes, armour-piercing bombs and gunfire were compared. The report which resulted summed up the Navy's views: 'The battleship of today, while not invulnerable to airplane attack, still possesses very effective structural protection. . . . The battleship of the future can be so designed as to distribution of her armour on decks and sides, and as to interior subdivision, that she will not be subjected to fatal damage from the air. . . . It cannot be said therefore that air attack has rendered the battleship obsolete.'

Mitchell, it is said, asked for his court-martial and got it, when in 1925 he accused the Navy of 'almost treasonable' incompetence leading up to the loss of the airship *Shenandoah* in a storm. He had done a great deal of good, and in the long run assured the future of the carrier, but he had also done a great deal of harm. Apart from the divisive effects of the quarrel, he focused attention, not only in the United States but elsewhere, on high-level precision bombing at the expense of torpedo attack. All the experience of World War II and since has shown that no major warship of any navy has been sunk while under way by high-level bombing. In World War II the RAF's faith in high-level bombing proved totally misplaced, as did that of the Italian *Regia Aeronautica*. Only those air forces which showed an interest in dive-bombing and torpedo-dropping showed any yield for the effort involved.

The exponents of naval aviation might have had to take second place to the battleship enthusiasts for the moment, but other events were in train which were to give them great encouragement. In November 1921 President Harding convened a naval dis-

armament conference in Washington to discuss ways of bringing the incipient arms race between Japan, Great Britain and the United States to a halt before it could trigger off another war. The main bone of contention was the number of battleships building in Japan and the US, and the delegates addressed themselves to the task of persuading the three major powers to cut back the size of their fleets, both in being and under construction. The result was that the United States and Great Britain agreed to retain 15 capital ships each, Japan accepted a limit of nine and France and Italy accepted a total of five ships each. Largely as a sop to their collective pride the navies concerned were allocated tonnage totals for aircraft carriers, 135,000 tons to the US and Great Britain, 81,000 tons to Japan and 60,000 tons to France and Italy. This was specifically to permit the British, Americans and Japanese to convert cancelled hulls to avoid unemployment in their shipyards but it provided the excuse to build carriers at a time when funds would have been extremely hard to find.

The fine print of the Washington Naval Disarmament Treaty provided the first formal definition of an aircraft carrier: a warship with a displacement in excess of 10,000 tons standard displacement but not more than 27,000 tons, designed for the specific and exclusive purpose of carrying, launching and landing aircraft. Guns were to be restricted to 8-inch calibre, with not more than ten carried. As a special exception the Japanese and Americans were each permitted to convert two carriers of 33,000 tons to make use of existing hulls. These were the rules which were to govern carrier design for nearly two decades, and only Pearl Harbor would sweep them aside.

5 THE BIG CARRIERS

The US Navy's Bureau of Construction and Repair had, as we have already seen, considered the modification of an existing battlecruiser design as early as 1919. Since the six battlecruisers of the *Lexington* Class (CC.1–6) were prime targets for the axe at the Washington Conference, the' chief of Preliminary Design on his own initiative ordered a study to be made for converting one of them to an aircraft carrier in July 1921. And so, when the delegates reached their momentous decisions early in 1922 the Bureau was well advanced in the preparation of the design.

The biggest headache was the arbitrary limit of 33,000 tons, which suited the Japanese. The original figure had been 41,000 tons, but it came down to 39,000 and finally to 36,000 tons. There was no way to reduce this figure any more, and so the General Board decided on a 'white lie'. The Treaty allowed all existing capital ships to be modified and modernized to improve defence against air attacks up to a limit of 3000 tons over their original standard displacement. It was argued, rather unconvincingly, that the clause covered the carriers which were to be converted from capital ships, and therefore the 3000 tons of modifications had been added to the original design. Therefore the standard displacement for the ships converted would be announced at 33,000 tons, when they were actually 36,000 tons.

The ships chosen for the conversion were the *Lexington* (CC.1), building at Bethlehem's Quincy Yard in Massachusetts and the *Saratoga* (CC.3) building at the New York Shipbuilding Company at Camden, New Jersey. The reason for choosing these two was that they were the most advanced of the six ships under construction, and so would need less money spent on their conversion. Even so, the cost was estimated at $22.4 million, excluding the money already spent, and as costs increased so did the hostility of Congress, which kept the ships on 'drip-feed'.

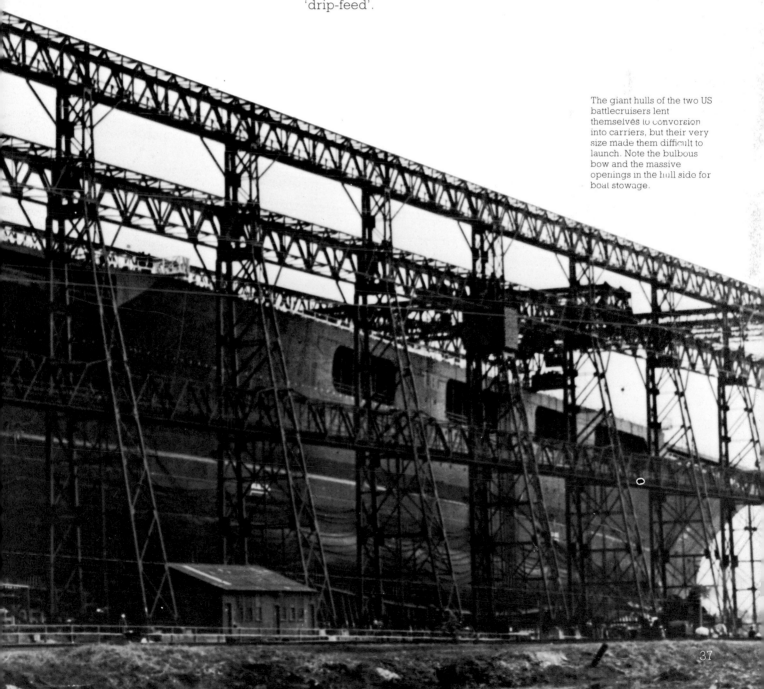

The giant hulls of the two US battlecruisers lent themselves to conversion into carriers, but their very size made them difficult to launch. Note the bulbous bow and the massive openings in the hull side for boat stowage.

Right: USS *Lexington* (CV.2) in dry dock, showing the massive bulbous bow, intended to reduce hull resistance at high speed. The third 15-ton anchor was provided because of the huge 'sail area' of the hull, which made mooring difficult.

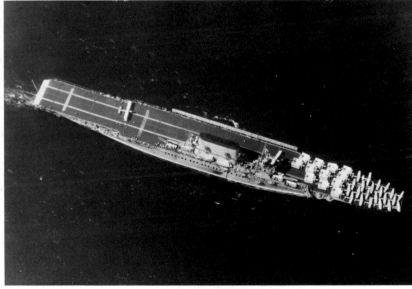

Above: Martin T4M-1 bombers on the *Lexington* during exercises in January 1929.

Right: The 8-inch guns in the *Lexington* and *Saratoga* were of little value, since their blast damaged the aircraft and the wooden deck. Time was to show that the carriers' aircraft were the best defence against surface attack.

When *CV.2* and *CV.3* commissioned at the end of 1927 they were derided as white elephants. Their critics claimed that they should be replaced by a greater number of small carriers, and particularly that more aircraft should be spread throughout the fleet, using catapults aboard battleships, cruisers and even destroyers, to provide greater flexibility. Time was to show how wrong these criticisms were, for the size of 'Lex' and 'Sara' permitted a designed aircraft complement of 78 (in practice as many as 80 or 90 could be carried), and this in turn made for a flexible air group. It was possible to vary the mix of bombers, scout planes and fighters in a series of 'Fleet Problems' or war-games held annually from 1928. Often the two sisters were matched against one another to test theories of carrier-employment. If they had a serious flaw in their design it was the inclusion of the four twin 8-inch gun turrets, for they encroached on hangar space in return for a very dubious contribution to the ships' defence against hostile cruisers. However, this only became obvious some years later, and when the design was conceived aircraft did not offer as certain a counter to enemy surface ships.

Everything about the two ships was on a colossal scale. Their turbo-electric machinery developed 180,000 shaft horsepower and drove them at over 33 knots. They carried a total of 6668 tons of oil, which enabled them to steam nearly 10,000 miles at 15 knots. But above all their appearance was majestic, with a massive funnel combining the uptakes from all 16 boilers. They retained much of the grace of the original battlecruiser design, as well as its massive freeboard. When the city of Tacoma ran short of hydro-electricity during a drought in December 1929 the *Lexington* was sent from Bremerton Navy Yard in Puget Sound to generate electricity for the city's 100,000 inhabitants. In a berth dredged in the harbour she lay for a month, coupled to the shore by power-lines, like a mighty oil-tanker, and supplied the incredible total of 4.25 million kilowatt hours. In fact she supplied rather more than was needed, and for a while Tacoma's electric clocks gained ten minutes, until the frequency was reduced.

Carrier tactics developed at a rapid pace. In Fleet Problem VIII in 1928 planes from the *Langley* raided Pearl Harbor, taking the garrison and the naval defenders by surprise. In Fleet Problem IX the following year the *Lexington* and *Saratoga* participated, with fascinating, if slightly confusing results. The *Saratoga*'s aircraft claimed a successful attack on the Panama Canal, but she had been judged 'sunk' by a battleship force previously and was subsequently 'sunk' by her sister; Navy land-based bombers then sank

Boeing F3B-1 fighters and
Martin T4M-1 torpedo-
bombers ranged on the
Saratoga's flight deck *circa*
1929–30. Unlike the British
the Americans produced
aircraft which matched the
potential of their carriers.

their own carrier, the *Lexington* instead of
the hostile *Saratoga*. If these war-games
sound childish, we must remember that their
most important dividend was the formulation
and exercise of procedures rather than win-
ning or losing. What was being evolved was
technique, on the flight deck, in the hangar,
in the air, and most important of all, on the
flag bridge. Only by playing such exuberant
games would the admirals and captains learn
to handle carriers with the same dexterity
and confidence enjoyed by battleship-
commanders.

The Japanese were busy with their own
plans as well. Under the Washington Treaty
they were permitted to convert the hulls of
two 41,200-ton battlecruisers, the *Akagi* and
Amagi. However on 1 September 1923 the
Amagi's newly launched hull was badly
damaged in the great Tokyo Earthquake,
and the slightly smaller battleship *Kaga* was
substituted.

The *Akagi* and *Kaga* struck the same bizarre note as other classes of Japanese ships,
with flying-off decks forward on three levels,
one forward, part of the flight deck and the
others serving the two hangars. They carried the idea of cruiser-sized guns to an even
greater length, with ten 8-inch guns each.
Their most grotesque features were the funnels; in the *Akagi* the forward funnel curved
downwards and a second one stuck out horizontally, while in *Kaga* it was carried right
aft horizontally. Their aircraft capacity was
rather less than the American carriers, 72

aircraft, a penalty paid for the heavier armament. They were only partially successful,
and were rebuilt along more conventional
lines within ten years, but nevertheless they
served the same purpose as the *Lexington*
and *Saratoga* in developing the concept of
fast carrier striking forces, working as a
major component of the Fleet rather than a
mere ancillary. The Japanese also had their
problems with diehards who refused to
countenance the importance of aircraft, but
the United States' Navy was the obvious rival,
and so its progress had to be matched.

The other runners in the race lagged far
behind. The British lacked very large hulls
for conversion, and had only two half-sisters
of the *Furious*, the light battlecruisers *Courageous* and *Glorious* available. They were
thin-skinned and fast, so did not suffer the
same penalties of weight as the conversions
from battleships and battlecruisers. The
Furious, herself recommissioned in Septem-

Top: Two of the *Kaga's* six twin 4.7-inch AA guns.

Above left: The *Akagi* under way.

Above left: The *Kaga* was similar but vented her funnel-smoke aft.

Below: The British *Glorious* did not complete her conversion until 1930.

ber 1925, was completely rebuilt with a flush flight deck and smoke ducts running right aft, as in the *Argus*. When the *Courageous* rejoined the Fleet in 1928 she had an island flight deck, following the favourable comments on *Eagle* and *Hermes*, and her sister *Glorious* was ready two years later.

The three carriers formed an homogeneous group, and demonstrated the advantages claimed for having a bigger number of small carriers, as against giants like the *Lexington* or *Akagi*. But for obvious reasons they could carry nothing like the same number of aircraft. Between them the three new British carriers normally operated 108 aircraft, whereas *Lexington* and *Saratoga* could operate 160–180, and on at least one occasion packed in 240 between them. *Kaga* and *Akagi* could also outmatch them, with over 140 aircraft. Another problem with smaller carriers was the amount of fuel they can carry, both for themselves and for their aircraft. The *Lexington* and *Saratoga* carried some 132,000 gallons of high-octane aviation gasoline (avgas) in specially protected tanks deep within the hull, as well as lubricating oil. *Furious* could only store 24,000 gallons of avgas and 4000 gallons of lube oil, while on a similar tonnage the *Eagle* could only manage the miserable total of 8000 gallons.

The only other nation to put an aircraft carrier into service was France. She too had battleship-hulls to spare, the five *Normandie* class laid down in 1914 but suspended during the war. The design was obsolescent by 1920, and plans were drawn up to convert the hull of the *Béarn* into a carrier. The Washington Treaty clinched the matter, and in April 1922 the decision was made to go ahead with the conversion. Co-operation between the British and French was rare, but in this instance the French seem to have been sufficiently desperate to ask the British for some technical assistance, and accordingly the details of the *Eagle*'s conversion were made available. The *Béarn* therefore reflected a number of British features, but she suffered from the same drawback, a speed of 21.5 knots, which was too slow for efficient flying. Aircraft were getting heavier year by year, and the speed of the wind over the deck was becoming more and more vital to aircraft when landing and taking off. It gave them more lift when taking off and provided better handling at low speed when coming in to land.

The *Béarn* had a starboard island, and was unique in having a special ventilating system to dilute hot funnel-gas with cold air, to reduce the turbulence over the flight deck. Another unique feature was the provision of huge hinged doors over the lift-wells in the flight deck; in all other carriers the lift-platform itself served as part of the deck when in the 'up' position. She was provided with three such lifts, serving two hangar decks, the upper one for storing 40 aircraft and the lower one for workshops and spares.

The French Navy operated the *Béarn* successfully from 1927 but lack of funds prevented any serious effort to improve the quality of aircraft. Another important brake on progress was the fact that France's only likely naval rival, Italy, had no carriers, and so the incentive was lacking to keep abreast of developments. The Italians had tried to form a naval air arm, but the influence of General Giulio Douhet, recalled in 1917 to head the Central Aeronautical Bureau, was paramount. In 1923 Mussolini took Italy down

the path of the RAF and decided to unify the Army and Navy air forces into a new independent air service. Mussolini could not see the need for carriers, when in his own words, Italy was a big unsinkable aircraft carrier, and in 1925 he 'encouraged' his admirals to endorse a decision not to build any carriers. It was to be bitterly regretted.

Several distinct features of design were now well established. Flight decks were planked, usually with teak, and the whole structure of the hangar was built on top of what a naval architect refers to as the main or 'strength' deck. This deck was usually armoured against bombs, unless the ship was a mercantile conversion, such as HMS *Argus*, its purpose being to protect the machinery and other vital parts of the ship from damage, rather than the aircraft. Anti-aircraft guns were disposed around the edge of the hull in some carriers, but in the *Lexington* and *Saratoga* they were sited at the edges of the flight deck to give them better arcs of fire. Guns in carriers caused two problems: first, the ammunition supply was tricky because the overhang prevented deep hoists from being positioned close to the guns, and second, cross-deck firing caused blast damage to the deck and to the aircraft. In the early days the problem of ammunition was disregarded as nobody could foresee the weight of air attack which would develop, but the positioning of the guns remained a constant headache.

The policy about stopping aircraft once they had landed was erratic, to say the least. Following their unsuccessful schemes tried in the *Furious* in 1917–18 the British had gone for a system of longitudinal wires, but this had been abandoned in 1926. The Americans had adopted a similar system for the *Lang-*

ley, *Lexington* and *Saratoga*, but abandoned it after 1929. The big carriers in particular had such long flight decks that it was felt there would be no need for arresting gear. It was left to the French to revive and improve a device first tried in the *Furious* in 1917, a series of transverse wires, one of which engaged a tail-hook on the aircraft. This device was adopted by the Japanese and the Americans, and then by the British in HMS *Eagle* in 1933, and soon became the standard deck-landing method. At the same time the crash-barrier was introduced, a transverse screen which would stop any aircraft which missed a wire, and prevent it from crashing into aircraft parked forward. This simple innovation enabled flying-off and landing to proceed simultaneously, and did much to speed up flight-deck operations.

The most frightening danger was fire, with thousands of gallons of avgas stored within the ship, giving off explosive vapour if allowed to leak. In the *Lexington* and *Saratoga* it

Top: An Aeromarine 39-B aircraft testing the longitudinal arresting device for the US Navy in 1921. The 'skis' are intended to stop the aircraft from pitching on its nose in an emergency landing on water.

Above: The final solution was athwartships arresting wires, seen here aboard the *Saratoga* in 1936. It is still in use.

was stored in two single and six double tanks having a total capacity of 21,790 cubic feet, and fuelling points were provided in the hangar and on the flight deck. The British were even more worried, and in the *Eagle* tried out a new scheme which later became standard. The avgas was stored in bulk tanks, clear of the main structure of the ship and surrounded by air-spaces.

As part of their fire precautions the British also developed the concept of the 'closed' hangar, in which the ventilation of the hangar was sealed off from the system provided for the rest of the ship. This enabled the hangar to be cleared of avgas fumes without the risk of dispersing them through the rest of the ship. The integrity of the closed hangar was preserved by air-locks in the bays through which personnel entered the hangar. The higher-octane fuel created problems too, for it was corrosive, and had to be stored in tanks made of special steel. The disadvantage of the closed hangar was that it encroached on aircraft stowage, and so when the US Navy came to build carriers to follow the *Lexington* and *Saratoga* there was considerable support for the idea of an 'open' hangar extending out to the side of the ship. The problem of ventilation would be coped with by roller shutters which could be opened to allow a through draught to assist the ventilation system. It should be noted, however, that the heart of the British method was the provision of a separate ventilation

system, and attention to the fuel-lines from the bulk tanks to the hangar and flight deck.

To control fires in the hangar steel fire-curtains were provided, in the hope that these would isolate the blaze. In 1929 the British introduced salt-water sprays in HMS *Eagle*, as the only way in which a hangar fire could be effectively subdued. Although salt water corroded the light alloy frames and the fabric wing-covering, fire was by far the greater hazard, and this marked the beginning of much better damage-control in carriers, and did away with the need to have firefighting parties in the hangar. It was the *Eagle* which introduced flight-deck fire precautions in 1933, when she was refitted with four sets of foam-generators capable of covering the whole flight deck with a carpet of foam.

Despite their great length the *Lexington* and *Saratoga* were fitted with a huge flywheel-driven catapult, 155 feet long. It was set in the forward part of the flight deck, flush with the upper surface, and could launch a five-ton aircraft at the somewhat ludicrous speed of 48 knots. Like the two catapults in the *Langley* they were seldom used, as the aircraft of the day were light enough to take off unaided, and they were removed in 1934 (*Langley*'s were taken out in 1928).

The US Navy was well aware of the need to build more carriers to exploit the knowledge gained from the three existing carriers, and in 1927 the General Board prepared plans for

Left: A Curtiss F6C-3 Hawk fighter takes off from the *Lexington* in April 1928. Note the photographer filming the take-off at the edge of the flight deck and the chocks lying alongside the 8-inch gun turret.

Below: Man, aircraft, and lives were expended in landing accidents as new techniques were learned. This Martin T4M-1 has come to grief on the flight deck of the *Saratoga*.

Right: The *Ranger* (CV.4) was
launched on 25 February
1933 at Newport News. She
was nearly two-thirds the
displacement of the
Lexington and *Saratoga* to
test the concept of small
carriers.

Far right (above): The *Ranger*
shows off her clean lines in
dry dock.

Far right (centre): The
Japanese *Ryujo* on speed
trials in 1934.

Far right (bottom): The *Ryujo*
in 1939 after modification to
rectify the poor seakeeping
and lack of stability. The
forecastle has been raised.

a five-year programme. As a reaction to the
size of *CV.2* and *CV.3* and to take advantage
of the tonnage available under the Washington Treaty, it was proposed to build 13,800-ton
carriers, laying down one a year from 1929
to 1933. This would use up the total of 135,000
tons and provide a total of nine carriers.

The public reaction was unfavourable, for
the political mood in America was isolationist
and reactionary. Then came the Depression
and with it retrenchment on defence spend-
ing. In all probability, had the need for work
in shipyards not been evident, the eventual
approval of even one carrier would have
been withheld. In September 1931 the keel
was laid of *CV.4*, eventually to be named
Ranger.

The new carrier was not an outstanding
success, and her shortcomings were only too
evident. The restrictions on displacement
meant that she could only make 29 knots,
although she was given a good air group for
her size, 75 planes. The original plan for a
flush deck had been modified, and instead
she had a small island, with six folding
funnels further aft, as in the Japanese *Hosho*.

These funnels were interconnected to allow
funnel-smoke to be directed to the lee side,
so as to cause minimum disruption of flying
operations, and as in the *Hosho* they could be
hinged downwards.

With the benefit of hindsight we can see
that the General Board was lucky not to have
been allowed to proceed with its plans for
four more *Rangers*. Before she was completed thinking on the subject had changed,
and the new minimum size was raised to
20,000 tons.

As usual the Japanese tried to go one
better, and took advantage of the clause in
the Washington Treaty which exempted carriers below 10,000 tons. In November 1929
they laid the keel of the *Ryujo*, designed to
displace only 8000 tons and carry 48 aircraft.
Despite her restricted dimensions the designers crammed in a two-storeyed hangar
and a dozen 5-inch anti-aircraft guns, while
providing the same speed as the USS *Ranger*.
If the *Ranger* was not a total success the *Ryujo*
was nearly a disaster. Too much had been
attempted on the displacement, and she was
nowhere near her intended standard dis-

placement of 8000 tons. Shortly after she was commissioned there were two disasters at sea in which a new torpedo boat capsized at sea and the Combined Fleet suffered severe damage in a typhoon. The new carrier's stability figures came under severe scrutiny, and as a result four guns were removed, with as much other weight as possible, but it was also necessary to add a deck-level to the forecastle to improve seakeeping, and this cancelled out most of the weight-reductions. Finally some 2500 tons of ballast had to be added to rectify stability, a load which impaired her speed considerably.

Considering that this activity was taking place against the backdrop of the world-wide depression and within the restrictions of the Washington Treaty, it is surprising how much progress was made between 1922 and 1933. These second-generation carriers all had their faults but in one respect or another they tested theories and converted them into practice. All of them survived to serve in World War II, some with great distinction. Without them the next generation would not have been nearly as effective.

6 THE THIRD GENERATION

Shipbuilding was one of the major industries to receive government support as the long haul out of the Depression started, and when the US Navy proposed the construction of two 20,000-ton carriers in 1932 approval was given. They would be part of the 1934 building programme, but would be funded by the Public Works Administration.

The Bureau of Aeronautics was particularly anxious that there should be no repetition of the mistakes made in the *Ranger*. The minimum displacement should be 20,000 tons, speed should be increased to 32.5 knots, protection against bombs and torpedoes should be increased, and above all the aircraft-handling facilities should be improved. Under this last heading were included such matters as having a hangar deck devoted entirely to aircraft storage, more and faster lifts, better bomb-handling and even the possible use of two flying-off decks.

Below: The USS *Yorktown* (CV.5) just two months before commissioning at Newport News.

Above: Stern of the *Yorktown* three months later.

49

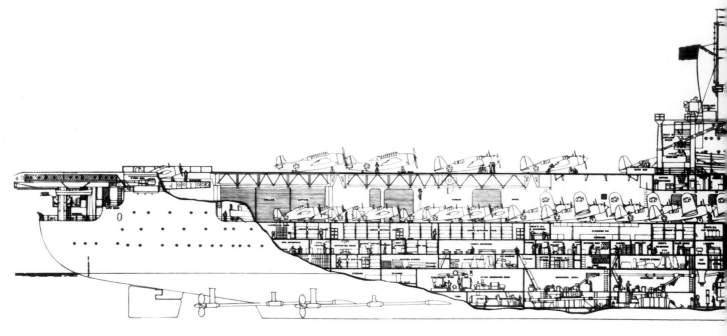

Above: Longitudinal section
of the *Yorktown* Class,
showing the single hangar
and the roller-shutters which
closed off the hangar
openings.

Not all these recommendations were incorporated into the *Yorktown* (*CV.5*) and *Enterprise* (*CV.6*), but they were still a remarkable improvement over all carriers of similar tonnage. They reverted to the starboard island configuration, carried 80 aircraft, had three centreline lifts and could steam at 33 knots. There was provision for three catapults, two flush-mounted on the flight deck, and one mounted athwartships in the hangar. In theory this would allow more aircraft to be launched quickly, but in practice it hampered movement of aircraft in the hangar and was never used in wartime.

The hangar was of the open type, and the flight deck was covered with 6-inch teak planks laid athwartships. To assist in securing aircraft metal tie-down strips were provided at 4-foot intervals, running the full width of the deck. It was still believed that aircraft could be landed at either end of the flight deck; and so two sets of arrester wires were provided. As with the hangar catapult this feature owed more to theory than practice, and it was soon dropped.

The Japanese had reached much the same conclusions as the Americans, and when they laid down the *Soryu* in November 1934 she

Below: The capacious hangar
of the *Lexington*, with aircraft
of VB-2 in the foreground.

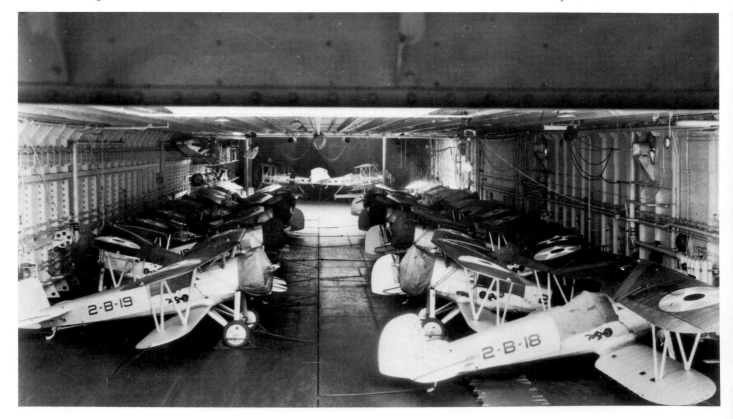

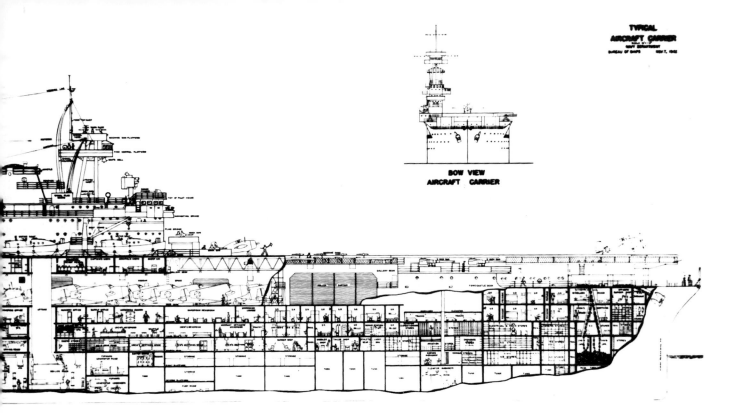

BOW VIEW
AIRCRAFT CARRIER

displaced 18,800 tons and carried 53 aircraft, but had slightly higher speed than the *York-town*, 34 knots. The restrictions of the Washington Treaty had been extended by the London Naval Treaty of 1930, but the Japanese worked on the theory that it would not be cheating if their next carrier was completed after the expiry date of the Treaty. As Japan had no intention of signing any more treaties, the sister of the *Soryu*, called *Hiryu* was given a number of improvements and worked out heavier.

The disastrous experience of the Combined Fleet in a typhoon in September 1935 also had its bearing on *Hiryu*'s design, but her most unusual feature was recommended by the Navy's Aeronautical Bureau. Observing that the ideal position for a carrier's island superstructure was as close to the midpoint of the hull as possible, the Bureau recommended that *Hiryu*'s island should be as near amidships as possible. When the designers reported that this was also the best position for the funnels someone had the brilliant idea of putting the island on the port side.

Human nature being what it is, a second reason was now thought up to justify the idea,

Below: The new *Enterprise* (CV.6) commissioned in May 1938. Note that the deck recognition letters EN are painted at both ends to permit landing on from the bow in an emergency.

Top: The *Shokaku* at Yokosuka on 23 August 1941, only three-and-a-half months before Pearl Harbor.

Above: The *Zuikaku* and her sister *Shokaku* were completed in 1941 and fought in all the carrier battles except Midway.

Why not run the two near-sisters in line abreast when together, so that aircraft landing on the left-hand ship (*Soryu*) would adopt a left-hand circle when picking up their formation or returning to land; the right-hand ship (*Hiryu*) would have her aircraft adopt a right-hand circle, and the two aircraft flying patterns would not conflict. It may have been logical but experience in British carriers had already shown that pilots for some reason tended to veer left if anything went wrong during a landing approach, and the portside island caused twice as many landing accidents as the starboard one (on *Soryu*).

The idea was taken a step further when *Akagi* and *Kaga* were taken in hand for rebuilding. They lost their unique triple flying-off decks forward and were rebuilt on more conventional lines in the late 1930s. The *Akagi* was fitted with a port-side island to allow her to operate with *Soryu*, while her sister would operate with the *Hiryu*, permitting all four carriers to operate in a compact formation. In fact the *Akagi* finished her modernization before the *Hiryu* was completed, and landing trials showed that the system would be unworkable, but it was too late to do anything about it.

Fortunately the problem showed itself in time to be cured in the next pair of Japanese

carriers, to be ordered under the 1937 Fleet Replenishment Programme. There was no intention of building to any treaty limits, and so the designers were given permission for the first time to build to whatever size was dictated by the specifications.

The *Shokaku* and *Zuikaku* displaced 25,675 tons standard, embarked a total of 72 aircraft and could steam at 34 knots. No catapults were fitted as the ultra-light Japanese aircraft could still take off unassisted, but 11 arrester wires were provided, three forward of the crash barrier and eight aft. There were two hangars, served by three lifts; the foremost was on the centreline and the other two were staggered to port and starboard. Although originally intended to have funnels on both sides of the ship the problems with the *Hiryu* caused a review of the design, and two starboard curved uptakes were provided on the starboard side, with a small island to starboard.

The *Shokaku* and *Zuikaku* were in most respects the best carriers built by the Japanese, and they were the basis for several other designs. There was no lack of freeboard, as in the *Ryujo*, and so they were dry forward. They were unusual in having a large Type O hydrophone or passive sonar under the bow, enabling them to detect

Left: The *Soryu* off Tokyo Bay in January 1938 on her trials. The faults of the *Ryujo* were rectified and she became the basis for future designs.

Left: The *Hiryu* off Tateyama in April 1939. She was basically a sister of the *Soryu* but slightly enlarged to take advantage of Japan's decision not to renew the London Naval Treaty limits on tonnage.

hostile submarines, although this was only usable when going dead slow. The defensive armament was heavy, eight pairs of a new pattern of 12.7-cm (5-inch)/40 calibre anti aircraft gun called the Type 89, and 12 triple 25-mm close-range AA guns.

The Japanese had evolved a different system of flight-deck operations to the Americans and British. An Air Operations Officer and two junior officers were positioned on the bridge. On the flight deck was another officer responsible for movement of aircraft, such as taxiing. The take-off procedure was simple; the Air Operations Officer or his assistant held up a white flag, the signal to pilots to take off at 20-second intervals. No further instructions followed, and when the Air Operations Officer wished to end flying he lowered the flag. When the aircraft had to be recovered they flew downwind, about 400 to 600 yards away from the carrier. When the flight deck was ready to receive them the Flight Deck Officer, known as the Seibiin, signalled by flashing lamp to the aircraft. The pilot nearest the island then turned to arrive at a point about 800 yards astern of the carrier, at an altitude of about 200 metres. There was no system of signals from the flight deck to help the pilot judge his approach, and so he had to make his own judgement. To help

him he had a steam jet at the forward end of the flight deck, which indicated the direction of the wind across the deck, a row of lights down the centre of the deck and lights at the deck-edge to indicate his height.

The Americans and the British had already adopted the idea of the Landing Signals Officer (LSO), Deck Landing Control Officer or 'Batsman'. This was an experienced officer who held two 'paddles' like table tennis bats and signalled to the pilot to correct his altitude, alignment and attitude as he approached the arrester wires with the 'sting' hook extended. If the aircraft was not likely to make a touchdown the batsman could give him a 'wave-off' in time, allowing the pilot to swing clear and make another circuit. This reduced the risks considerably, although there was still a chance that the hook would not engage a wire, in which case the aircraft would plunge into the barrier.

The United States now took what would appear to be a retrograde step. Despite the recommendations of the Bureau of Aeronautics the General Board sanctioned the building of a 14,500-ton carrier, similar in size to the unsuccessful *Ranger*. The reason was that under the London Naval Treaty of 1930, which in effect extended the provisions of the Washington Treaty, the United States could only build a further 14,500 tons, bringing the total up to 135,000 tons.

The new ship would, however, avoid some of the *Ranger*'s faults. She was virtually a diminutive of the *Yorktown* design, sacrificing speed to enable her to carry the same number of aircraft. She was intended to have three centreline lifts in the flight deck, but while building the forward one was replaced by a new type, a deck-edge lift on the port side opposite the island. It was a T-shaped platform just big enough to accommodate an aircraft, with the undercarriage placed just below the cross-bar and the tailwheel at the bottom of the upright. The platform folded vertically when not in use, and its purpose was to speed up the transfer of aircraft from the hangar to the flight deck. The athwartships catapult seen in the *Enterprise* and *Yorktown* was also provided, proof that the Bureau of Aeronautics was looking at ways of improving the handling of aircraft. Although these experimental solutions were not all successful the basic premise that carrier aircraft are only effective when they become airborne was grasped more firmly by the US Navy than by anyone else.

The contract to build *CV.7* was awarded to the Bethlehem Steel Company in 1935 and she was launched on 4 April 1939 as the USS *Wasp*. Time was running out for the United States, and the *Wasp* was commissioned only a year later. The number of modern carriers now met peacetime requirements and so in 1937 the veteran *Langley* was downgraded to a seaplane carrier, with nearly half her flight deck removed. She had served the Navy well but her slow speed made her virtually useless for work with the Fleet.

The British were also becoming uneasily aware that they would have to rearm as soon as possible to match the rise of Germany. The Fleet Air Arm had gone from bad to worse under Air Ministry management. The worst shortfall was in aircraft; the RAF controlled aircraft design and procurement and would not sanction the procurement of a dive-bomber as it believed implicitly in high-level bombing. Nor was the Navy encouraged to develop aircraft of similar performance to land-based types. The 'defection' of so many air-minded officers to the RAF in 1918 was now making itself felt, and there was a predominance of senior officers who still thought in terms of subordinating air-power to the needs of the battle fleet.

The Fleet Air Arm was partly to blame for the poor performance of aircraft, for its overriding requirements were for an observer to assist primarily in the complex job of navigating, and ruggedness to stand up to the stresses of deck-landings. But these were also requirements laid down for US Navy

aircraft, and there is no question that the specifications written under RAF supervision placed the aircraft designers under no great pressure to reconcile them with high performance. It is hard to believe that an aircraft industry which produced the Hurricane and Spitfire could not have produced something comparable for use at sea.

The story of the Swordfish illustrates this sorry state of affairs. In 1933 the Fairey Aviation Company produced a design for a biplane Torpedo-Spotter-Reconnaissance designated TSR.1, as an alternative to the same company's S.9/30, designed to an Air Ministry specification. It had a maximum speed of 138 mph with a torpedo on board and its defensive armament comprised a single .303-inch machine gun fired by the observer and one firing forward through the propeller. By comparison, the US Navy a year earlier had ordered a prototype from Curtiss called the XF12C-1, a two-seat fighter intended to be capable of dive-bombing. Its parasol wing failed to be strong enough for dive-bombing, and like the prototype Swordfish it crashed during testing. In 1935 it reappeared as a biplane, now designated

XSBC-2, capable of scouting and bombing, with a top speed of 220 mph. Even the Douglas T2D twin-engined torpedo-bomber, which flew experimentally off the USS *Langley* in 1927 had a top speed nearly as great as that specified for the Swordfish six years later. More to the point, the Japanese Aichi D1A biplane dive-bomber, also ordered in 1933 for the Navy, had a top speed of 174 mph.

The problem of designing a suitable carrier-borne fighter was not simple. It had to comprise several characteristics in order to get a balance in one airframe; it needed sufficient speed to intercept and destroy hostile aircraft but also had to have sufficient range to escort its own dive- and torpedo-bombers. Add to these conflicting requirements the need for ruggedness and a limitation on size, and the aircraft designer had a difficult task. For those reasons naval fighters were always heavier than their land counterparts, but they were also considerably more flexible aircraft in every way. Gradually technology came to the aid of the designer. Folding the wings not only permitted the aircraft to fit onto the lift, it allowed greater wing area for better lift, which compensated for the high weight. As early as 1923 the little Fairey Flycatcher had landing flaps to improve its low-speed flying on take-off and landing, and these became essential for carrier aircraft.

It was against this confused background of good ideas but poor performance that the British returned to the aircraft carrier business. The first fruit of that effort, HMS *Ark Royal* was not only a remarkable technical achievement but was destined to become one of the most famous carriers of World War II. In 1930 when the British and the Americans locked the shackles of the Washington Treaty firmly around their wrists for another five years the Admiralty laid down a new policy for the Fleet Air Arm. Five large carriers, each with a capacity of 72 aircraft, were to be built to replace the *Argus, Furious, Eagle, Courageous* and *Glorious* by 1955. As a part of a general British desire for retrenchment they were campaigning for a limit of 22,000 tons on carriers, rather than the new 27,000-ton limit imposed by the London Naval Treaty and favoured by the Americans. When the first of the new British car-

55

This stern view of the *Ark Royal* shows how the designers gave her maximum flight deck length but minimum hull length, with a massive overhang. The small island and the funnel are streamlined to produce a smooth airflow.

rier programme was authorized in 1934, she was therefore deliberately kept to the lower figure.

Sad to relate the need for the new ship was bitterly disputed by the Royal Air Force, which feared that any increase in naval air strength would tempt the politicians to compensate by cutting back on numbers of land-based aircraft. A broader-minded approach might have been to make common cause with the Navy against the politicians to put the case for both services, but the RAF always suffered from the inferiority complex of being the 'Junior Service', and devoted a great deal of its energy to nurturing the myth of the indivisibility of airpower, purely to ensure its survival as an independent force. Needless to say that the doctrine of naval airpower clashed violently with the de-

mands of bombing. Although there were many sweeping claims about the ability of aircraft to sink ships very little was done to develop dive-bombing, very little about sinking submarines, and nothing about torpedo-bombing.

The financial situation was also parlous, and it was not until 1935 that the new aircraft carrier could be ordered. The name *Mercury* had been tentatively earmarked in 1930, but it was finally decided that she should bear the name of the first seaplane carrier, which had done so well in the Dardanelles. Accordingly, the day before she was launched the old *Ark Royal* was renamed *Pegasus*, and the new name was bestowed on 13 April 1937. At a time when Japan and the United States had laid down six ships designed as carriers the British

were only starting their second.

Uppermost in the minds of the designers was the need to provide the maximum area of flight deck on the limited displacement, and so the ship was given a remarkable degree of overhang forward and aft, 80 feet more than the waterline length. The machinery was designed for the abrupt accelerations and decelerations which carriers need to make to adjust the speed of the wind over the deck; this means in effect that the *Ark Royal*'s machinery needed power to drive a battleship but characteristics more appropriate to a destroyer. Tank tests showed that a shorter and beamier hull would be appropriate, and so instead of the length: beam ratio of 9 or 10:1 favoured in the *Yorktown* and *Hiryu*, the *Ark Royal* had a ratio of 7.6:1. This gave a good turn of speed

without sacrifice of stability or seakeeping.

The machinery was an unusual 3-shaft layout, last seen in German battleships, and the results gave a top speed of 31.75 knots, not far behind the *Hiryu* but on 65 per cent of the power. The system of stowing fuel was the same as in previous British carriers, with 380 tons in cylindrical tanks separated from the main structure to prevent rupture of tanks from the whipping of the hull. However, for the first time the salt water displacement system was replaced by compressed air to avoid the risk of salt water contaminating the fuel.

As in American and Japanese carriers the flight deck and hangars were left unprotected, but the magazines, avgas stowage and machinery were protected by a 3.5-inch armoured deck at the level of the lower

hangar deck. Protection against shellfire and torpedoes was provided by 4.5-inch side armour, a shallow bulge and a 1.5-inch internal anti-torpedo-bulkhead. The ship was calculated to be safe against 6-inch shellfire from cruisers at ranges of 7000 yards or more, 500-lb bombs dropped below 7000 ft, and a hit from a 750-lb torpedo warhead.

Two hangars were provided, with good overhead clearance and the usual excellent fire-precautions, including steel-slat fire curtains, salt water sprays and air locks to prevent vapour from seeping out of the hangars into the rest of the ship, in short, all the advantages of the closed hangar system. But a penalty had to be paid, and by the time the design was finalized the capacity had dropped from 72 to 60 aircraft.

Unlike the American and British carriers the *Ark Royal* had a steel flight deck, with a typically British 'round-down' or downward curve at the after end, and a similar downward slope at the forward end. Ever since the wind tunnel tests carried out on the *Eagle*'s superstructure in 1918 the British had paid great attention to aerodynamic factors in the design of carriers, and in *Ark Royal* even the island superstructure was aerofoil shaped to reduce turbulence. This was very necessary with the somewhat fragile British aircraft then in vogue, whereas US carriers in particular paid no attention at all to such problems, and had squared off flight decks and rectangular islands. One British constructor was later to comment that US carriers

seemed designed to *create* turbulence rather than dissipate it, but the simple reason for this discrepancy was that American aircraft were built to withstand the buffeting, and did not need quite the same delicate treatment.

In one respect the *Ark Royal* harked back to the *Lexington* and *Saratoga*, in that her flight deck formed the 'strength' deck or upper girder of the hull. This was made possible by doing without the big openings in the hull sides which were essential to the open hangar, but it led to the provision of rather small lifts, as it was undesirable to pierce the main girder with large centreline openings. Two lifts, forward and aft and to starboard, were only 22 feet wide, while the third, to port opposite the island, was 25 feet wide. The long (45 feet), narrow type of lift made it possible to move aircraft around the open spaces when the lifts were being used, but here British ingenuity overreached itself. Each lift had an upper and lower platform, so that the 'travel' of the upper platform was from the upper hangar to the flight deck, and that of the lower platform could only be from the lower to the upper hangar. The reasoning behind this bizarre arrangement was that the lower hangar would be used to repair and maintain aircraft, while the upper hangar would be used to accommodate the aircraft ready for flight. Which was all very sound, but it ignored the fact that to get a damaged aircraft down to the workshops it would be necessary to send it down to the

vided with a comprehensive system. This included a system to outline the edge of the flight deck as well as systems to indicate the angle of descent and depth perception. A further refinement was a system of recognition lights along the ship's sides, by which it was hoped that returning pilots would be able to identify their own carrier, but it proved quite useless.

The amount of effort put into the design and building of the *Ark Royal* reflected a profound change within the Royal Navy. Growing disillusionment with RAF control had led to the resurgence of air-mindedness and a new generation of admirals led a prolonged fight to regain control of naval flying. What made the eventual surrender of the RAF possible was paradoxically the airmen's obsession with strategic bombing; naval aviation was becoming a tiresome distraction from the exciting task of building up a force of bombers. When in the summer of 1937 the government announced that responsibility for naval aviation was to be handed back to the RN over a period of two years, there was almost a sigh of relief, for it meant that the RAF could take back a large number of its pilots and maintenance men.

The worsening situation in Europe meant that the original leisurely programme of laying down a carrier every five years had to be thrown out. Only two years after the approval of the *Ark Royal* the 1936 Naval Estimates contained provision for two 23,000-ton carriers. Common sense would have dic-

upper hangar, move it off the lift, raise the lift again, put the aircraft on the lower platform and then lower it another deck. Which all took time and slowed down movement of aircraft. The narrowness of the lifts also meant that any aircraft had to be folded before they could be 'struck down' to the hangar.

The *Ark Royal* was fitted with two hydro-pneumatic catapults at the forward end of the flight deck, but they differed from the type in the *Yorktown* Class in being 'accelerators', which used a trolley to raise the aircraft to its flying attitude and then pushed it forward at a speed of up to 66 knots on its own wheels. In contrast the US pattern of catapult launched aircraft in the tail-down position, but the net result was the same. Eight arrester wires were provided, as well as a safety barrier, the first installed in a British carrier.

The British had first tried a night landing on *Furious* in May 1926, and *Ark Royal* was pro-

The French seaplane carrier
Commandant Teste,
launched in 1929, could
launch her 26 floatplanes
from four catapults. These
were positioned amidships,
with the hangar doors on the
quarterdeck.

tated an order for two slightly enlarged *Ark Royal* types, for the design of carriers is complex and time-consuming, but instead the new carriers were to be a new type, with armoured hangars and flight decks.

The decision was made by Rear-Admiral Reginald Henderson, Third Sea Lord and Controller of the Navy. Henderson had once commanded the *Furious* and had also commanded the first British squadron of aircraft carriers in 1931, and he was only too well aware of the appalling lack of modern naval aircraft. Since 1933 the German Navy had been re-created and was growing fast; it was also likely to be joined by the Italian Navy. The French had only one carrier, it was certain that British ships would be fighting within range of shore-based aircraft in the North

Sea and Mediterranean, and there was as yet no British naval fighter capable of taking on high-performance land fighters. It also reflected the RAF's obsession with the pre-eminence of the bomber.

The solution was to provide as much protection for the aircraft as possible. This meant in practice trying to keep out 1000-lb bombs by building an armoured box with 4.5-inch sides and a 3-inch roof. It was envisaged that in the face of a heavy bomb attack the air group would land on deck, be struck down into the hangars and then leave the defence of the ship to the exceptionally heavy battery of 16 4.5-inch AA guns and six 8-barrelled pompoms.

The technical problems of building an armoured hangar on virtually the same dis-

60

placement as the *Ark Royal* were great. Whereas the *Ark Royal* had been given a long and spacious flight deck and two hangars the new ships would have 60 feet less on the flight deck and have only one hangar. This in turn meant only 36 aircraft, divided in a ratio of 5:1 between torpedo-bombers and fighters. This was not as serious a drawback as might be imagined for the Royal Navy did not yet possess sufficient aircraft or pilots to provide bigger air groups, and later revised ideas on aircraft handling would lead to an increased aircraft capacity. To improve the air defence the 4.5-inch AA guns were sited flush with the edge of the flight deck in twin mountings at the four corners, providing the heaviest battery of all pre-war carriers.

Despite the complexities of the design

Henderson was able to push it through in just three months and the two ships, *Illustrious* and *Victorious* were laid down early in 1937 and launched in 1939. Two more ships of this type, *Formidable* and *Indomitable* were ordered under the 1937 Estimates, the former being launched ahead of *Victorious* and the latter in the spring of 1940. There was strong criticism of the small aircraft capacity and so the design of the *Indomitable* was modified during construction to incorporate an additional half-hangar below the main one. This was achieved by thinning the side armour of the hangar box and reducing the clearance in the hangars from 16 feet to 14 feet. At the same time plans to build a fifth and sixth ship of the class under the 1938 and 1939 Estimates were shelved.

Although all reference books still refer to the third group of the *Illustrious* Class (*Indomitable* and *Formidable* forming the second group), the design for the *Implacable* and her sister *Indefatigable* was completely new. For one thing the British had invoked an escape or 'escalator' clause in the naval treaties to allow them to increase displacement to 27,000 tons. This allowed an armoured deck version of the *Ark Royal*, with two full-length hangars, the same heavy armament as *Illustrious* and a capacity of 72 aircraft. This should have combined the best of both worlds but in fact the *Implacable* Class were not as successful as the *Illustrious* Class. For one thing they were not ready when they were needed as they suffered from wartime delays and diversion of equipment to more urgent ships. For another the rapid preparation of the design had failed to allow sufficient space for the additional crew needed to man the larger machinery and boilers, and to work on the extra aircraft. In the end the forward half of the lower hangar had to be used for accommodation, leaving them no better off than the *Indomitable* despite all the work done on their redesign. Considering the tremendous achievements of the *Ark Royal* in the same European and Mediterranean waters that were thought to be so dangerous for carriers it is a great pity that the British did not save their scarce resources by building six more improved editions of the *Ark Royal*. Certainly more of them would have been ready sooner.

The French also tried to get back into the carrier game, but they cut things finer than the British, which ultimately proved too late. In 1935 the French Navy looked at proposals to convert the fast but flimsy heavy cruisers *Duquesne* and *Tourville* to carriers. Mercifully the plans were turned down as impractical, for the three different schemes considered would have got only 12 to 14 aircraft

to sea. This would have turned them from indifferent cruisers into useless carriers, and it was decided to build proper carriers instead. Under the 1938 Programme two carriers were ordered, to be named *Joffre* and *Painlevé*.

As the first French carriers to be built from the keel up they were unusual, to say the least. On a displacement of 18,000 tons there were to be two hangars, a heavy battery of four twin 5.1-inch AA guns, but only 40 aircraft. The 656-foot flight deck was offset to port to counterbalance the very big island, which resembled the superstructure of a cruiser. On the dimensions there could be no heavy armouring, although deck protection was given to the magazines and a 4-inch belt protected the machinery. The *Joffre* was laid down in November 1938, and was only 28

per cent complete when Germany invaded France. Her sister had not been laid down, and all materiel was destroyed apart from the *Joffre*'s main machinery, which was completed in 1946 for an underground power station at Brest Arsenal.

In 1935 the Germans had authorized an aircraft carrier, launched on 8 December 1938 as the *Graf Zeppelin*. A second ship was authorized the following year but never progressed very far. If the Royal Navy had problems with the RAF they paled into insignificance when compared with the rivalry between the *Kriegsmarine* and the *Luftwaffe*. The reserved Admiral Raeder was no match for the bombastic Reichsmarschall Göring when it came to court politics, and so there were endless difficulties in deciding what aircraft would fly from the two carriers. To add to this the German constructors had no experience of designing a carrier, and so the 23,000-ton design was a hotch-potch of other navies' ideas, some old, some new, some good and some bad. Light splinterproof armour was provided on the flight deck as well as heavier armour on the hangar deck, and a 4-inch waterline belt.

Below: The German carrier *Graf Zeppelin* slides down the ways on 8 December 1938, amid all the panoply of Nazi banners and salutes. Even if she had been completed squabbles between the Luftwaffe and the *Kriegsmarine* over her aircraft would have made her a white elephant.

The *Enterprise* (CV.6) painted in her wartime dark grey colour-scheme, some time in 1942.

The armament was heavy, six twin 10.5-cm (4.1-inch) AA mountings forward and aft of the island, backed up by sixteen single 15-cm (5.9-inch) low-angle guns in casemates low down, as a defence against surface attack. On her displacement she was grossly overpowered, with 200,000 shaft horsepower for 33.75 knots, but only carried 40 aircraft.

The United States was still officially isolationist in its attitude to the growth of Axis military power, but in May 1938 Congress passed the Naval Expansion Act. Under this legislation 40,000 tons of new carrier construction was authorized, for the 1930 naval treaty had now expired. The United States

was permitted to build carriers of 27,000 tons, but was still limited to a total tonnage of 175,000 tons. Unlike the British Admiralty, the General Board decided to save time by ordering a repeat of the *Yorktown* Class, and to continue design work on a new class. The ship was the *Hornet* (CV.8), authorized just five days after the commissioning of the *Enterprise* and laid down in September 1939.

The decision to save time with *CV.8* was a wise one, not only because it produced another fast carrier in time for the war against Japan but because it gave BuC&R time to prepare a new design which was to raise carriers to a peak of perfection never reached again. In June 1939 the Bureau pro-

would constitute a major offensive weapon in their own right. It must also be remembered that the British and American admirals of the 1930s were trying to find cost-effective solutions on severely limited budgets. They had to plan for war but without the political support of a nation prepared to spend money on defending itself.

The US Navy eventually decided on the big carrier. This decision influenced the outcome of history as much as any made in that decade. The prime requirement of the General Board was to improve aircraft capacity, with additional requirements for more speed and protection. This resulted in a rapid escalation from the 20,400-ton *CV.9A* design to the 25–26,000-ton *CV.9E* and *CV.9F*.

Comparison between *Yorktown* (CV.5) and *CV.9F*

	CV.5	CV.9F
Standard Displacement (tons):	19,800	26,000
Length (wl):	761 feet	820 feet
Beam:	83 feet	91 feet
Draught:	21 feet 9 inches	26 feet 6 inches
Power (SHP):	120,000	150,000
Speed (knots):	33	33
Aviation Fuel (gals):	178,000	220,000
Aircraft:	81	90

As the British were finding, increasing the size of the air group brought in its train a whole host of new problems. A mere 10 per cent increase in the number of aircraft called for 10 per cent more deck area. Bigger and heavier aircraft would need more fuel, and the increased fuel stowage would automatically require more armour to protect it, even if new enemy weapons did not call for a heavier scale of armouring. Another consequence of bigger aircraft was the need for bigger lifts and more powerful catapults, as well as improved flight deck refuelling. In fact the designers soon realized that even to operate the same air group as the *Yorktown*, 80 aircraft, with the same efficiency would call for a bigger ship. And acting as a long-stop against any temptation to keep expanding the design was the United States' Navy's overriding need for its ships to be able to pass through the Panama Canal, which meant a limit of 108 feet on the maximum beam.

The final decision to be made in designing these new carriers concerned the theatre in which they were expected to fight. Fortunately this had simplified itself as the British were no longer regarded as a likely enemy in Washington. Design for the Pacific meant

duced a set of Ship's Characteristics for the new *CV.9*. These then resulted in a set of sketch-designs numbered *CV.9A* to *CV.9F* prepared between July 1939 and January 1940 by the various bureaux. The initial intention was to produce a 'warmed over' version of the *Hornet* at 20,400 tons, to keep inside the remaining 21,000 tons allowed by statute. Another proposal by Captain John C McCain of the *Ranger* was to build two 10,000-ton 'scout carriers'. The choice was the same one that had bedevilled carrier tactics and design for 20 years, whether to build a large number of less battleworthy carriers which relied on other ships for protection, or to go for big ships with big air groups which

quite different seakeeping characteristics from the Atlantic, and made the Panama Canal limitation even more important. But above all it meant long legs to cover the vast distances, with an endurance of 15,000 miles at an economical speed (about 15 knots). Carriers need maximum endurance, both for the ship and for her aircraft. A carrier has to do a lot of extra steaming, away from a fleet to a launching point, then back to the protection of the fleet at high speed. Launching an air strike requires steaming for as much as an hour into wind at high speed, and when recovering aircraft she often has to take a course directly opposite to that of her consorts, and then steam at high speed to catch up.

Something had to go to resolve all these conflicts, and eventually the requirement for 35 knots was dropped and the air group was left at 80 aircraft. A requirement to carry engines and knocked-down airframes equivalent to 50 per cent of the air group was reduced to 25 per cent. Again this was related to the Pacific theatre, for a carrier

would be operating a long distance away from home, and could not easily replace aircraft lost in battle.

The final design of *CV.9* worked out at 27,100 tons, but by the summer of 1940 Congress had thrown out the statutory limit, with the 11 Percent Fleet Expansion Bill and the Two-Ocean Navy Bill. The former authorized three 27,100-tonners and the latter reinforced it with an order for eight more. The ships which resulted from this programme were to be the weapon which would eventually destroy Japan, although they would not be ready for another two years or more. Their names were chosen from the roster of history: *Essex* (CV.9), *Bonhomme Richard* (CV.10), *Intrepid* (CV.11), *Kearsage* (CV.12), *Franklin* (CV.13), *Hancock* (CV.14), *Randolph* (CV.15), *Cabot* (CV.16), *Bunker Hill* (CV.17), *Oriskany* (CV.18), *Ticonderoga* (CV.19) and *Bennington* (CV.20). Half of them would be renamed before completion to commemorate losses in the war which was now only 18 months away.

Left: The starboard side of the island of the *Yorktown*, showing the gallery of 20mm Oerlikon AA guns added for close-range defence.

Above: A 'stand easy' on the flight deck of the USS *Enterprise*. It is late in the War, with large numbers of AA guns and radar antennae visible.

7 BAPTISM OF FIRE

Below: A flight of Fairey
Swordfish torpedo-bombers
over their parent carrier,
HMS *Ark Royal* in 1939.
Despite their slow speed
these 'Stringbags' achieved
remarkable successes and
were still in production late
in the War.

When the British ultimatum to Nazi Germany expired on 3 September 1939 the strategic situation remained very much what it had been at the beginning of the previous conflict. The Home Fleet was based in the Orkneys at the same base in Scapa Flow, guarding against a German attempt to break out into the Atlantic, while defence of the Mediterranean was largely left to the French Navy. The main difference was the existence of air power, and there were many who looked to German and Italian shore-based air power to wipe out the traditional British advantage of a superior fleet.

First events seemed to bear this out. In a mistaken attempt to take the offensive against the U-Boats the Admiralty formed 'hunting groups' of one aircraft carrier and four destroyers. This meant that the *Hermes, Courageous, Furious* and *Ark Royal* were released from working with the Fleet, and were sent to patrol in the Western Approaches and other

Below inset: This view of an American carrier's island superstructure shows how narrow it had to be to avoid encroaching on the flight deck.

likely areas in the hope that their aircraft could support convoys attacked by U-Boats. There were two snags in this line of reasoning: the British simply dared not risk their few carriers in submarine-infested waters, and the aircraft were very badly equipped to sink submarines, as they only had an ineffective anti-submarine bomb.

On 14 September the *Ark Royal* was operating west of the Hebrides when her lookouts spotted the tracks of torpedoes passing astern. Her destroyers counterattacked with depth-charges, and *U.39* was blown to the surface, but the carrier was extremely lucky. Three days later the *Courageous* paid the penalty when *U.29* scored three torpedo hits and sent her to the bottom with the loss of her captain and 518 of her crew. The remaining carriers were immediately withdrawn, and time was to prove that the big fleet carrier was not suited to such work. This sinking of a relatively modern carrier was a far greater loss than the much-publicized loss of the old battleship *Royal Oak* a month later.

The Admiralty had other problems, for two large surface raiders had slipped out into the Atlantic a week before war was declared. They were the 'pocket battleships' *Admiral Graf Spee* and *Deutschland*, and they threatened to wreak havoc on the trade routes. The *Deutschland* returned to Germany after sinking only two ships but the *Graf Spee* disappeared into the wastes of the South Atlantic. The Admiralty reacted vigorously, and in concert with the French formed eight hunting groups. Three of these had aircraft carriers:

Group I: operating around Ceylon, with the
  Eagle and two cruisers,
Group K: operating off Pernambuco, with the
Ark Royal and the battlecruiser *Renown*,
Group L: operating out of Brest, with the
  Béarn, the battlecruiser *Strasbourg* and
  three cruisers.

Other measures included sending the *Furious* and capital ships to Halifax to cover convoys from Canada, and sending the *Glorious* from the Mediterranean through the Suez Canal to the Indian Ocean. None of the carriers saw the *Graf Spee*, but the imagined arrival of the *Ark Royal* and *Renown* was one of the factors which influenced Hitler in his decision to scuttle the *Graf Spee* off Montevideo after the inconclusive Battle of the River Plate in December.

The German invasion of Norway in April 1940 marked a sharp change in the tempo of the war, and although it seemed a cheap victory at the time, the losses incurred by the German Navy were to prove irreparable. It also provided the aircrews of the Home Fleet carriers with invaluable experience. The first into battle was the *Furious*, which had landed her aircraft for intensive training. Pausing only to embark two Swordfish torpedo-bomber squadrons, she sailed from the Clyde on 9 April, two days after the invasion, and two days later her aircraft made their first attack, an unsuccessful attempt to torpedo a destroyer off Trondheim. Next day they attacked shipping and destroyers at Narvik and reconnoitred the fjord to gain information for the impending destroyer action.

The *Ark Royal* had been sent to the Mediterranean on 22 March to work up her aircrews after a short refit and to give them a chance to practise night-flying. She and the *Glorious*, home from hunting raiders in the Indian Ocean, were lying at Alexandria when orders came to return to the Home

Left: The first of the new generation of British carrier aircraft, the Skua dive-bomber was too slow. But in April 1940 Skuas sank the cruiser *Königsberg*, the first major warship to be sunk by aircraft in World War II.

Centre left: The old carrier *Furious* was modernised in 1939 and served successfully until 1944.

Centre right: Swordfish flying over the *Ark Royal* and the *Argus*, brought back to operational duty in 1939.

Fleet on 10 April. Both carriers set a course for Gibraltar at maximum speed, and from there to Scapa Flow. They left for Norway on 23 April, to relieve the *Furious*, whose ability to continue operations was limited by her lack of fighters. Incidentally when *Ark Royal* went to the Mediterranean in March she left 15 of her Skua fighter/dive-bombers behind in the Orkneys to provide additional defence against air attack, and on 10 April they had made their own contribution to the Norwegian Campaign by flying all the way to Bergen, just about their maximum range, and sinking the light cruiser *Königsberg* with three 500-lb bombs. It was the first occasion on which a major warship was sunk by aircraft alone.

The operations in Norway were trying, to say the least. With only the most primitive navigation aids the aircrews had to fly over mountains, dodge electric cables strung across fjords, fly in fog and snow squalls and then return to a flight deck covered in icy slush. In 14 days the *Furious'* aircraft flew a total of 23,870 miles, dropped 18 torpedoes and 15 tons of bombs. Both *Furious* and *Glor-*

ious were used to ferry additional RAF aircraft, Cladiators and Hurricanes, to the temporary RAF base at Bardufoss, while the *Ark Royal* was used to provide cover for other operations further North.

Above: RAF Hurricane fighter being taken up to the flight deck of HMS *Argus*.

Above: Even large carriers could 'take it green' over the flight deck, as with HMS *Illustrious* in the Atlantic. Note how the 4.5-inch guns are trained aft to avoid damage.

Above centre: HMS *Illustrious* returns to Malta on 21 August 1943 with her sister *Formidable* (foreground), two-and-a-half years after leaving with heavy battle damage.

The collapse of the Norwegian Campaign was inevitable, for already the Battle of France had been lost. On 7 June the *Glorious* was ordered to recover the surviving RAF Gladiators and Hurricanes from Bardufoss. Despite the fact that none of the aircraft was fitted with a tail-hook and none of the pilots had ever landed on a carrier, all landed safely. But next day the unlucky *Glorious* was intercepted by the battlecruisers *Scharnhorst* and *Gneisenau* West of Narvik. Despite the devotion of her two escorting destroyers, which laid smokescreens and even hit the *Scharnhorst* with a torpedo, the carrier was a sitting duck. With her deck still crowded with the Gladiators and Hurricanes there was no time to fly off a strike of Swordfish before 28-cm shells started to fall on the flight deck from a range of about 28,000 yards.

By about 1720 the carrier was burning, and twenty minutes later she rolled over and sank. The loss of a second carrier was bad enough, but with her she took her trained aircrews and those RAF aircrews who had managed to land on her deck rather than be destroyed on the ground. The two destroyers were also sunk, and only 46 men from the three ships were saved.

Five days later the *Ark Royal*'s Skuas, not knowing of the torpedo hit by *Glorious'* escorts, tried to dive bomb the *Scharnhorst* at Trondheim, followed by an attack by land-based Swordfish from Hatston in the Orkneys. Neither was successful. Despite the missed opportunities and the tragic losses the *Ark Royal* emerged from the Norway débâcle with a considerable reputation for efficiency. She had already become well-known to the public, both in England and Germany, as the German propaganda broadcasts plaintively repeated the question, 'Where is the *Ark Royal*?' As early as October 1939 a Luftwaffe pilot had been awarded the Iron Cross for sinking her and the *Völkischer Beobachter* had even published an imaginative painting of the sinking. The question became a British catch-phrase, and the ship a symbol of the British refusal to accept defeat.

The '*Ark*' went back to Gibraltar little more than a week after the end of the Norwegian Campaign, to form the nucleus of a new striking force under Vice-Admiral Somerville, 'Force H'. Being such a fast ship her escort was the battlecruiser *Hood*, and the purpose of Force H was to prevent any move of the Italian Fleet out into the Atlantic and to cover the areas formerly left to the French Fleet. The French were, of course, out of the war by this time, as Marshal Pétain had concluded an armistice, but a powerful fleet of six capital ships, a seaplane carrier, ten cruisers and a number of destroyers were in North African harbours. According to the conditions of the armistice these ships were to be disarmed and demobilized 'under German and Italian control', an ominous phrase which, given the reputation of both Hitler and Mussolini for mendacity, meant whatever anybody chose. While the British might believe the assurances given by the head of the French Navy, Admiral Darlan, that no French warships would fall into German hands, they doubted the ability of the French to honour that pledge if German or Italian forces were

close enough to coerce the crews.

Whatever the correctness of this view, the British were determined to settle the outcome quickly, and on 3 July, following the expiry of an ultimatum to the French at Mers-el-Kebir, *Ark Royal*'s Swordfish went into action against the former Allies. They had several tasks, including spotting for the bombardment by the capital ships of Force H, laying mines at the harbour entrance and bomb- and torpedo-strikes against ships trying to escape the destruction. Two attempts to torpedo the battlecruiser *Strasbourg* failed, but a hit on an ammunition-barge alongside her sister *Dunkerque* caused considerable damage.

The little *Hermes* was at that moment shadowing the new battleship *Richelieu*, which had escaped from Brest to Casablanca and from there had headed for Dakar in Senegal. On 8 July six Swordfish achieved a single torpedo hit on the battleship, damaging her propeller shafts and steering. This success was enough to put the *Richelieu* out of action for a year, but this was not known in London and so Operation 'Menace' was launched, an Anglo-French amphibious assault on Dakar. *Ark Royal* had to provide the air cover as the *Hermes* had been damaged in a collision, but the task was beyond her aircraft. The Swordfish proved too slow to attack defended targets in daylight, and the Skuas were outclassed by the modern French fighters defending Dakar. As the Skuas were forced to carry out the reconnaissance missions normally left to the Swordfish there were soon not enough fighters left for fighter patrols and strikes.

The inherent flexibility of the carrier was amply demonstrated when *Ark Royal* was able to provide cover for an operation in the Western Mediterranean after the Mers-el-Kebir attack and before the Dakar operation. With Italy now in the war it was essential to reinforce Malta, and the old *Argus* was brought out to the Mediterranean with a dozen Hurricanes embarked. These fighters were flown off her deck when within flying distance of Malta, while *Ark Royal*'s Swordfish attacked targets in Sardinia and her Skuas shot down shadowers. This provocation was not enough to stir the Italian Fleet to defend what Mussolini had claimed as *Mare Nostrum*.

Life was becoming uncomfortable for the Italians, and the presence of a hostile aircraft carrier in *Mare Nostrum* accounted for many of their problems. The *Eagle* had been refitted at Singapore and was sent to join Admiral Cunningham's Mediterranean Fleet at Alexandria, where she embarked three Sea

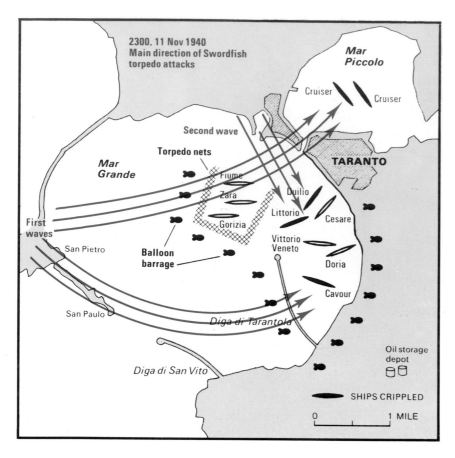

2300, 11 Nov 1940
Main direction of Swordfish
torpedo attacks

Mar Piccolo

Cruiser   Cruiser

Second wave

Torpedo nets

Mar Grande

Fiume

Zara

Duilio

Gorizia

Littorio

Cesare

First waves

San Pietro

Balloon barrage

Vittorio Veneto

Doria

San Paulo

Cavour

Diga di Tarantola

Diga di San Vito

TARANTO

Oil storage depot

SHIPS CRIPPLED

0   1 MILE

Gladiator biplane fighters to supplement her 18 Swordfish torpedo-bombers. With such a small air group there was little enough that she could do, but Admiral Cunningham was a man capable of immense mischief with limited resources. On 9 July 1940 he encountered the Italian Fleet in the Battle of Calabria, during which the hard-worked aircrews of the *Eagle* had to shadow the enemy, spot for the battleships, defend their own ships against high-level bombing and try to mount strikes against the Italian ships. Not surprisingly they failed to slow down the Italians, who were lucky to escape with minor damage, but the determination shown by the *Eagle*'s pilots convinced Cunningham that he could take the offensive with a modern carrier.

Cunningham's request was granted, and on 30 August the brand-new armoured carrier *Illustrious* and a powerful escort of the battleship *Valiant* and two anti-aircraft cruisers left Gibraltar. Her air group was small, only 15 Fulmar fighters of 806 Squadron and 18 Swordfish of 815 and 819 Squadrons, but she had one of the first production air-warning radars, known as Type 79Z, and this gave her a big advantage in fleet defence as she could detect and track hostiles and give her Skuas time to gain altitude. Another improvement was the provision of long-range fuel tanks for the Swordfish, to enable them to strike at ranges up to 200 miles from the carrier. The Fairey Fulmar, although slow (it was developed from an unsuccessful light

bomber and could fly at only 247 mph) had four hours' endurance and could dive at 400 mph. Provided it could be got up to its modest height (16,000 feet) it had a fair chance of shooting down Italian bombers but it could never hold its own against enemy fighters. But, in spite of the drawbacks, the 15 Fulmars of 806 Squadron enjoyed a period of unbroken supremacy from September 1940 to January 1941, when they destroyed or damaged 40 Italian aircraft.

With *Illustrious* under his command Cunningham could now take the offensive, and the *Eagle* and *Illustrious* rampaged through the Central Mediterranean, bombing airfields, hitting shipping between Italy and North Africa and mining harbours. All this was achieved for trifling loss, and more important, not a single major RN warship was hit by a daylight air attack. But these were pinpricks, and Cunningham and his staff were eager to revive the plan formulated at the end of the previous war, a torpedo strike against a fleet in harbour. Code-named Operation 'Judgement', the plan was to attack the main fleet base at Taranto with aircraft from both *Eagle* and *Illustrious* on Trafalgar Day, 21 October. But a fire broke out in *Illustrious*' hangar, fortunately while her air group had been flown ashore for maintenance, and then *Eagle*'s fuel-supply started to give trouble, a legacy of previous damage from near-misses. The damage to *Illustrious* was not serious, and so it was decided to transfer five Swordfish and eight crews from *Eagle* to strengthen her air group for the attack. With another Swordfish from the shore pool *Illustrious* mustered a total of 22 Swordfish, 14 Fulmars and four Sea Gladiators for the attack, now scheduled for the night of 11/12 November.

Only 21 Swordfish finally took off for the attack on Taranto, in two waves an hour apart. Contrary to popular belief the defenders were not taken by surprise when the first six Swordfish arrived over the harbour, and heavy flak met them. But the co-ordination of the attack was good, with flares dropped to illuminate the anchorage and dive-bombing of subsidiary targets to create a diversion. Two 18-inch torpedoes ripped into the new battleship *Littorio* and a third hit the *Conte di Cavour*. An hour later the second wave of eight aircraft arrived, and they hit the *Littorio* a third time and damaged another battleship, the *Duilio*. The subsidiary attacks were also successful as oil-storage tanks were set alight and the seaplane base was wrecked.

The shallowness of the harbour meant that the stricken battleships would be raised and repaired, but the powerful *Littorio* was out of action for more than six months, the *Duilio* would not be fit for action inside eight months, and the *Conte di Cavour* proved to be beyond repair, all for a total of 11 torpedoes and the loss of two Swordfish (only one crew was lost). But the biggest blow was to Italian morale, for half the Fleet was out of action. The surviving heavy units were withdrawn to more Northerly bases, and were ever afterwards handled with great caution, especially if the presence of a carrier was suspected. Coming at a time when Great Britain was under aerial bombardment from the Luftwaffe and the threat of invasion had barely receded it was a great fillip for British morale. At a crucial stage it tightened Cunningham's grip on the Mediterranean and marked a strategic setback to the Axis which would ultimately prove fatal.

The benefits of Taranto were seen quite quickly, for on 27 November Force H met the Italian Fleet off Cape Spartivento, with two of the battleships which had escaped damage at Taranto. The British were initially in a tricky position, with a convoy passing through to Malta and their heavy forces divided. The *Ark Royal* flew off three strikes to slow down the Italians, and even though none of the tor-

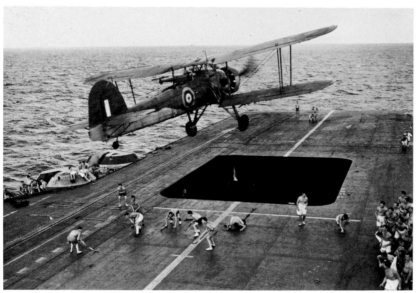

pedoes found a target Admiral Campioni decided that the threat of air attack was too great and ordered his forces to withdraw. Although disappointing from the British point of view in that they missed an opportunity to bring the enemy to battle, the Italians had even less cause for congratulation. The performance of *Ark Royal*'s air group had not been brilliant for her Swordfish crews were still short of practice, but in spite of this their intervention had been decisive.

The pressure from the Mediterranean Fleet and Force H was now so severe on the Italians that their German allies were forced to lend a hand. During the Norwegian cam-

paign a special force of Ju-87 Stuka dive-bombers had been formed to attack shipping. Known as *Fliegerkorps X*, the group had learned from its experience, and it was moved to Sicily in January 1941 with the specific task of sinking the *Illustrious*. What followed was an outstanding example of a co-ordinated attack catching the defence off balance. When the carrier was sighted about 55 miles west of Malta a pair of Italian Savoia-Marchetti SM-79 torpedo bombers made a feint attack to draw off the air patrol of four Fulmars. The British fighters took the bait and pursued the Italians for 20 miles, before the fighter controller in the *Illustrious* realized that another attack was developing, in the opposite direction and at a height of 12,000 feet. Although another four Fulmars were 'scrambled' they had no hope of intercepting this new force, the Stuka Ju-87Rs of *Stuka-gruppe 1* and the Ju-87Bs of *Stukagruppe 2*. Rule 1 of carrier defence had been broken: don't send the whole air patrol after an unimportant target, especially when only 65 miles from the enemy coast.

Illustrious paid dearly for her over-confidence. Within ten minutes six bombs of various sizes hit her, three forward and three aft. The hits forward did relatively little damage, but two of the three bombs aft nearly sank her. They hit the after lift and started serious fires in the hanger. With her steering gear crippled the carrier was a sitting duck for further air attacks, but her armoured deck had limited the extent of the damage, and when the steering was repaired she was able to shape a course for Malta. The fires continued to burn and the engine rooms were filled with smoke and fumes, but she worked up to 18 knots and even managed to avoid most of the subsequent dive-bombing attacks. With a fierce AA barrage from the battleships *Valiant* and *Warspite* providing some protection the battered *Illustrious* finally crawled into Malta late that night. The fires were not extinguished for another five hours, by which time 126 of her crew were dead and 91 wounded, but she had survived the worst punishment, and although damaged while lying alongside Parlatorio Wharf she was ready for the breakout to Alexandria by 23 January. From there it was a relatively quiet trip through the Suez Canal, around the Cape of Good Hope and across to Norfolk, Virginia for massive repairs which lasted until November.

The Mediterranean Fleet now faced the combined resources of the Luftwaffe and the *Regia Aeronautica* without the help of an armoured carrier. Fortunately the second of the *Illustrious* Class, HMS *Formidable* had just completed her workup, and on 10 March she passed through the Suez Canal and joined the Fleet. The effect was immediate: on 28 March Cunningham was at sea with his fleet, hunting for the Italians, who had been sighted by a Malta-based flying boat. In the afternoon came the exhilarating news that one of the *Formidable*'s Albacore torpedo-bombers had scored a hit on the battleship *Vittorio Veneto*, and that her speed had dropped to eight knots.

Here was the opportunity Cunningham had been seeking for nearly a year, and he pushed his ships forward at maximum speed in the hope of catching the crippled battleship. What nobody knew was that although the *Vittorio Veneto* had managed to effect some repairs and had increased her speed to 19 knots, an Albacore had managed to torpedo the heavy cruiser *Pola* at dusk. Thanks to the efficient air patrol of the carrier's Fulmars the Italian Admiral Iachino had received no reports of the whereabouts of the British main fleet, and he felt safe in ordering the *Pola*'s sisters, the *Fiume* and *Zara* to turn back with an escort of two destroyers to try and help her. The result was the Battle of Cape Matapan, in which the three hapless Italian cruisers were surprised by Cunningham's three battleships and destroyed. But the credit was entirely due to the *Formidable*, for her aircrews had accomplished all that was asked of them; they had found and immobilized the main enemy units, they had defended their own fleet and

had denied intelligence to the enemy.

This was the zenith of British carrier operations, for events were in train which would all but sweep the British from the Mediterranean. The *Formidable* was badly damaged during the battle for Crete, this time by Stukas flying from North African airfields. Her damage was less extensive than *Illustrious'*, but it was beyond the capacity of Alexandria to repair, and so she too left via the Suez Canal, bound for Norfolk Navy Yard for repairs. It is useless to speculate on what might have been achieved, but the chronic shortage of spares and the unsuitability of the aircraft meant that *Illustrious, Formidable* and *Ark Royal* made considerably less impact on operations than they could have. The two decades of dual control had much to answer for.

While the *Formidable* was taking part in the disastrous attempt to hold Crete events had taken an even more serious turn in the North Atlantic. On 22 May news was received that the new battleship *Bismarck* had sailed from Bergen, bound for the shipping routes

Top. An Albacore torpedo-bomber and a Fulmar fighter on board HMS *Victorious*, with the battleship *Duke of York* in Northern waters.

Above: The Grumman Wildcat, known in the RN as the Martlet 6, provided a much-needed high-performance fighter from 1941 onwards.

of the North Atlantic. Immediately the newly-commissioned carrier *Victorious*, which had just taken on a load of RAF Hurricanes bound for Malta, was told to prepare a torpedo strike. This was harder than it looked, for her only aircraft were nine Swordfish of 825 Squadron and six Fulmars of 800 Squadron. There was a squadron of Albacore torpedo-bombers in the Orkneys which could have been embarked, but the local RAF Coastal Command officer refused to release them in time – another example of poor inter-service co-operation.

The *Victorious* was intended as a stopgap, but on 24 May it was learned that the *Bismarck* and her escorting cruiser the *Prinz Eugen* had sunk the battlecruiser *Hood* and had shaken off the battleship *Prince of Wales*. It was not known that the *Bismarck* was losing oil from two hits inflicted by the *Prince of Wales*, and it was imperative that some effort be made to slow her down. At about midnight the nine Swordfish found her and attacked. Considering their lack of training it was only by outstanding luck that they managed to

score a single hit amidships, but what demanded even more skill and a large measure of luck was to find the carrier again and land safely. But it was all in vain, for the 18-inch torpedo did not carry enough explosive to inflict more than superficial damage on a battleship's main belt, and the *Bismarck* was no more than shaken by the blast.

There was one more trump to play, the *Ark Royal*. She had just returned to Gibraltar after covering an operation to fly Hurricanes into Malta, and with her faithful consort *Renown* she steamed north at full speed. As Force H was positioned to prevent a possible breakthrough to Brest it was ideally placed for the next move of the *Bismarck*, and so as soon as the position was reported by a Catalina flying boat on the morning of 26 May she was ready to fly off a strike of Swordfish.

What followed was nearly tragic, but it turned out to be beneficial. The first strike of 15 Swordfish, unaware of a change of dispositions, mistook the cruiser HMS *Sheffield* for the *Bismarck* in thick visibility, and attacked her. The torpedoes were all fitted with a

Inset below: The new carrier *Indomitable* at Rosyth in 1941. Luckily she missed the disastrous mission of the *Prince of Wales* and *Repulse*, and did not reach the Indian Ocean for another six months.

Duplex exploder, using either a magnetic (non-contact) fuse or a conventional contact type. The weather was so bad during the attack that the torpedoes plunged wildly to a depth at which the Earth's magnetic field set off the sensitive magnetic fuse. Eleven torpedoes were fired at the *Sheffield*, and although the cruiser was somewhat affronted at having to dodge 'friendly' torpedoes she was able to signal to the *Ark Royal* that several of the 11 torpedoes dropped had detonated prematurely, and to signal sardonically to the Swordfish 'Thanks for the kippers'. It was then an easy matter to change the Duplex setting to Contact, a safer method in such conditions, and to rearm the Swordfish for a second strike.

This time the Swordfish made no mistakes, and with the *Sheffield* directing them towards the *Bismarck* they picked up their target on their own radar. The conditions were even worse than those experienced by the *Victorious'* aircrews, with low cloud and bad visibility, and so the Swordfish attacked individually. Despite fire from a flak-battery of 68 guns ranging from 105-mm down to 20-mm the biplanes lumbered on, seeming to fly almost into the *Bismarck*'s superstructure in some cases, to make sure of dropping their torpedoes at the right point. One theory put forward to explain the German gunners' failure to destroy the Swordfish is that the lead-angle computation for the fire-control directors had assumed a minimum flying speed of 100 mph, and so the *Bismarck*'s gunners were shooting slightly ahead each time! Whatever the truth of that story, the *Ark Royal*'s Swordfish escaped the hail of tracers and shell-fragments and dropped 13 torpedoes. One hit the main belt, as before, and did little damage, but the second hit right aft and wrecked the rudders. This single hit made the German ship impossible to steer, and sealed her fate. Next morning a third strike of Swordfish was airborne, but was kept clear of the gun-duel between the *Bismarck* and the two battleships of the Home Fleet which finished her off.

Below: The stricken *Ark Royal*, whose luck finally ran out on 13 November 1941, when *U.81* torpedoed her 50 miles from Gibraltar.

Right: Carley rafts and boats take off the crew of the *Ark Royal*, and the destroyer *Legion* stands by to provide power. Although only one life was lost the ship was prematurely abandoned, and was an unnecessary loss.

Far right: The 'batsman' or Landing Signals Officer aboard the USS *Wasp* (CV.7) in June 1942. His signals were a vital aid to the pilot in judging his approach.

The *Ark Royal* returned to the Mediterranean, where she fought in the repeated attempts to get aircraft and supplies into Malta. When her luck finally ran out it was almost an anticlimax. On 13 November 1941 she was less than 50 miles away from Gibraltar when *U.81* slipped through the screen and hit her on the starboard side with a single torpedo. She started to list, but being a modern ship with good subdivision there was every reason to think that she could be towed to safety. But flooding in the centre boiler-rooms put the main electrical switchboard out of action, by which time the key electrical ratings had all left the ship and were ashore in Gibraltar. As power was lost the pumping failed to keep pace with the flooding, and next day the ship had such a heavy list that it became clear that she was going to go down. Finally she gave up the struggle and lay on her beam ends before sinking. She had stayed afloat for 14 hours, and was less than 30 miles from Gibraltar, but it was not enough. This was a classic case of how not to cope with torpedo damage.

The loss of the '*Ark*' was a shock to the British, for it revealed weaknesses, not in the design of their carriers, but in their damage-control procedures. A searching enquiry revealed what had gone wrong and the mistakes were not repeated. It brought to an end a string of brilliant victories in the Mediterranean, often against heroic odds. The bitter lesson of 1942 was to be that without carriers and without adequate aircraft the Mediterranean was almost untenable.

WARTIME CARRIERS

Left: F6F-3 fighters and SBD-4 dive-bombers ranged on the flight deck of the USS *Essex* (CV.9), first of the new fast carriers.

Left: Curtiss SB2C Helldivers on board the new *Yorktown* (CV.10) during her trials in May 1943.

Below: The crowded flight deck of the escort carrier *Santee* (CVE.29) during the invasion of North Africa at the end of 1942.

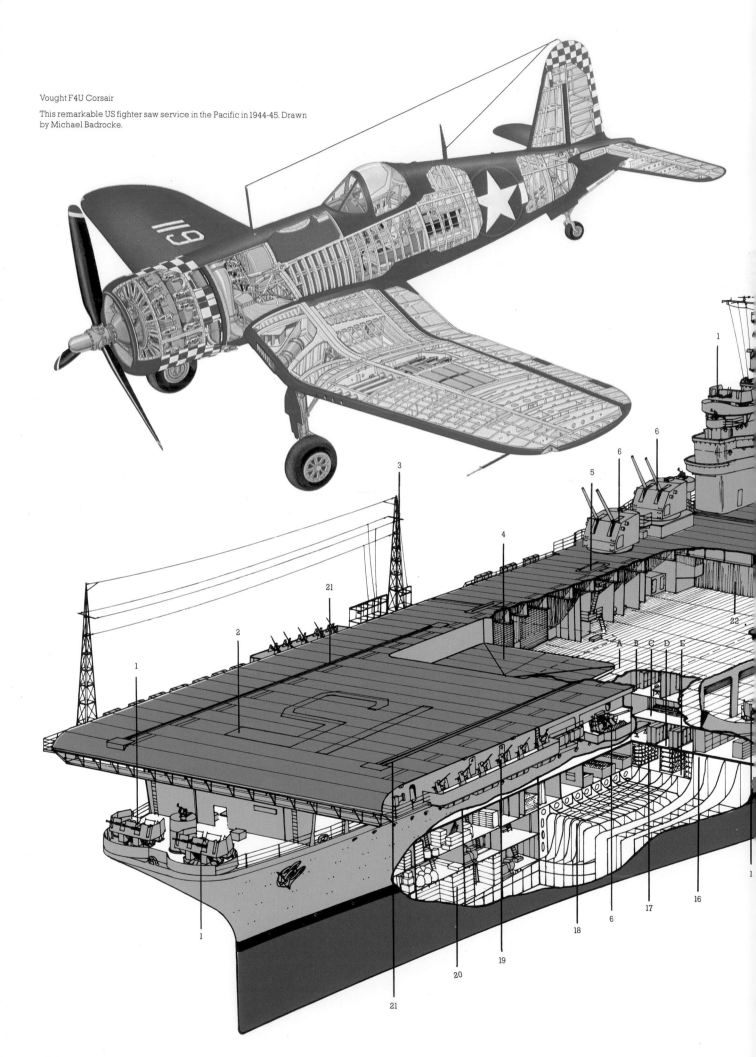

Vought F4U Corsair

This remarkable US fighter saw service in the Pacific in 1944-45. Drawn by Michael Badrocke.

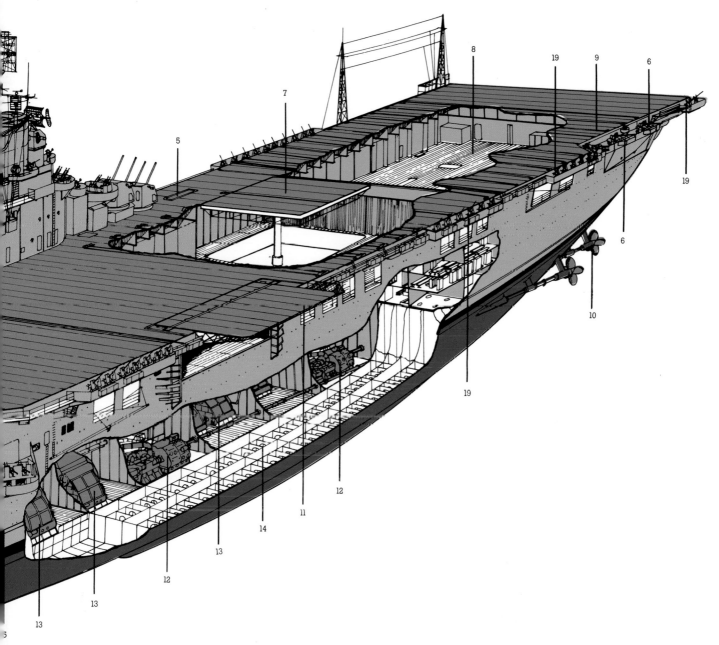

The USS *Randolph* (GV.15), an *Essex* Class carrier commissioned in
October 1944.

1	Quadruple 40mm Bofors AA guns	15	Side armour
2	Deck recognition number (also aft)	16	Deck armour
3	Radio masts (horizontal during flying)	17	Bomb magazines
4	Forward aircraft lift (lowered)	18	Aviation fuel stowage (duplicated aft)
5	Bomb lift	19	Single 20mm Oerlikon AA guns (port and starboard)
6	5-inch dual-purpose guns (twin and single)	20	Stores
7	After aircraft lift (raised)	21	Catapults (port and starboard)
8	Aircraft hangar (full length)	22	Fire screens
9	Arrester wires	A	
10	Port propellors and shaft	B	
11	Side lift	C	Deck levels
12	Forward and after Engine rooms	D	
13	Boilers (port and starboard)	E	
14	Anti-torpedo protection (liquid-air-liquid filled)		Drawn from the original plans by John A Roberts.

Right: The nuclear-powered
USS *Nimitz* (CVN.68) in the
English Channel in
September 1975.

Top right: The new British
V/STOL carrier,
HMS *Invincible* nears
completion in mid-1978.

Bottom right: The
conventionally-powered
Constellation (CVA.62)
makes a turn to port.

Below: Men of the *Coral Sea* (CV.43) form an anchor to commemorate her fourth 'Golden Anchor' award for retaining personnel.

Right: Sunrise over the vast flight deck of the *Coral Sea*, with F-4 Phantoms in the deck park.

Far right: Although the 'batsman' has been replaced by automatic landing lights the LSO is still in voice-communication with an incoming pilot.

Below: Carriers require basic seamanship in addition to the skills of aircraft handling, as this scene aboard the *Lexington* (CVA.16) shows.

Right: The *Lexington*'s Catapult Control Officer supervising launches from the two steam catapults.

Bottom: A Skyraider landing aboard the *Lexington*. During the Vietnam War these propeller-driven veterans proved more suitable for ground attack than the big jets.

91

Below: HMS *Ark Royal* paid a visit to the United States in the Bicentennial Year.

Far right: HMS *Invincible* put to sea on her trials on 26 March 1979, only three months after the *Ark Royal* paid off for scrapping. Her sister is to be named *Illustrious*, and a third ship will take the name *Ark Royal*.

Right: The last British fleet carrier, HMS *Ark Royal* at sea in August 1978.

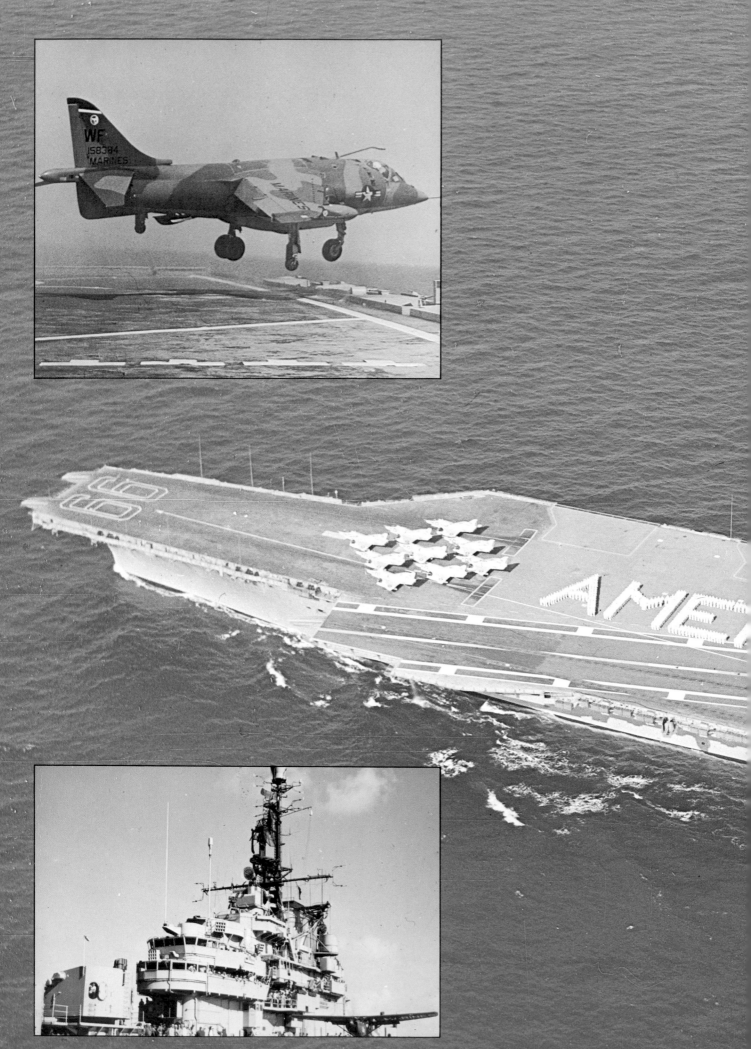

Right: The USS *America* (CVA.66) off Guantanamo Bay, Cuba in June 1965 during her shakedown cruise.

Top left: A Marine Corps NV-8A Harrier V/STOL aircraft carries out landing trials aboard the amphibious ship *Coronado* (LPD.11). The Marines now operate the Harrier from small carriers as a support aircraft.

Bottom left: A light observation plane takes off from the support carrier *Boxer* (CVS.21).

Below: The crew of the *America* spell out her name during her 1965 shakedown cruise.

Below: In 1977 the Soviet Navy unveiled its new aircraft carrier *Kiev*. Although not a fleet carrier the deployment of a flight of V/STOL *Forger* aircraft on board shows that the Russians have grasped the potential of naval air power.

Inset: Apart from the US Navy, France is now the only country to maintain attack carriers. The *Foch* and her sister *Clemenceau* are equipped with all the latest aids, and will serve to the end of the 1980s.

8 T E RISING SU

The lesson of Taranto had been studied with great interest by the Japanese. It gave them the encouragement that they needed to put the finishing touches to their plans for dealing with the American Pacific Fleet, which had been a long time maturing.

The arguments for a surprise attack on the American Fleet were strong ones. For one thing there was the disparity in strength, and major reductions in American strength were needed to put the two surface fleets on an equal footing. For another there was the historical precedent of the war against Russia, in which the Japanese had established a moral ascendancy over the Russians by a surprise attack. The third and clinching argument was the need to keep the war short, partly to prevent America from mobilizing her industrial might and partly to capitalize on what was believed to be the American public's unwillingness for war.

Secure in their ignorance of America, the Japanese proceeded with their plans. Admiral Isoroku Yamamoto, Commander-in-Chief of the Combined Fleet, was sceptical of the theories about America's decadence but he believed implicitly that the war had to be a

Below: Weary machine gunners on board a US aircraft carrier after repelling a Japanese air attack. The .50 calibre was soon replaced by the more effective 20mm gun.

short one, and so he backed the plan to knock out the US Pacific Fleet in its forward base at Pearl Harbor in Hawaii. In April and May 1940 two war-games were staged to test the effectiveness of a raid by carriers, and the results were conclusively favourable. Then came the news of Taranto in November, and Yamamoto ordered naval attachés in London and Rome to find out as many details about the attack as possible.

The planning was entrusted to Rear Admiral Shigeru Fukudome, who brought in Rear Admiral Takijiro Onishi and Commander Minoru Genda, the Navy's most experienced pilots. Between them they de-vised new methods of dropping torpedoes fitted with wooden fins, to avoid the risk of hitting the bottom of Pearl Harbor, while as much intelligence was gathered about the dispositions of the enemy as possible. In September 1941 full-scale practice began in Kagoshima Bay, and at the beginning of November Yamamoto announced that his plans were ready. The politicians having failed to settle their differences with the United States, there was then virtually no alternative to war, as Yamamoto had carried the whole Navy with him in his plans, even the somewhat sceptical carrier commander, Admiral Chuichi Nagumo.

Right: The battleship *Nevada* burns following the attack at Pearl Harbor. Shortly after the picture was taken the *Nevada* was run aground.

Right: The *Akagi* at sea in the summer of 1941, exercising her air group for the Pearl Harbor strike.

Right: Aircraft leaving the *Akagi*, bound for Pearl Harbor.

As everyone knows the attack on Pearl Harbor was a devastating success. Taken completely by surprise, the US battleships were rapidly put out of action. The *Arizona* blew up, the *Oklahoma* capsized, the *California* and *West Virginia* sank in shallow water, and the *Nevada, Maryland, Tennessee* and *Pennsylvania* all more or less seriously damaged. A second strike destroyed numerous aircraft on the ground and caused many casualties; a third strike might have inflicted further damage on the ships but the cautious Nagumo would not allow it.

Fortune favours the bold, and certainly the Japanese deserved their success. The skill and devotion of the carrier pilots of the *Akagi, Kaga, Hiryu, Soryu, Shokaku* and *Zuikaku* had been matched by extraordinary lethargy on the part of the naval and army commanders at Pearl Harbor. Considering the size of the air groups, 132 A6M2 'Zero' fighters, 129 D3A1 'Val' dive-bombers and 143 B5N2 'Kate' torpedo-bombers the damage was comparatively restricted. For one thing, faulty intelligence meant that the carriers *Enterprise* and *Lexington* were not caught in harbour. Another failure was the omission of two vital strategic targets from the battle-plan: the machine shops and the oil storage tanks. The ships could be repaired and the defences could be replaced, but if the fuel stocks had been destroyed Pearl Harbor could not have sustained a fleet for another year or more. And of course, psychologically the attack was an appalling miscalculation, for its very destructiveness shook America out of its isolationism more effectively than a small disaster further away might have done.

It is opportune at this point to lay one ghost firmly to rest. Because of the success of American cryptographers in cracking the Japanese cyphers it has in recent years been rumoured that the battleships of the Pacific Fleet were deliberately sacrificed to provide a target to tempt the Japanese to strike, as the only way to shock the citizens of the United States into war. The evidence for this assertion is flimsy, and rests principally on the failure by Washington to alert the Army and Navy commanders to the possibility of a Japanese attack, and the absence of the carriers.

The truth is that the cryptographers knew

Below: A Japanese pilot's eye view of 'Battleship Row', Pearl Harbor on 7 December 1941. The ominous pools of oil indicate major damage to those ships still afloat.

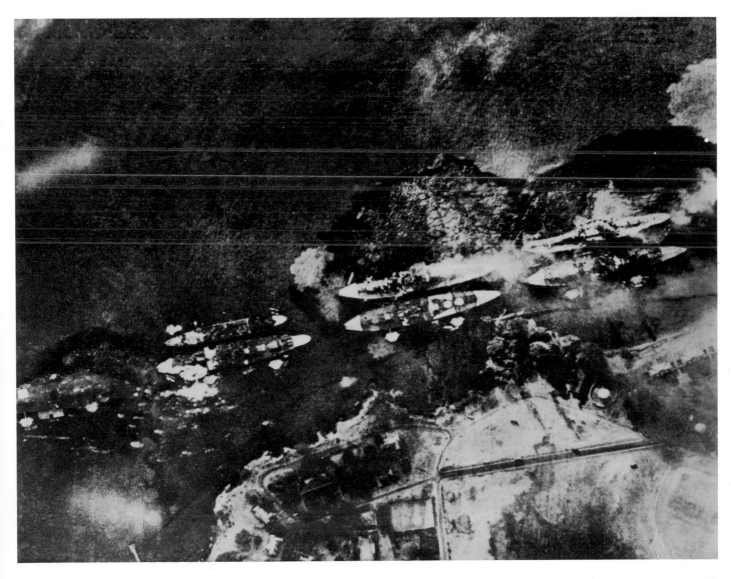

RUSSIA

Kamchatka

ATTU

MONGOLIA
ULAN BATOR

MANCHURIA
(MANCHUKUO)
HARBIN
MUKDEN

Sakhalin

Kurile Is

26 Nov 1941
Nagumo's fleet
sails

Hokkaido

C H I N A

PEKING

Hwang Ho

Yangtse-kiang

NANKING
HANKOW
SHANGHAI

CHUNGKING
CHANGSHA
Burma Road
KUNMING   CANTON

VLADIVOSTOK

KOREA
SEOUL

SEA OF
JAPAN

Shikoku
Kyushu

Honshu

TOKYO
JAPAN

NAGASAKI

7 Dec 1941

16 De
Part o
to Wa
suppo

DELHI

NEPAL
Ganges   IMPHAL

KARACHI

I N D I A

CALCUTTA

BOMBAY

BAY OF
BENGAL

MADRAS

LASHIO
MANDALAY

BURMA!

RANGOON

ANDAMAN
IS

TRINCOMALEE

Maldive
Is

COLOMBO
Ceylon

NICOBAR
IS

HANOI

THAI-
LAND

BANGKOK

FRENCH
INDO-CHINA

SAIGON

Ryukyu Is
OKINAWA

Formosa
(Taiwan)

HONG KONG

HAINAN

SOUTH CHINA
SEA

KHOTA BHARU

MALAYA

SARAWAK

N BORNEO

BONIN IS

IWO JIMA

Luzon

MANILA

PHILIPPINE
ISLANDS

LEYTE

Mindanao

DAVAO

PALAU IS

P A C

8 Dec
Wake I
23 Dec
surrende

WAKE

Marianas
Islands
SAIPAN

GUAM

ENIWETOK

TRUK

YAP

Caroline   Islands

O   C

KWAJALEIN

M
Is

MAJURO

SINGAPORE

Equator

Sumatra

DUTCH   EAST   INDIES

BATAVIA

Java

Borneo

Celebes

FLORES

TIMOR

I N D I A N

O C E A N

TIMOR SEA
DARWIN

HALMAHERA

ARAFURA SEA

New Guinea

ADMIRALTY
IS   NEW
IRELAND

RABAUL

PAPUA

PORT
MORESBY

NEW
BRITAIN

BOUGAINVILLE

NEW
GEORGIA

Solomon Is

GUADALCANAL

NAURU

OCEAN I

TARAWA

NEW
Caledonia

NOUMEA

CORAL   SEA

CAIRNS

New
Hebrides

EFATE

SANTA CR

ESPIRITU-

NANU

ROCKHAMPTON

A U S T R A L I A

BRISBANE

NORFOL

PERTH

ADELAIDE

SYDNEY
CANBERRA

MELBOURNE

TASMAN

SEA

AUCKLA

NEW ZEALAND

WELLINGT

CHRISTCHURCH

JAPANESE EMPIRE, 1933

OCCUPIED BY JAPAN, JULY 1937/DECEMBER 1941

MILITARY BASES ESTABLISHED BY JAPAN, SEPTEMBER 1940

ABDA (American, British, Dutch, and Australian) COMMAND

MERCATOR'S PROJECTION

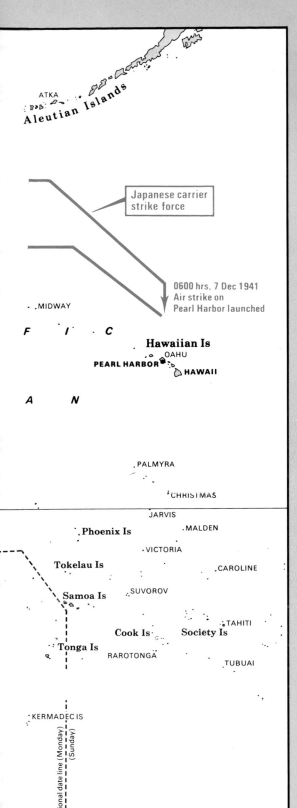

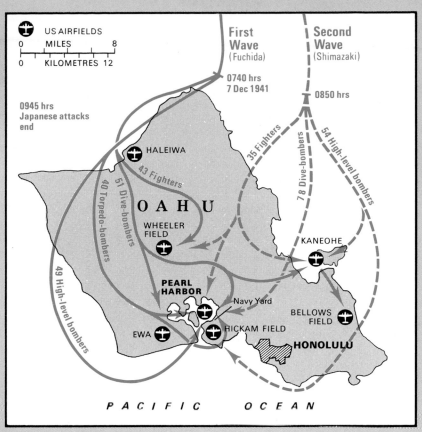

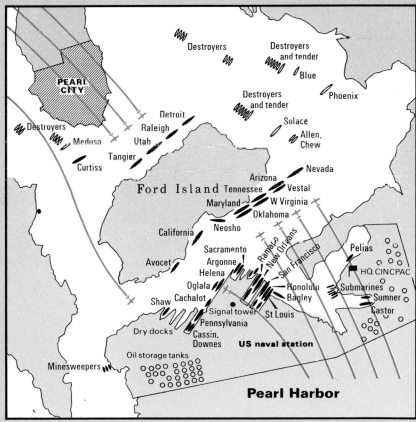

only that a surprise attack was planned, not the destination; Pearl Harbor was considered but rejected on the grounds that a well-defended base would either not be overwhelmed or would be considered too tough a nut by the Japanese. Nobody foresaw that the two commanders Kimmel and Short would between them allow the Japanese to wreak such havoc. The carriers were on the move frequently because Rear Admiral 'Bull' Halsey was anxious to bring the air groups up to scratch as fast as possible. He lost no opportunity for flying, and as a result the carriers were on the move in and out of Pearl Harbor before the Japanese attack. Their absence was fortuitous, and it was the sole advantage left to the US Navy as it surveyed the devastation on Oahu.

Although it is dangerous to over-simplify the history of ideas, there can be no doubt that Pearl Harbor was a milestone in the history of American carrier-warfare. Without a battle-fleet there was no longer any possibility of 'battleship tactics' taking precedence over pure 'carrier tactics', for there was no other way of taking the offensive against the Japanese. Henceforward the Americans would have to base everything on the carrier task force rather than the battleline – an idea that naval aviators had envisaged and had even experimented with, but which had never been official doctrine.

But all this was hidden at the time, and for nearly six months after Pearl Harbor it seemed as if the Japanese were unstoppable. A futile attempt was made to stop Admiral Nagumo's carriers from battering Wake Island into submission with all three American carriers (the *Saratoga* had arrived from San Diego a week after the attack on Pearl Harbor), but perhaps it was fortunate that they did not meet Nagumo's confident battle-hardened air groups so soon. The next target was the Philippines, for which the *Ryujo* and four seaplane carriers were allocated. No carriers were provided for the fleet covering the invasion of Malaya, for the slender British naval forces had no carrier with them. The capital ships *Prince of Wales* and *Repulse* were sunk with relative ease by shore-based torpedo-bombers as they had not even a vestige of shore-based air support.

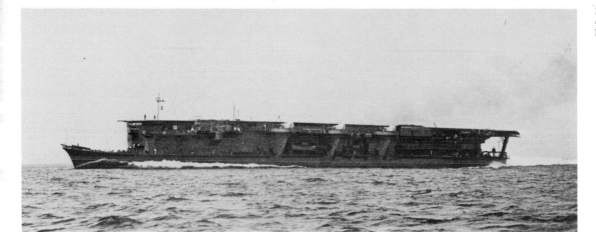

Left: The small carrier *Ryujo* did not take part in the Pearl Harbor attack.

Left: Admiral Husband E Kimmel USN (centre) with his staff at Pearl Harbor before the attack. He and the Army commander, General Short, were dismissed from their posts for negligence.

Far left: The shattered wrecks of the destroyers *Cassin* and *Downes* ahead of the battleship *Pennsylvania* in the flooded 'Ten-Ten' dock, with the damaged cruiser *Helena* behind.

Inset: Admiral Isoroku Yamamoto, C-in-C of the Combined Fleet and architect of the Pearl Harbor plan, was ironically an opponent of war with the United States.

The British were spared an even bigger disaster, for they had planned to send their third armoured carrier, HMS *Indomitable* out with the *Prince of Wales* and *Repulse*; it is highly doubtful that her slow aircraft would have been a match for the Japanese, and she would probably have gone down as well.

As soon as Nagumo could get his fast carriers back into action he struck at the East Indies. On 20 January they struck at Rabaul in New Britain from their new base at Truk in the Carolines. Despite heroic efforts by the Australian defenders, which caused Nagumo to order a second strike, Rabaul was invaded three days later. The *Hiryu, Soryu* and *Zuiho* covered the invasion of Ambon, while *Ryujo*'s aircraft attacked the ABDA force of American, Australian, British and Dutch cruisers off Sumatra. On 15 February the fast Carrier Division 1 struck at Australia itself, with an attack by 188 aircraft on Darwin and Broome on the North coast. The results for Darwin were catastrophic and virtually destroyed it as a base for some time to come. The Australians were lucky that the raid was only to pre-empt any attempt to interfere with the invasion of Java.

The only Allied carriers in striking distance of Java were HMS *Indomitable*, which had delivered 50 Hurricanes but was without half her air group, and the USS *Langley*, which was also transporting aircraft. The *Indomitable* was prudently withdrawn, for she could not have faced even the small *Ryujo* without her full air group, but the *Langley* was caught by the land-based bombers on 26 February and was sunk *en route* to Tjilatljap with crated P-40 fighters on board. From 1 to 3 March the Japanese carrier aircraft roamed at will, sinking warships and merchant ships trying to escape to Australia. When they finally withdrew to their base in the Celebes they could rest content in the knowledge that they achieved all they had set out to do. What surprised them was the small cost: three destroyers, less than 100 naval aircraft and a number of transports and naval auxiliaries, a trifling price to pay for the oil, rubber and mineral wealth of the Philippines, Malaya and the East Indies.

On 26 March Nagumo's carriers went on the rampage again. This time it was the turn of the British in the Indian Ocean, who had so far escaped their attentions. The *Akagi, Hiryu, Soryu, Shokaku* and *Zuikaku* struck the Royal Navy's main base at Trincomalee and the big commercial harbour of Colombo, while the *Ryujo* and four cruisers hunted for shipping around the coast of India.

There was on paper a balanced Eastern Fleet to defend India and Ceylon, three carriers and five battleships under Vice-Admiral Sir James Somerville, formerly commanding Force H. Two of the carriers were the modern *Formidable* and *Indomitable* but the third was the *Hermes*, which carried only a dozen Swordfish. The *Formidable* had 16 modern Martlet fighters acquired from the United States under Lend-Lease, while the *Indomitable* had 21 Fulmars and Sea Hurricanes, scarcely enough to defend against the Japanese, let alone escort an attack by the Albacores and Swordfish against over 100 Zeroes. Nor were the battleships any sort of match for the Japanese surface fleet.

Somerville had no intention of indulging in heroics, for the events of the past three-and-a-half months had instilled respect, not to say dread, for the air groups of Nagumo's Striking Force. He intended to stay out of reach by day and only to close with the Japanese by night, using the advantage of radar. He also had the advantage of having a new base at Addu Atoll in the Maldive Islands, nearly 500 miles West-South-West of Columbo, whose existence was to remain unknown to Nagumo until long after the danger was past.

The art of night-flying from carriers had been developed to a much higher pitch by the British than either the Japanese or the Americans, largely because of the recognized limitations of their existing strike aircraft. The big convoy battles in the Mediterranean had also given them valuable experience in using radar to aid the defence against daylight attack. The principle was to concentrate the fighters where they could do the most damage, and the technique was to get the fighters aloft to a 'holding' position and then vector them out to a position at right-angles to the approaching enemy, preferably with the sun behind them. This

Right: Vice-Admiral Chuichi Nagumo, whose fast carriers devastated Pearl Harbor but failed to knock it out.

avoided the head-on approach, with its time-consuming turn of 180° in full view of the opposition. The refinement of Identification Friend or Foe (IFF) equipment also made it possible for the Fighter Direction Officer (FDO) on board the carrier to distinguish friendly aircraft from hostile on the radar plot, and saved valuable time.

Until radars with Plan Position Indicators (PPI) were available the radars had to be trained in specific sectors to establish height, range and bearing, and so to save time the course of the defending fighters was plotted by dead-reckoning, until the FDO was ready to begin the attack, at which point they were 'gathered in' by the radar. The normal technique for using these early air-warning radars was for another ship to maintain an all-round search, leaving the carrier's radar free to track the raid. The biggest danger was still the low-level approach by land-based torpedo-bombers, which could come in 'under' the radar.

Unfortunately the plan went wrong. When Nagumo's carriers failed to show up at the estimated time on 2 April Somerville interpreted it (somewhat optimistically) as evidence that his information was false or that Nagumo had withdrawn in the face of his concentration. He therefore sent his Fast Division, the two armoured carriers and the battleship *Warspite*, to refuel at Addu Atoll, leaving the *Hermes* and two destroyers in the vicinity of Trincomalee. He was thus caught on the wrong foot when the Japanese arrived over Colombo on 5 April. Damage to the port was relatively light, but the heavy cruisers *Cornwall* and *Dorsetshire*, hurrying South to Addu, were sunk by D3A 'Vals' from *Akagi*, *Hiryu* and *Soryu*.

The Eastern Fleet was caught out of position again three days later. While refuelling at Addu Nagumo's carrier-aircraft struck at the naval base at Trincomalee, on the other side of Ceylon. As at Colombo, there had been sufficient warning from reconnaissance aircraft to disperse shipping, and so comparatively light damage was done to the base. But a second wave of aircraft was held back when a floatplane from the battleship *Haruna* sighted HMS *Hermes* and a number of ships, only 65 miles from Trincomalee, heading for safety. Within two hours 85 dive-bombers were attacking the *Hermes* and the other ships, sinking her, a fleet oiler and two escorting warships. Again the loss was trifling; even when eight naval Fulmars attacked the 'Vals' and shot down four, the dive-bombers were able to turn on their pursuers and destroy two of them, being lighter and faster. The Japanese carriers were attacked, too, by nine RAF Blenheim bombers, but this medium-height level attack was completely unsuccessful and lost more than half its aircraft.

Meanwhile, in the Central Pacific, American attempts to regain the initiative were getting underway. The *Yorktown* was sent through the Panama Canal early in January 1942; she rendezvoused with the *Enterprise* and the two carriers accompanied a convoy of troopships to Samoa. This brought the total of US carriers to four, but on 11 January the *Saratoga* was damaged by a torpedo from a Japanese submarine southwest of Oahu, and had to be sent back to the United States for repairs. She was, however, quickly replaced by the *Hornet*, and so the planned raid

Left: The British carrier *Hermes* on fire and sinking by the bow. She was caught without fighter protection on 5 April 1942 off the coast of Ceylon by Nagumo's dive-bombers and sank within ten minutes.

against airfields in the Gilbert and Marshall Islands was not held up.

The carriers were now grouped in three task Forces, TF 8, built around *Enterprise* under Admiral Halsey, TF 11 under Rear-Admiral W A Brown in the *Lexington* and TF 17 under Rear-Admiral Frank F Fletcher in the *Yorktown*. TF 8 and TF 17 were to effect the strike while TF 11 was to cover them from a position east of Wake island. The first strike was by TF 8 against Kwajalein Atoll in the Marshalls group, and inflicted slight damage on shipping in return for light losses from defending Zeroes. The strike by TF 17 on the Gilberts accomplished even less, and lost seven aircraft. The raid was later described as an extremely expensive form of pilot training, but it showed up several weaknesses in the US Navy's carrier tactics. The worst was the lack of IFF in the F4F Wildcat (the same aircraft known to the British as the Martlet), which prevented the FDOs from distinguishing even the strike aircraft from the patrol aircraft and 'friendlies' from 'hostiles'. Another was the lack of good long-range radios, which meant that two-way radio contact could not be guaranteed outside a range of 30 miles.

The new carrier *Hornet* was earmarked for an unusual task. As early as 10 January a submariner on the staff of the Chief of Naval Operations (CNO) had suggested the idea of flying Army bombers off a Navy carrier, to drop bombs on Tokyo as a reprisal for Pearl Harbor. When Admiral King's Air Operations staff studied the problem they discovered that a Mitchell B-25 two-engined bomber could just manage a take-off; there was no question of landing again, and it was hoped that America's ally China would provide a landing strip for the bombers at the end of their mission.

The Chief of the Army Air Forces, General 'Hap' Arnold was enthusiastic about the plan and selected the well-known pre-war flying personality, Lieutenant Colonel James Doolittle to lead the raid. On 2 February the *Hornet* launched two B-25s experimentally off the Virginia Capes, and final approval was given for the operation. After a hectic period of preparation the *Hornet* left San Francisco on 2 April 1942 with no fewer than 16 B-25s lashed to her flight deck. There was no way of concealing them, and it was put about that the carrier was employed on a ferrying mission. She carried most of her normal air group stowed in the hangar, but would have had difficulty in defending herself as most of the aircraft had to be dismantled to leave room for the Army Air Corps maintenance teams.

The *Hornet* would have her sister *Enterprise* as an escort for the most dangerous part of the mission, and the two carriers made their rendezvous North of Hawaii 11 days later, forming Task Force 16 under Halsey's command. On 15 April Halsey signalled:

'Intention fuel heavy ships 1000 miles to Westward X Thence carriers and cruisers to point 500 miles east of Tokyo launch Army bombers on *Hornet* for attack X DDs and tankers remain vicinity fuelling point rejoin on retirement X Further operations as developments dictate'

For the last part of the mission the two carriers would leave behind their destroyers, as they lacked the high-speed endurance to keep up with the carriers and the four cruisers.

On 18 April the B-25s were spotted ready for take-off, leaving only 467 feet of flight deck for Doolittle's take-off. A 40-knot gale was blowing, making the *Hornet* pitch violently,

but at 0820 Jimmy Doolittle opened the throttles, and keeping his wheels within the 'tramlines' painted on the deck to guide the Army pilots, took off safely. The rest of the B-25s lumbered off at four-minute intervals, and as soon as they were seen to be safely in formation and shaping course for Japan Task Force 16 withdrew at high speed, pausing only to sink as many patrol vessels as possible.

The Japanese were aware of the impending raid, partly from analysis of American radio traffic and partly from a signal flashed by a small patrol vessel before she was sunk by TF 16's escorts. But the use of B-25s was unsuspected, and basing their estimates on

Left: The B-25s of 17th Bombardment Group ready for take-off on 18 April 1942.

Left: With its engines revving at full power a B-25 lumbered into the air from the *Hornet*'s flight deck. The white lines were specially painted to help the pilot align the B-25's tricycle undercarriage.

Far left: B-25 Mitchell twin-engined bombers on the flight deck of the *Hornet*, on the way to the take-off point for the Tokyo raid.

the range of single-engined aircraft the Japanese defences expected the raiders a day later. They arrived on a spring afternoon and 15 of the bombers dropped their bombs on their chosen targets. A stunned defence failed to intercept them, and they headed for mainland China. The sequel was tragic; because of bad weather over Chungking most of the crews had to bail out in darkness. Four B-25s crash-landed and the crew of one was interned by the Russians after landing near Vladivostok, but only 3 of the aircrew out of the original 80 were killed.

The military results of the 'Doolittle Raid' were negligible, but it provided a tremendous boost to morale after the unbroken run of defeats. President Roosevelt, when asked where the raid had started from, referred to James Hilton's novel, and claimed that the B-25s had flown from a secret base called Shangri-La. To commemorate the exploit one of the new *Essex* Class carriers was renamed *Shangri-La*.

Task Force 16 spent five days at Pearl Harbor for a brief refit before sailing on 30 April for the southwest Pacific. This time they were under the command of Rear Admiral Raymond A Spruance, but they were too late for the Battle of the Coral Sea as they were still a thousand miles away from TF 17.

The Battle of the Coral Sea came about because Admiral Yamamoto's cherished decisive battle had not yet come about. His strategy had worked almost perfectly so far, the US Pacific Fleet had been destroyed and a chain of island bases had been established to protect the new conquests. But still the American carriers eluded him, as the Doolittle raid on Tokyo showed only too clearly. It was recognized that Australia was an important base for any counter-offensive, and that any such attack would be aimed at their own base at Rabaul. Yamamoto did not believe that the southwestern Pacific would provide the de-

cisive battle, and his staff was planning for that in a strike against Midway, but he acquiesced in the Army's plans. Like the other Japanese commanders it all looked so easy to him after the staggering series of victories; the Japanese were drunk with success.

The operation, code-named Mo by the Japanese, included an amphibious invasion of Port Moresby and the capture of Tulagi in the Solomons. The Carrier Strike Force under Rear-Admiral Takeo Takagi, comprising the *Shokaku* and *Zuikaku* left Truk on 1 May and by the afternoon of 5 May it was in a position to attack any American strike against the Port Moresby invasion. Its opposition was Task Force 17 with *Lexington* under Rear-Admiral Aubrey W Fitch and *Yorktown* under Rear Admiral Frank F Fletcher. The Americans had a slight edge, with the same number of fighters as the Japanese, fewer torpedo bombers but more dive-bombers. They also had radar, and *Yorktown* had just received the first IFF equipment for some of her fighters, but above all they had the benefit of superior intelligence about the Japanese dispositions. Not only had the Americans broken the code, so that Admiral Nimitz and his staff knew exactly what the Japanese objectives would be, but there was a constant flow of reports from the Australian 'coastwatchers', who reported sightings of Japanese forces.

Inferior in equipment and knowledge the Japanese may have been, but their grasp of carrier tactics was at that stage of the war still superior to the Americans. Instead of operating each carrier as the nucleus of a task force, with an admiral commanding each one, the Japanese carriers operated as a single unit. This meant that above all the carriers contributed the maximum cover against both air and submarine attack, while receiving the maximum benefit of the anti-aircraft defences of the supporting warships. It also

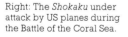
Right: The *Shokaku* under attack by US planes during the Battle of the Coral Sea.

Left: SBD-3 Dauntless dive-bombers on the flight deck of the *Yorktown* during the Battle of the Coral Sea.

meant that fighter patrols and bomber strikes could be properly co-ordinated – the arrival of two carriers' strikes at the target simultaneously doubled the enemy's problems. The American doctrine allowed each admiral full freedom of operation as he saw fit, so long as he conformed to the overall plan, but in practice it led to poor tactical co-ordination and increased the screening problems; each carrier had to provide its own fighter patrols and escorts for strikes, while the surface warships had to divide themselves to afford AA and A/S screens for them.

First blood went to the Americans, when the invasion transports in Tulagi harbour were sighted. On the morning of 4 May the *Yorktown*'s aircraft swept over Tulagi, and in three strikes they sank a destroyer, a transport and two patrol vessels, and dam-

aged a minelayer, a transport and another destroyer. An important bonus was the destruction of five H6K 'Mavis' flying boats – these were an important source of intelligence to the Japanese, and any reduction in the number of shadowers would benefit the Americans. On 6 May an Army bomber sighted the small carrier *Shoho*, which was refuelling at Bougainville while acting in support of the invasion forces. Before noon the next day the *Yorktown* and *Lexington* air groups had sunk her with bombs and torpedoes. It was realized too late that this could not be the Strike Force, and that the attack had revealed the presence of Task Force 17, but this could not be helped.

Admiral Takagi, meanwhile, was operating well to the north of TF 17, but equally unaware of its position. Early on the morning of

Left: *Lexington* recovers her aircraft on 8 May, with a Devastator taxying on deck and a Wildcat coming in to land. Note the wreckage in the gun-gallery on the port side.

Right: The *Shoho* shrouded in smoke from bomb hits from the *Yorktown*'s aircraft. Within minutes she was hit by torpedoes and more bombs, and sank quickly.

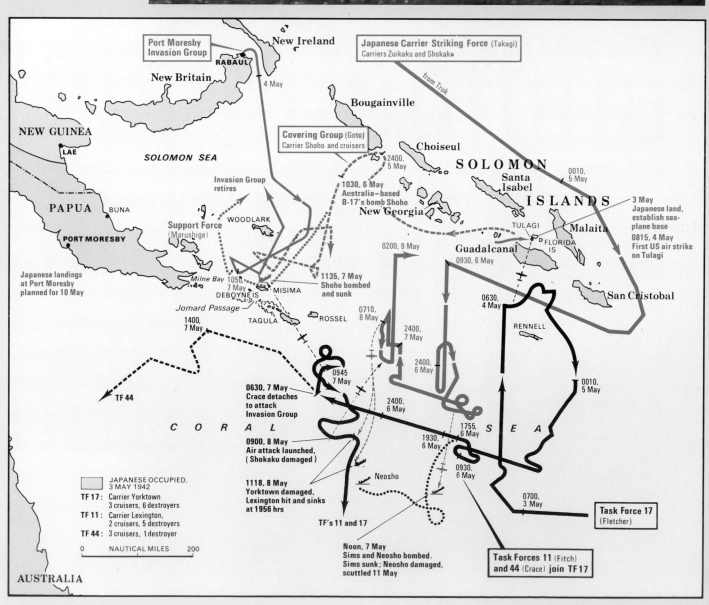

Port Moresby Invasion Group

New Ireland

RABAUL

4 May

New Britain

Japanese Carrier Striking Force (Takagi)
Carriers Zuikaku and Shokaku

from Truk

NEW GUINEA

LAE

SOLOMON SEA

Bougainville

Covering Group (Goto)
Carrier Shoho and cruisers

Invasion Group retires

2400, 5 May

Choiseul

SOLOMON

Santa Isabel

0010, 5 May

1030, 6 May
Australia–based B-17's bomb Shoho

New Georgia

ISLANDS

3 May Japanese land, establish sea-plane base

PAPUA

BUNA

PORT MORESBY

Support Force (Marushige)

WOODLARK

TULAGI

FLORIDA IS

0815, 4 May First US air strike on Tulagi

Guadalcanal

0930, 6 May

Malaita

Japanese landings at Port Moresby planned for 10 May

Milne Bay 1050, 7 May

DEBOYNE IS

MISIMA

0200, 9 May

0630, 4 May

San Cristobal

1135, 7 May Shoho bombed and sunk

Jomard Passage

1400, 7 May

TAGULA

ROSSEL

0710, 8 May

RENNELL

2400, 7 May

0010, 5 May

TF 44

0945 7 May

2400, 6 May

0630, 7 May Crace detaches to attack Invasion Group

2400, 6 May

1755, 6 May

S E A

0900, 8 May Air attack launched (Shokaku damaged)

1930, 6 May

C O R A L

0930, 6 May

0700, 3 May

JAPANESE OCCUPIED, 3 MAY 1942

TF 17: Carrier Yorktown 3 cruisers, 6 destroyers

TF 11: Carrier Lexington, 2 cruisers, 5 destroyers

TF 44: 3 cruisers, 1 destroyer

0   NAUTICAL MILES   200

1118, 8 May Yorktown damaged, Lexington hit and sinks at 1956 hrs

Neosho

Task Force 17 (Fletcher)

TF's 11 and 17

AUSTRALIA

Noon, 7 May Sims and Neosho bombed. Sims sunk ; Neosho damaged, scuttled 11 May

Task Forces 11 (Fitch) **and 44** (Crace) **join TF 17**

Left: The *Lexington* shows little sign of damage from the four torpedoes which hit her at 1120 hours on 8 May, but she has already suffered a major explosion. Just after this photograph was taken she was shaken by a second series of explosions and sank.

7 May he received a sighting report of a carrier and a cruiser and ordered an all-out strike from the *Shokaku* and *Zuikaku*. The targets turned out to be the oiler *Neosho* and her escorting destroyer, USS *Sims*, and they put up such a defence that 15 B5Ns and 36 D3As took two-and-a-half hours to sink them. In all five precious hours were lost in this uncharacteristically inept affair and Takagi lost his chance to locate and engage TF 17, which was at that moment in the process of preparing to sink the *Shoho*. In a belated attempt to save the day the Japanese launched another strike at the *Yorktown*, but an error in calculating the target's position led the strike astray. On their way back they were hammered by the *Yorktown*'s Combat Air Patrol (CAP), which shot down nine aircraft for the loss of two of their own. The survivors then lost their way, and four even tried to land on *Yorktown* in error, until the carriers opened fire. The American radar operators could see the survivors milling around as they tried to locate the *Shokaku* and *Zuikaku*. The final loss was 21 aircraft out of the 27 which had taken off. The Japanese had wasted 17 per cent of their strength on the first day of battle, all for an oiler and a destroyer, and still the American carriers had not been located.

The Japanese carriers turned northwards, while the *Yorktown* turned southeast to clear a patch of bad weather which was hindering flying, but during the night the Japanese reversed their course so as to be able to engage shortly after dawn. They kept in touch with the *Yorktown*'s movements, and were able to launch a dawn search in the right sector next morning at 0600, with a strike to follow as soon as the target was located.

Rear-Admiral Fletcher had no such confidence, for he had no idea where Takagi's carriers were. He handed over tactical command to Rear-Admiral Fitch in the *Lexington*, who ordered a big search to be flown off at 0625. At about 0800 a Japanese plane radioed a sighting report which was intercepted by the Americans and passed to Fitch, but almost immediately this disquieting news was followed by a report from a Dauntless that the Japanese carriers had been found. A combined strike of 84 aircraft was put up by the *Lexington* and *Saratoga*, but half-an-hour earlier the Japanese had launched their own strike, 69 aircraft. The world's first carrier-versus-carrier battle had started.

The American organization meant that the two carriers' strikes were about 20 minutes apart, and so *Yorktown*'s CVG-5 struck first, nine TBD Devastator torpedo-bombers and 24 SBD Dauntless dive bombers. The torpedo strike was a failure as the torpedoes were released too soon, but two bombs hit *Shokaku*, one forward which started an avgas fire, and one aft which wrecked the engine repair workshop. *Lexington*'s CVG-2 made a navigation error and so failed to find the target; after nearly an hour's search only four dive-bombers and 11 torpedo-bombers had sufficient left for an attack when they sighted the smoke from the burning *Shokaku*. Only one bomb hit, on the starboard side of the bridge, which caused little damage and five aircraft were shot down.

The Japanese attack began at 1118, 51 bombers and 18 fighters operating as a single unit. The raid was detected at nearly 70 miles' range on *Lexington*'s radar, but a series of errors by her FDO put the eight Wildcats of the CAP at 10,000 feet, between the dive-bombers at 18,000 feet and the Zeroes and torpedo-bombers at 6000 ft. To make matters worse they were not stationed at a reasonable distance from the carrier, so that only three fighters made contact before the attack developed. There were also 12 Dauntlesses stationed at 2000 feet three miles outside the screen to try to break up the torpedo-bombers' attacks. Unfortunately the B5Ns were flying much higher than anticipated, and they simply flew over the SBDs to take up their dropping height inside the carriers' destroyer screen.

The *Yorktown* was lucky not to be hit by a torpedo, and her manoeuvrability helped here, but a 250 kg bomb hit inboard of the island and penetrated three decks before bursting. The longer and less manoeuvrable

Lexington was attacked by six torpedo-bombers, three converging on each bow, and had little chance to dodge them. She was hit once on the port side forward and a second time amidships, and subsequently by two hits from 60-kg bombs, which caused only slight damage. Exact figures are not available, but about 20 aircraft were lost in these attacks.

The *Lexington* appeared to be holding up well despite her torpedo hits. Three fires were burning, but these were being dealt with by fire-parties, and the real damage had been done to her avgas system by the colossal 'whip' of the hull under the blast. Many leaks were caused by the distortion and slowly avgas fumes permeated the lower part of the hull; about an hour after the

attack a spark set off a big explosion, followed by several minor explosions and a further fire. Despite this she continued to recover 39 aircraft and even flew off a CAP, but the fires were now gaining on the firefighters, and at 1445 a second big explosion shook the ship. Half-an-hour later she suspended flying operations and asked the *Yorktown* to take whatever aircraft she could. After 1700 she was abandoned and three hours later a destroyer scuttled her with torpedoes.

The *Yorktown* had been lucky. Her fires were soon brought under control and at no time was her operational efficiency impaired. But the elated Japanese pilots had seen her burning furiously and reported that both she and the *Lexington* had been sunk. The *Shokaku* was badly damaged by the fire,

and could not recover her aircraft. She limped back to Japan but with so much water on board that she nearly capsized in a gale. Her sister *Zuikaku* also needed attention for minor defects, and so the two best Japanese carriers were out of action for some time. In fact *Zuikaku* was ready in a month, but had to work up a new air group before becoming operational again, while the *Shokaku* was not ready until late in August.

The Americans had won an important strategic victory on the first day of the battle, but then suffered a tactical defeat on the second. They had stopped the invasion of Port Moresby, but had lost a big fleet carrier in exchange for a small carrier. The Japanese had performed better because of their experience, but they had been reckless with their aircraft and their superb aircrews. At a crucial stage Admiral Yamamoto was robbed of the services of his two most seasoned and battleworthy carriers. The Coral Sea marks the high-water mark of Japanese naval aviation, the last in that chain of success which had started just five months before at Pearl Harbor.

Top: Two destroyers alongside the blazing *Lexington*, helping to fight fires and evacuate wounded.

Inset: An explosion in the *Lexington* flings aircraft and debris in the air.

Above: The final agony of the *Lexington*, as the fires reach her magazines.

9 PRIDE GOES BEFORE A FALL

The Coral Sea operation had been in Japanese eyes little more than a sideshow. Although the Army still wanted to capture Port Moresby as a prelude to the invasion of Northern Australia, Admiral Yamamoto and the Navy saw their prime task as the annihilation of the American carriers.

Yamamoto saw the small island of Midway as the key to his plans. Its name indicated its position, almost exactly in the centre of the Pacific. By itself it was of little importance, but the little atoll, actually two islands totalling just over 1100 acres, was an important advanced post for the Americans from which reconnaissance aircraft could watch the Central Pacific. In Japanese hands it would drive a wedge into the American defensive triangle which had its base on the west coast and its apex at Pearl Harbor, and Yamamoto knew that they must come out to defend it.

Fighting at such a distance from Japan would pose certain logistic problems, but the Combined Fleet staff knew that the chance of luring the American carriers into a trap was well worth the risk. The Doolittle Raid added weight to the argument, for although the US carriers had achieved very little so far it was clear that nothing but mischief would follow if they were not disposed of.

The plan was complex but sound. Four fast carriers would provide air strikes on Midway, with a powerful surface force backing it up. To make doubly sure the Aleutian Islands, 1500 miles to the north were to be attacked and two islands occupied to provide bases for aerial reconnaissance in case the Americans should try to attack the Kurile Islands, to the north of Japan. This force would have two light carriers, and a covering force comprising three battleships and a light carrier would be in position 500 miles

Above: The *Yorktown* during the approach to Midway, with a fleet oiler in attendance.

Left: TBD Devastator torpedo-bombers on the flight deck of the *Enterprise* during the Battle of Midway.

southwest of Kiska in the Aleutians and 1150 miles northwest of the Midway carrier force. This covering force also had the task of watching for any American force trying to outflank either the Aleutian or the Midway striking forces. The plan called for a rapid occupation of Midway to allow bases for reconnaissance aircraft to be set up, and so two seaplane carriers were allocated to the sur- face forces covering the assault. It was expected that the Americans would take a day to react to the first attacks, leaving a good two days for occupation and preparation for the decisive battle.

There were two major snags to the plan. The first was that it all hinged on surprise, and the second was that the Japanese had poor intelligence on the number and whereabouts

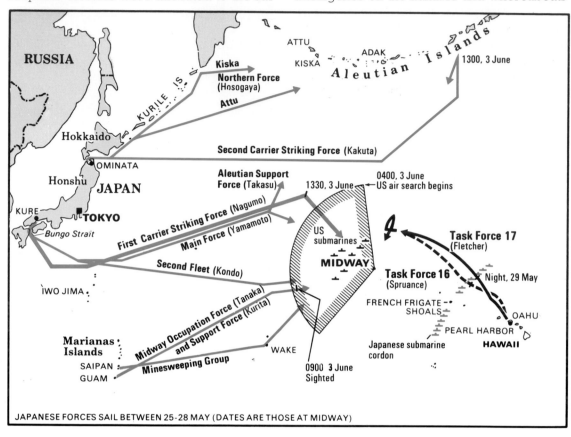

JAPANESE FORCES SAIL BETWEEN 25-28 MAY (DATES ARE THOSE AT MIDWAY)

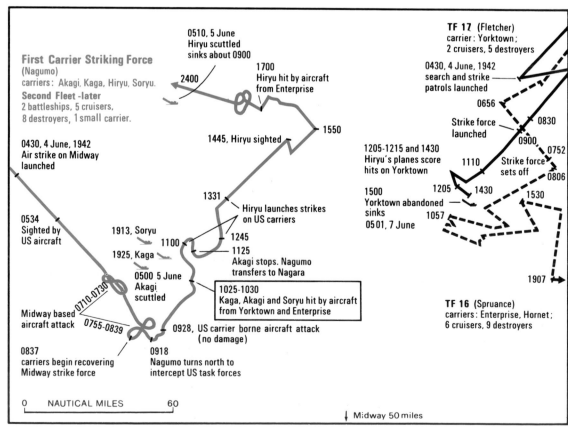

of the US Navy's carriers. The Japanese naval code, JN-25 had been broken some months before, and so Admiral Nimitz knew that a major operation was planned for the Central Pacific. Possession of this code also helped the Americans to foil a plan for Japanese Operation K, which involved a submarine stationed at French Frigate Reef, where it could refuel a large seaplane for reconnaissance flights over Pearl Harbor to check on ship movements in and out. As soon as this operation was detected the US Navy sent an oiler and two destroyers to French Frigate Reef to keep the submarine down. Operation K was suspended on 30 May, and as a result the Japanese had no news from that source. Complacency about the time available led to a bad slip, when the patrol line of 13 submarines was positioned between Pearl Harbor and Midway after TF 16 and TF 17 had passed on their way to Midway. This was the last chance that the Japanese had of finding out the strength of the Americans and they assumed that only two carriers were operational in the Pacific.

The most important piece of information which eluded the Japanese was the fact that the *Yorktown* was not only afloat but in fighting trim. She had arrived at Pearl Harbor on 27 May bearing the scars of her bomb-damage in the Coral Sea Battle, and it was estimated that it would take three months to repair her. With the knowledge that the Japanese were heading for Midway, Nimitz ordered the Navy Yard to make every effort, and the *Yorktown* sailed *three days* later,

after 1400 men had worked on her round the clock. She was not 100 per cent repaired but was battleworthy. A similar effort by Bremerton Navy Yard to get *Saratoga* away to Pearl Harbor in time, after repairs to the torpedo damage which she had suffered in January, was just too late.

The Americans had been forced to make changes in their command. Rear-Admiral Fletcher continued to fly his flag in the *Yorktown* as commander of TF 17, but Halsey had fallen ill and the command of TF 16 passed to Rear-Admiral Spruance. Although not an aviator Spruance had commanded the screen under Halsey and backed up by Halsey's highly competent air staff he was to prove an able task force commander. Fletcher was also a non-aviator, but his touch was not as sure as that of Spruance. Although in overall command Fletcher allowed Spruance considerable freedom of action in accordance with US Navy doctrine.

The Japanese could muster the *Akagi*, *Kaga*, *Hiryu* and *Soryu* for the Carrier Strike Force. The battle-hardened *Shokaku* and *Zuikaku* would have been invaluable, but as we know they were repairing damage after the Coral Sea action. Vice-Admiral Nagumo protested that the four carriers allotted to him had been driven without respite since the beginning of the war, and needed refitting. But nobody took his complaints seriously, for the tetchy admiral had been just as pessimistic about the Pearl Harbor attack. Yamamoto was ill at this time, but even if he had been in peak condition the fatal mis-

Left: Only one of the Midway-based TBFs survived the first strike against the Japanese carriers.

calculations had been written into the battle plan, and nobody would have been able to compensate for them.

The small carrier *Hosho* was to sail with the main body of the fleet, the *Ryujo* and a new light carrier the *Junyo* were with the Aleutian invasion force, and the light carrier *Zuiho* was to accompany the Support Force. The Aleutian diversion robbed the Midway force of the *Ryujo*'s air group (37 aircraft) and the 77 aircraft carried by the *Junyo* and *Zuiho* between them.

The early warning of the attack enabled TF 16 and TF 17 to be in position covering Midway, 400 miles to the northeast, and also enabled Admiral Nimitz to ignore the diversionary attack on the Aleutians. On 3 June a Catalina sighted the invasion force under Admiral Kondo about 800 miles west of Midway and that afternoon a series of air attacks started from the aircraft based on Midway, most of them ineffectual. By nightfall the two opposing carrier forces were closing on Midway, neither aware of the other's whereabouts, and by dawn on 4 June they were only 248 miles apart, the Americans to the east of the Japanese. The only difference was that the Americans knew they were looking for carriers; the Japanese were not even certain that any US carriers could be in the vicinity. Admiral Nagumo launched 108 aircraft for the first softening up of Midway's defences, but he cautiously held back *Kaga*'s air group in case any American ships were sighted. Fletcher took much the same precaution by launching only ten SBDs from the

Right: The first attack on the *Yorktown* left her dead in the water. The aircraft are F4F Wildcat fighters.

Right: The *Yorktown*'s firefighters and repair parties get to work to repair the damage to her flight deck.

118

Yorktown to search to the North, just to make sure that the Japanese task force had not turned his flank.

At 0602 Admiral Fletcher learned from a Catalina that the Japanese carriers had been sighted 207 miles northeast of Midway, and five minutes later he ordered Spruance to launch a strike from *Enterprise* and *Hornet.* He himself would launch *Yorktown's* aircraft as soon as the SBDs had been recovered and refuelled. Spruance's Chief of Staff decided not to fly a reconnaissance mission to confirm the Catalina's sighting, but to attack straight away to catch the Japanese carriers in the middle of recovering and refuelling the Midway strike. It was a rash move, for as we know, Nagumo had kept back over 90 aircraft, but as yet he had no idea that the two carriers were so close.

Although the American attacks were made piecemeal their frequency and tenacity kept up the pressure on Nagumo. At 0707 four B-26 bombers and six Avenger TBF torpedo-bombers attacked *Akagi* and *Hiryu* but the Japanese CAP mauled them severely and seven aircraft were lost without scoring a hit (one TBF actually bounced off the *Akagi's* flight deck). Nagumo now reached the conclusion that Midway's defences had not been silenced sufficiently and ordered a follow-up attack using the 93 aircraft held back for strikes against ships. This meant striking down the B5Ns to the hangars for removal of

the torpedoes and rearming with bombs. Then at 0728, just 14 minutes after the fateful order had been given, came a report from a float-plane to say that TF16 had been sighted. The report was vague and did not mention carriers or the fact that they were flying off aircraft. Nagumo hesitated, asked the float-plane to amplify its report and then suspended the bombing-up of the remaining B5Ns.

Meanwhile the attacks from Midday started again. The first was at 0755 on the *Hiryu* and *Soryu*, the second came at 0810 and the third at 0830. They achieved nothing but the

Top left: Vice-Admiral Frank J Fletcher, who commanded Task Force 16 and flew his flag in the *Yorktown* at Midway.

Top right: The second bomb hit on the *Yorktown* damaged her funnel and tripod mast, and the blast blew out the fires in five out of six boilers.

Above: The *Yorktown's* damage control parties find it harder to cope with the increasing list.

119

third attack by SB2U Vindicators coincided with the return of the first Midway strike aircraft, and this delayed the recovery of the aircraft to such an extent that ditchings and crashes of damaged aircraft pushed the total losses up to 36 aircraft, or 33 per cent of the strike. The final aircraft was not safely back on board until 0917. The delay was fatal, for at 0820 Nagumo received his first intimation that the mystery task force sighted at 0728 *might* include a carrier.

Nagumo had been outmanoeuvred and knew it, but he finished the recovery of his aircraft and resolutely turned his carriers 90 degrees north to get in position for a strike against TF 16. Even the arrival of the first wave of attackers at 0925 had little effect on these preparations for as usual they were unco-ordinated. The first wave of 15 TBDs from *Hornet* was shot down by the CAP and flak. Then *Enterprise*'s VT-6 went in with 14 TBDs, scored no hits and lost 10 aircraft. Finally *Yorktown*'s 13 TBDs attacked and were beaten off with the loss of 10 more. The TBD Devastator was inappropriately named, for

out of the 41 which had attacked that morning only six survived. Of the other aircraft in the strike, 35 Dauntless dive-bombers of CVG-8 and 10 escorting fighters failed to find the Japanese ships. All the fighters had to ditch when they ran out of fuel and only 11 bombers reached Midway. Another 50 SBDs of CVG-6 and VB-3 had overflown the estimated position and had turned back towards *Enterprise* when they sighted a lone Japanese destroyer heading back to the carriers. The Air Group Commander, Lieutenant-Commander McClusky correctly interpreted her movements and sighted the carriers at about 1005. They were in a diamond formation, with *Hiryu* leading.

McClusky led 12 aircraft of VB-6 in a diving attack on *Kaga*, while VS-6 and the remaining aircraft of VB-6 went for the flagship *Akagi*. The third squadron, VB-3 attacked *Soryu* four minutes later. Two of the three were armed with 1000-lb bombs, while VS-6 had the less effective 500-pounder.

The concentrated attack was a brilliant success. The *Akagi* was hit twice, once by a

Below: Nakajima B5N 'Kate' torpedo-bombers finish an attack on the *Yorktown* at Midway.

Bottom left: One of a pair of torpedoes hits the *Yorktown* on the port side amidships, sealing her fate.

Bottom right: A firefighting detail in the inferno aboard the *Yorktown*.

Left: The crippled *Yorktown* with a heavy cruiser standing by to provide AA fire. The cross is a mark on the negative.

Left: Once the carrier strikes were over attention could be given to saving the *Yorktown*, but the next day she was sunk by two torpedoes from a Japanese submarine.

1000-pounder which hit the edge of the centre lift and burst in the hangar, and by a 500-pounder which burst on the after end of the flight deck and set fire to parked aircraft. The *Kaga* was hit by four 1000-pounders which hit the flight deck and three penetrated the hangar. The *Soryu* took three 1000-pounders in a line down the centre of the flight deck and two penetrated the hangar. All the dive-bombers survived the attack, although 18 of the aircraft from the *Enterprise* were either shot down on the way home or had to ditch because they could not find their ship.

Aboard the three stricken carriers a terrible holocaust ensued. The *Kaga* was the worst hit, with the forward part of the ship set on fire. The third bomb hit just in front of the island and killed nearly everyone on the bridge, including the captain. The Flight Officer, the only surviving officer on the bridge, took over command and tried to fight the fires but nothing could make any impression on them. When the time came to abandon ship about three hours after the attack the fires raging below were so fierce that it was impossible to reach the engine rooms; about 800 men died. The *Soryu* was set on fire from end to end, and shortly after 1040 lost rudder control. Her captain realized that the fires were out of control and gave the order to abandon ship at 1045, but the blazing hulk continued to drift for another eight hours before sinking with the loss of about 718 of her crew. The *Akagi* was racked by fire and explosions but stood up better to the damage. Her captain took energetic

measures to fight the fires and gained time for Admiral Nagumo to shift his flag to a light cruiser. At 1130 all survivors except the damage-control parties were evacuated, and even when forced to move to the cable deck Captain Aoki continued the fight to save his ship. Although finally forced to abandon ship at 1915, Aoki lost only 221 men, a remarkably low total in the light of the number of explosions on board.

Despite the disabling of three of his carriers Nagumo still had a trump card in the undamaged *Hiryu*. She was ordered to launch an immediate counter-strike, with the certain knowledge that the Americans had used all but 17 of their strike aircraft, and that the 60 TBDs and SBDs which had just departed would need at least four hours to refuel and rearm for a second strike. *Hiryu* had her problems as well, for she had lost 10 out of the 27 bombers sent to Midway, and the survivors needed repairs and servicing before they could take off. Thus she could not launch a co-ordinated bomb- and torpedo-attack.

The *Yorktown* was the only US carrier with search aircraft left, and so she launched ten SBDs at 1130 before recovering her strike aircraft. Half an hour later her radar detected the *Hiryu's* strike and her defending Wildcats were vectored out to intercept at 15–20 miles at about noon. Aboard the carrier last-minute precautions were taken; refuelling was stopped and the avgas supply system was flooded with carbon dioxide gas to damp down the deadly vapour.

A lethal dogfight developed over the *York-*

town, with many of the attackers jettisoning their bombs, but eight of the D3A 'Vals' did not, and broke out of the dogfight to streak in through the screen. Six were shot down but three bombs hit the carrier. One burst on the flight deck and set aircraft ablaze, the second burst in the funnel and blew out the fires in five out of the six boilers, while the third penetrated three decks before bursting. An avgas fire was started, but fortunately the magazines were promptly flooded and the cofferdams surrounding the fuel tanks were flooded with carbon dioxide gas, and the fire did not spread. But the ship had lost nearly all power and by 1220 was stopped.

Admiral Spruance detached two cruisers and two destroyers from TF 16 to provide extra AA cover for the crippled carrier, and by 1320 she had three boilers working and could make 20 knots. The fire was still burning but was under control. She had flown her CAP to the other carriers, but was now able to resume the fuelling and arming of her remaining strike aircraft. About an hour later one of the screening cruisers reported that it had detected *Hiryu*'s second strike, the ten B5N torpedo-bombers and six escorting Zeroes. They were heading for the *Yorktown* rather than the two undamaged US carriers, and so once again fuelling was stopped and the fuel system was flooded with carbon dioxide, but there was time to fly off eight fighters.

This time the CAP was not so successful in breaking up the attack, and only two 'Kates' were shot down before they reached an attacking position. The CAP then chased the 'Kates' through their own AA barrage and stopped them from dropping more than four

torpedoes, but two of these struck the *Yorktown* on the port side. Only five 'Kates' returned to *Hiryu* to report that they had sunk the carrier. The Japanese, well aware of what had happened to their own carriers that morning, could not believe that the carrier they had seen burning at noon could have been operational so soon, and so they jumped to the conclusion that they had just inflicted torpedo hits on a *second* carrier. As we know, they credited the Americans with having only two carriers fit for sea, and so they were now certain that they had wiped out both of them. By a coincidence the three carriers of TF 16 and TF 17 were sisters, virtually identical in appearance, and the confusion was understandable.

The *Yorktown* was battered but still afloat. Once again power was lost and the ship lay dead in the water. She had already diverted

Below: The carrier *Hiryu* near-missed by B-17 bombers of the 431st Bombardment Group, based on Midway. Neither she nor *Soryu* were hit by these high-level attacks.

Below right: The *Hiryu* ablaze on the afternoon of 4 June. Although she has no perceptible list bombs have blown out the roof of the hangar and destroyed her as an effective unit.

Right: Admiral Nimitz, the C-in-C inspects a bunker on Midway Island after the battle.

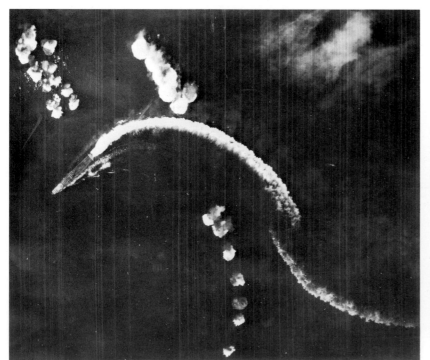

122

her SBDs to the *Enterprise*, and the fight continued to check the flooding. By 1500 she was listing 26° to port and the order was given to abandon ship.

While the attack on *Yorktown* was developing one of the ten SBDs which she had launched earlier reported the position of the *Hiryu*, and so TF 16 prepared a forlorn hope strike with all its remaining aircraft. These were pitifully few, 4 TBDs and 24 SBDs from *Enterprise* and 22 SBDs from *Hornet*, with 50 fighters. *Enterprise* started to launch her strike, 24 SBDs, at about 1530, followed half-an-hour later by 16 SBDs from *Hornet*. The Wildcats were all held back for the CAP, and none could be spared to escort the strike.

The *Hiryu* was preparing for a third strike against the *Yorktown* at 1630 but it had been postponed until 1800 to give time for the exhausted crew to have an evening meal. That meal was never finished, for without warning 13 dive-bombers attacked out of the sun, while others attacked her escorts. The first three bombs missed but then four hit, two forward of the island and two amidships. Once again there was a searing explosion of fire in the hangar, and the warheads and bombs stored in readiness for the next strike began to explode. Despite this damage the *Hiryu* continued to steam at 28 knots. Nothing could stop the flames for the bomb blast had destroyed the fire-fighting equipment, and the fires gradually spread through the ship. She burned through the night, and the order to abandon ship was not given until 0230 the next morning. Despite a torpedo from an escorting destroyer to scuttle her she was still afloat next morning, but she eventually sank at about 0900.

To Admiral Yamamoto on board his flagship, the giant battleship *Yamato*, the situation was surprisingly hopeful. Although stunned by the loss of the four magnificent carriers which had achieved so much in their short active lives, Yamamoto ordered the Second Mobile Force in the Aleutians and Admiral Kondo's Second Fleet to meet the Main Body northwest of Midway. This would give him in little over 24 hours a concentration of force, with the light carriers and the *Hosho*. Even after the sinking of *Hiryu* was confirmed the Japanese still had parity in aircraft with the Americans. But the Japanese had no experience of being on the losing side, and Yamamoto's estimate of the time needed to concentrate such a large force was too low; only Admiral Kondo's two battleships joined Nagumo by the morning of 5 June, and even the Commander-in-Chief himself was still out of touch. In any case Spruance had very prudently withdrawn his two carriers to the east at dusk, so there were no carriers to be sunk by the Japanese, although the reconnaissance aircraft had swung from one extreme to the other, and were now reporting four carriers present. Although this was obviously erroneous Nagumo and Yamamoto knew that the Americans were still dangerous.

At 0255 on the morning of 5 June Yamamoto conceded defeat by ordering the withdrawal of the invasion forces, although the covering forces to the north were told to devote their attention to the assault on the Aleutians. As soon as the withdrawal was noticed the American carriers gave chase, but inaccurate reporting resulted in the air-searches missing opportunities to inflict

Left: A B5N 'Kate' takes off with a Model 90 18-inch torpedo slung below the fuselage.

Right: During action off Guadalcanal, 15 September 1942 the carrier *Wasp* (CV.7) was hit by two torpedoes from a Japanese submarine. While she blazes part of a salvo from a second submarine aimed at the battleship *North Carolina* seven miles away hits the destroyer *O'Brien*.

Right: The *Wasp*'s avgas fuelling system was ruptured by the torpedoes, and shortly afterwards a small fire broke out on the flight deck forward.

further damage. It was a disappointment to Spruance and Fletcher but they had just won the most important single victory of the war in the Pacific, and had more than enough laurels.

The *Yorktown* was still afloat at dawn, and the destroyer watching her reported that she might still be saved, and so a fleet minesweeper was ordered to take her in tow. All day the fight went on, with destroyers standing by. At 0200 the next morning three more destroyers arrived, and at 0400 the destroyer *Hamman* came alongside to provide power for pumping. Hopes were beginning to rise as the carrier's list was reduced and the fires were extinguished, but at 1330 the following afternoon the Japanese submarine *I.168* arrived on the scene. She fired a spread of four torpedoes, three of which hit the *Yorktown* on the starboard side and a fourth which blew the *Hamman* apart. Still the *Yorktown* refused to sink, and she was afloat at dawn on 7 June, but she finally gave up the fight just after 0500.

The implications of the Battle of Midway were far-reaching. Although the war had not been won the Japanese had been given a severe shock. It is said that Imperial HQ was sunk in black despair for several weeks, fearing an immediate American attack on Japan itself. The loss of the carriers was bad enough, but at least 260 aircraft had been lost, and 45 per cent of the aircrews. These losses could have been replaced but now a fatal rift between the Army and the Navy opened up. Even when the losses became

known the Army continued to plan for further expansion as if Midway had not happened. It was this straw which started the slow breaking of the camel's back, for the Navy was forced to over-extend its resources at just the moment when it should have been resting and rebuilding its strength. For the Americans it was an obvious strategic victory, and although the loss of the *Lexington* in the Coral Sea and the *Yorktown* at Midway were hard blows the first of the new *Essex Class* were not far away from completion. The worst of Admiral Yamamoto's fears had come to pass: the decisive battle had been fought without accomplishing the destruction of the main American fleet, and now it was to be a war of industrial production, which in the long run the Japanese must lose.

There were in fact to be only two more genuine carrier-to-carrier battles, the Eastern Solomons on 24 August and Santa Cruz on 26 October 1942. These were brought about because of the Japanese Army's insistence on occupying the Solomons. That

Left: The abandoned *Wasp* continued to burn for three hours, and was eventually sunk by the destroyer *Landsdowne*.

125

precipitated the ferocious struggle for Guadalcanal, and the two battles were part of the struggle for domination of the area. In the first engagement the *Ryujo* was sunk and the *Enterprise* was damaged, and as at Midway the Americans won a strategic victory by preventing an invasion. Then on 31 August the *Saratoga* was damaged by a torpedo from a submarine and had to return to the United States for repairs. On 15 September the *Wasp* was also torpedoed, but this time the 'whip' of the hull ruptured avgas lines and fire mains and the carrier was gutted by fire. Within half-an-hour she was abandoned and sinking, leaving the *Hornet* the only carrier in the front line for a while. Fortunately the *Enterprise* returned to active duty only two days before the Battle of Santa Cruz, for the two carriers were faced by Nagumo's Striking Force, comprising the *Shokaku, Zuikaku, Zuiho* and *Junyo*. Their last success was to be the sinking of the *Hornet* in a classic attack by dive- and torpedo-bombers. Although the *Hornet* stood up

nearly as well as her sister *Yorktown* to the widespread damage she eventually had to be scuttled to avoid capture. In fact the *coup de grâce* was administered by Japanese destroyers, who sank her with four 'long-lance' torpedoes.

Santa Cruz was a technical victory for the Japanese, for on paper they had only suffered damage to the *Zuiho* and *Shokaku*. But they had lost over 100 aircraft and most of their crews, thanks to prodigal use of them over Guadalcanal. When the Guadalcanal campaign finally petered out at the beginning of February 1943 it was clear that turning point had been reached. Although the US Navy had lost two carriers, eight cruisers and 14 destroyers the Japanese Naval Air Force had lost a thousand front-line aircraft and with them most of the crews. In the long run these losses were to outweigh even the staggering losses on land. What makes it even more significant is the fact the Japanese Navy was pursuing no important strategic aim, but merely supporting the Army.

Below: During the Battle of Santa Cruz the *Enterprise* was attacked by 44 dive-bombers. The third bomb hit on the starboard side abaft the island and blew two SBDs bodily off the flight deck.

Left: A crippled Aichi D3A 'Val' is aimed by its dying pilot into the superstructure of the *Hornet*. At almost the same moment she was hit by two torpedoes below the island and completely crippled.

Below: A destroyer takes off survivors from the *Hornet* in the afternoon of 26 October. Her fires were under control, but a final strike from the carrier *Junyo* damaged her beyond repair. Even so the final sinking had to be done by Japanese destroyers.

10 THE PRODUCTION BATTLE

The Japanese knew that their industrial resources could easily be outstripped by the Americans and the British, which is why they had opted for a short war. But they had made a few contingency plans, particularly to make good their shortage of carriers. As early as 1931 a large submarine tender had been designed for rapid conversion to a carrier, followed by two fast oilers in 1934. The special features included special strengthening for the flight deck and armament. As a result the *Taigei*, *Tsurugizaki* and *Takasaki* (the latter was lying unfinished) in 1940–41 emerged as the *Ryuho* (13,360 tons and 31 aircraft), *Shoho* and *Zuiho* (11,262 tons and 30 aircraft). The *Ryuho* had too small a flight deck and so spent most of her time in home waters but the greater width of the flight deck in the *Shoho* and *Zuiho* made them effective fleet units. The *Shoho* had a short career as she was sunk in the Battle of the Coral Sea but her sister saw considerable active service from January 1942.

The Nippon Yusen Kaisha shipping line had three 17,000-ton luxury liners, the *Nitta Maru*, *Yawata Maru* and *Kasuga Maru* coming into service in 1940, and these were requisitioned by the Navy for conversion to carriers as the normal shipping links with Europe were suspended. The *Kasuga Maru* was still on the stocks, and she was launched in September 1940 and towed to Sasebo Navy Yard for a conversion which lasted until September the following year. In 1942 the *Nitta Maru* and *Yawata Maru* were also converted in about six months, and the three ships recommissioned as the *Taiyo, Chuyo* and *Unyo*. With a good speed, 21 knots and capacity for 30 aircraft they made adequate second-line or auxiliary carriers. Had the Japanese had any coherent policy of escorting convoys these three ships would have been the first escort carriers, but without arrester gear or catapults they were useless when working with the Combined Fleet. Most of their service was therefore restricted to ferrying aircraft and training aircrews.

Below: To cope with the enormous number of new pilots needed the US Navy converted two Great Lakes steamers. The SS *Seeandbee* became the USS *Wolverine*.

In October 1940 work began on converting two even larger NYK liners, the 27,000-ton *Idzumo Maru* and *Kashiwara Maru*. They were launched in June 1941 and joined the fleet in the summer of 1942 as the *Hiyo* and *Junyo*, 24,140 tons and 53 aircraft. They were the first Japanese carriers with a funnel built into the island superstructure, but in typical Japanese fashion it was angled out at 26° to take the smoke clear.

In 1939 the Fourth Reinforcement Programme was authorized and under it a new fleet carrier was ordered. Nobody knows to what extent her design was influenced by the British decision to build the *Illustrious* Class, but in much the same way the new ship was to be similar to the *Shokaku* Class in general performance but was to have an armoured flight deck. As a result she had to sacrifice one hangar but as her displacement was permitted to rise to 29,300 tons she could carry a total of 53 aircraft with spares for a further 21 on board and steam at 33 knots. With her enclosed or 'hurricane' bow and funnel she looked remarkably like the *Illustrious*, apart from the sharp angle to the funnel. Named *Taiho*, this carrier was laid down in 1941 but did not come into service until 1944.

No carriers were ordered under the 1940 Programme as the dockyards were fully engaged in the conversions mentioned previously but in 1941 it was proposed to build an improved edition of the *Hiryu* Class, with a sister ship to follow in 1942. Known as the *Unryu* Class, they were practically in-

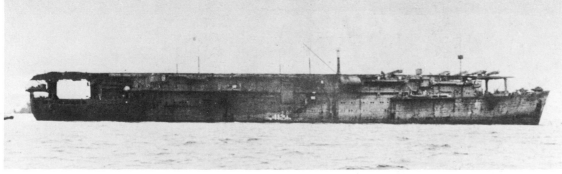

Top: The damaged *Junyo* as she was at Sasebo at the end of the War. She and her sister *Hiyo* were converted from liners in 1940–42.

Above centre: The *Shinyo* on her trials in the Inland Sea in November 1943, following her conversion from a German liner.

Above: The *Kaiyo*, another ex-liner, running her trials in the Inland Sea in October 1943.

Left: The *Unryu*, virtually a repeat of the *Hiryu* Class, seen in July 1944. She and the *Amagi* were sunk in 1944–45.

Below left: The *Taiyo* and her sisters *Chuyo* and *Unyo* were laid down as liners but completed as carriers in 1941–42.

Above: The capsized hulk of the 17,000-ton *Amagi*, sunk at Kure in the last days of the War.

distinguishable from the prototype apart from having only two lifts to simplify construction.

The loss of four carriers at Midway caused an immediate recasting of the carrier programme. The plans to build two more of the *Taiho* Class were replaced by orders for five ships. The German luxury liner *Scharnhorst*, lying at Kobe since September 1939 was taken over and converted on the lines of the *Taiyo* Class; she commissioned in December 1943 as the *Shinyo*. Two smaller liners, the *Argentina Maru* and *Brazil Maru* were taken over in December 1942; the former became the *Kaiyo* and was completed in November 1943 but her sister was sunk while still serving as a transport. The successful seaplane tenders *Chitose* and *Chiyoda* were also converted to carriers from the end of 1942.

Apart from the order for the extra three *Taiho* Class these additions to the strength were a reasonable if belated mobilization of resources, but further plans to order 13 more of the *Unryu* Class were wildly unrealistic. Even the conversion of the incomplete cruiser *Ibuki*, started in November 1943 was still only 80 per cent complete by the end of the war.

The most ambitious conversion of all was planned for the battleship *Shinano*, the third ship of the 64,000-ton *Yamato* Class battleships. She had been laid down in May 1940 but late that year work slowed down to release the work-force for other ships. By June 1942 she was complete up to the main deck, but with the decision to give priority to aircraft carriers work stopped completely. Two schemes were proposed for the 872-foot hull, one a full conversion to a fleet carrier and a

second 'partial' conversion to a maintenance or support carrier. This second role was becoming increasingly important as carriers ranged far and wide across the Pacific, and it was envisaged that the *Shinano* would be able to land aircraft for servicing and repair and then fly them off, back to their parent carrier. She would also be able to refuel and rearm aircraft operating at extreme range, and thus extend their operational radius.

Finally a compromise was agreed on, with the full maintenance facilities but a small fighter air group for self-defence. Work restarted in the summer of 1942 and as many of the original battleship features as possible were adapted. For example the barbettes for the 18-inch guns were provided with high-speed lifts to carry bombs and torpedo warheads from the magazines below. She was given an armoured flight deck and island like the *Taiho*, and had a colossal defensive armament of 16 5-inch guns, 145 25-mm guns and 336 anti-aircraft rocket-launchers.

Although this enormous number of carriers was a big strain on Japan's shipyards a much bigger strain was the shortage of pilots. At the start of the war the pilots of the *Koku Sentai* or air flotillas serving in the carriers were among the best-trained pilots in the world. Not only did they learn to fly but they learned the theory of flight and aircraft design as well. Very few were officers pre-war, and selection started at 14-year olds. After rigorous selection process the survivors were given an intensive eight-month course and about 100 flying hours. Officers selected were given an even more rigorous ten-month training and 150 to 175 flying hours; as leaders they were expected to have a higher standard than the ordinary naval pilot.

There were drawbacks. Such exhaustive training produced only about a 100 pilots a year, and it might take a man as much as five years from the time he started training to the time he joined an aircraft carrier. The heavy losses sustained in 1942 showed up the weakness of the system but it proved surprisingly hard to make reductions in the educational section of the trainee's syllabus. More reserve officers were admitted for training, but the strict physical conditions laid down for naval pilots meant that many enlisted men were not eligible.

At first the wastage of pilots at Midway was made good from the training schools, but in April 1943 naval pilots and their aircraft were put ashore at Rabaul to make up for the heavy losses suffered by the 11th Air Fleet. This exposed the pilots to attrition at an accelerated rate, and by the end of the year there was a grave shortage. This was remedied first by cutting the intermediate stage of training by 10 hours, and then by cutting out the advanced and operational training phases. The pilots were sent directly to combat units, where they received a brief conversion and tactical course before going into action. These inexperienced pilots had a short life expectancy.

There was also a lack of qualified instructors to show the pilots how to convert from the standard biplane trainer to the fast A6M3 'Hamp' fighter. Many pilots died in training accidents, reflected by the fact that accidental losses of fighters rose by more than 100 per cent in the second half of 1943. They were to rise even higher in the first months of 1944, when a worried Naval Staff decided to return to the old system of training.

The net result of this pilot-famine was that the existing carriers were manned by inexperienced pilots, while the new carriers had aircraft but no pilots. This came to a height in the Battle of the Philippine Sea in June 1944, when some of the pilots could fly off a carrier but had too little experience to count on being able to land again. Four months later at Leyte some carriers had no aircraft at all, for there was no fuel either.

The Americans operated on an entirely different system. Although they too recruited an elite force of naval pilots they cast their net wide, and with a large educated population had little trouble in finding volunteers of the right physical and mental physique for the job. Nor did the war reveal any grave shortage of candidates, and it proved relatively easy to expand the intake of training schools. In addition to the pre-war flying school at Pensacola, Florida two new schools were opened at Jacksonville, Florida and Corpus Christi, Texas, and by the middle of 1943 nearly 45,000 pilots were 'in the pipeline'.

This was an almost unbelievable increase over an intake of only 200 recruits a month in 1941, but it had been achieved without making any important sacrifices in quality. First, elementary training was delegated to a total of 92 flying schools. After three months of basic flying instruction the trainee was sent for a further three months of basic naval training, which included drill and theory. Thereafter he went to one of 16 Primary Training Schools for further flying, and if he passed (there was only a 15 per cent failure rate on average) he was sent to Pensacola or Corpus Christi for Intermediate Flight Training. Only at this stage would the young pilot be allocated to carrier aircraft, as against patrol bombers or observation. Each of these

training centres had six auxiliary stations, each with its own satellite airfields – the so-called 'pilot factories'.

Operational training started at Jacksonville, and after two months there carrier pilots went to Glenview, Illinois for training in deck-landing. For this purpose the US Navy operated the only fresh-water aircraft carriers in the world, two Great Lakes steamers called USS *Sable* and USS *Wolverine*. In winter, when Lake Michigan was frozen the pilots destined for the Pacific carried out their carrier-qualification landings ('Carquals') on board a carrier off the West coast. Either way a pilot logged from 360 to 450 flying hours. The real strength of the system lay in the high quality of the instructors. From basic training onwards the instructors were likely to be experienced carrier pilots, and operational training was always given by men who had seen combat flying.

Left: Like the *Sable*, the *Wolverine* was used to give Navy pilots practice in deck-landings without taking a precious carrier out of operational service.

Below: The ex-Great Lakes steamer *Greater Buffalo* became the training carrier *Sable* in 1943.

The qualified pilot now joined a shore-based squadron which worked up with the other squadrons which would make up the air group of a carrier as much as six months later. Once the air group was worked up it would fly out to its carrier or would be sent out to the forward area to take over the aircraft of pilots who had finished their tour of duty. In the former instance the pilots had the benefit of time to acclimatize themselves to shipboard routine and to gain experience by flying off the carrier. In the latter, the pilots could be in action only a day or two after joining the ship.

Having gone to such trouble to train its pilots the US Navy was miserly with their lives. Often at great risk submarines, flying boats and surface ships would be stationed on 'planeguard' duty to pick up aircrew. This attitude was in stark contrast to the reckless way in which Japanese commanders squandered pilots. It was not a sign of callousness but rather a reflection of a different outlook; a Japanese serviceman was expected to sacrifice his life for the Emperor without question.

The British had great problems with numbers of pilots when the war started in Europe. The Royal Navy had only 360 qualified pilots in September 1939, with another 332 under training. One of the sillier legacies of the period of RAF control was that the RN could not increase its pilot-strength unilaterally, and nothing could be done about this as training to the equivalent of the US Navy's Basic and Intermediate stages remained in RAF hands.

The problem was partially solved by moving the naval flying school to Canada, but things began to go right in July 1941 when under Lend-Lease the first RN trainee pilots were accepted for Pensacola. The RN was also able to take advantage of a surplus of Canadian and New Zealand Air Force candidates, and many of these would-be land pilots ended up as naval aircrew. By the middle of 1942 there were 1632 naval pilots.

The British and Americans could look forward to a point where they would have more aircraft and pilots than carriers from which to operate them. The British shipyards were full to capacity in 1941, and were hard put to cope with shortages of steel and interruptions from bombing but the USA had no such problems. A week after Pearl Harbor two more *Essex* Class were ordered, the *Bennington* (CV.19) and *Boxer* (CV.20). But it was estimated that it would be December 1944 before these two ships would be ready for service (in fact they did not commission until 1945). In a desperate attempt to get more carriers into service as fast as possible plans were hurriedly drawn up to convert

the 610-foot hull of a *Cleveland* Class light cruiser into a light carrier. Unlike the majority of the Japanese conversions from liners or auxiliaries, this would give a properly armoured and compartmented hull built to naval standards, with a speed of 30 knots or more. The idea was not a new one, but the pursuit of the best possible carrier had always caused the concept to be pushed aside; the best is often the enemy of the good.

In January 1942 the New York Shipbuilding Company at Camden, New Jersey received orders to suspend work on the light cruiser *Amsterdam* (CL.59), because she had been selected as the prototype for the so-called Light Fleet Carrier (CVL). The conversion was much more involved than anyone had imagined for the added topweight threatened to make the ship capsize. To offset this the hull had to be widened by 'blisters', with cement ballast in the port blister to offset the weight of the island. As in the Japanese carriers there would be only a small island, and the smoke was ejected through four small funnels projecting over the starboard side. Although two centreline lifts were provided there was only space for one catapult, a necessary addition in view of the restricted length. It was hoped to provide four 5-inch AA guns but these proved too much for them and they were never installed. In her new guise the ship was to be called *Independence* (CVL.22), and over the next six months the *Tallahassee, New Haven, Huntington, Dayton, Fargo, Wilmington, Buffalo* and *Newark* (CL.61, 76–78, 85, 79, 99–100) were reordered as the *Princeton, Belleau Wood, Cowpens, Monterey, Crown Point,*

Left: The new *Essex* Class *Ticonderoga* (CV.14) comes up astern of another carrier in 1944.

Below: The *Independence* Class CVLs betrayed their cruiser-origin, and were unique in having four diminutive funnels angled out on latticework sponsons.

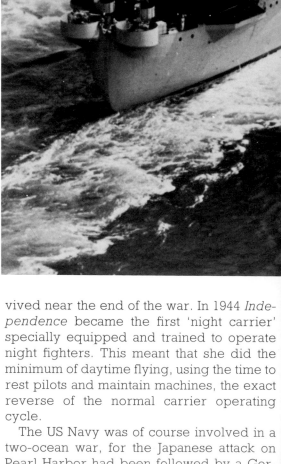

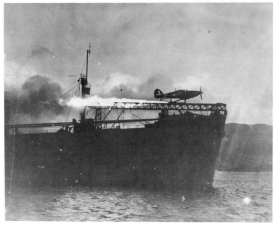

Above: A Hurricane fighter on its catapult, mounted on the forecastle of a British CAM-Ship.

Right: The CAM-Ship launches its Hurricane fighter with a searing sheet of flame. The pilot could only land on a shore airfield or come down in the sea.

Cabot, Bataan and *Reprisal* (CVL.23–30). In due course the *Reprisal* would be renamed *San Jacinto* and the *Crown Point* became the *Langley* to commemorate the old seaplane carrier sunk in the East Indies, and the class commissioned between January and December 1943.

The *Independence* Class were never more than stopgaps. They were a tight squeeze, both for the aircraft and the men, with cramped accommodation and limited workshop capacity. When they first appeared in the Pacific their air group was fixed at 24 Hellcat fighters and 9 Avenger torpedo-bombers. A suggestion to use them as fighter-carriers was turned down, but re-

vived near the end of the war. In 1944 *Independence* became the first 'night carrier' specially equipped and trained to operate night fighters. This meant that she did the minimum of daytime flying, using the time to rest pilots and maintain machines, the exact reverse of the normal carrier operating cycle.

The US Navy was of course involved in a two-ocean war, for the Japanese attack on Pearl Harbor had been followed by a German declaration of war on the United States. In response to an urgent request from the British early in 1941 the US Navy had begun a conversion of a merchant ship into a small aircraft carrier intended to accompany con-

answer to both shadowing and bombing was to have high-performance aircraft with the convoy. A further development was the Catapult-Armed Merchantman or CAM-ship, which was an ordinary freighter fitted with a catapult for launching an RAF Hurricane. The drawback to catapulting fighters in this manner was that each time an aircraft was lost and the life of a pilot was risked. Although every effort was made to rescue the pilot quickly it was a gamble, particularly in bad weather, and the CAM-ship pilots displayed a particular brand of courage each time they took off.

Before the war the Admiralty's Trade Division had put forward a scheme to convert small 'trade protection' carriers, and in 1938 there was even a plan to convert the giant ocean liners *Queen Mary* and *Queen Elizabeth* to carriers for service on the trade routes, but in each case the acute shortage of aircraft was sufficient to cause it to be pigeon-holed. The limited success of the catapult ships caused the idea to be resurrected and so approaches were made to the USN to build a prototype based on the standard C3 mercantile hull, while the British themselves undertook a prototype conversion.

The American prototype was the *Long Island* (BAVG.1), and she was commissioned at the end of June 1941. Her British counterpart was the ex-German banana boat *Hannover*, and she commissioned as HMS *Audacity* two months later. She was an immediate success, for her six Martlet II (alias Wildcat) fighters shot down, damaged or drove off nine Fw 200 shadowers in only three operations in addition to reporting nine U-Boats to the convoy escorts. The *Audacity* had a brief but hectic life, being sunk on her third convoy operation during a particularly fierce battle in December 1941 but she had proved the validity of the idea. Five improved versions of the *Long Island* were already in hand for the British, to be called *Archer, Avenger, Biter, Charger* and *Dasher* (BAVG.1–5), but they would not be ready until the spring of 1942 at the earliest.

Immediately after Pearl Harbor the USN ordered a further 25 CVEs, 24 for themselves and one for the RN. Instead of the slow diesel propulsion used in the first group these vessels would be steam powered to give a speed of 19 knots. Among the ships earmarked were four large Navy oilers, and these became the *Sangamon, Suwannee, Chenango* and *Santee* (AVG.26–29), the first really successful escort carrier conversion. They had twin shafts and carried twice as much fuel as the C3 conversions. In these small ships, as in the *Independence* Class CVLs, the catapult became a vital part of the equipment, for it enabled the new generation of

voys. Although this was the first escort carrier or CVE the origins went back to 1940, when convoys in the Western Approaches to the United Kingdom were suffering from the attentions of German long-range patrol aircraft operating from new bases on the Atlantic coast of France. These Fw 200 Condors scouted for the U-Boats and attacked merchant ships at a range far beyond any British-based aircraft.

The first answer to the 'Condor menace' was to use the old seaplane carrier *Pegasus* (the original *Ark Royal*) to catapult a land fighter off to intercept the Condor. With five converted merchantmen, known as Fighter Catapult Ships, the *Pegasus* showed that the

Left: The *Sangamon* Class escort carriers (CVE.26–29) were converted from fleet oilers. With powerful steam machinery they proved much more successful than the earlier CVEs.

Above: The *Charger* was ordered for the Royal Navy in 1941 but was retained by the USN for training British crews taking over CVEs. Even on a displacement of only 8000 tons she carried 21 aircraft.

heavy aircraft to be launched without having to encroach on the already limited landing area.

HMS *Archer* had her first deck-landing the day after the *Audacity* was sunk late in December 1941 but did not leave the United States until the following March. The third ship, *Charger* was eventually retained by the USN, but the others crossed the Atlantic in 1942, and more were ordered during the year. Eventually a total of 39 were transferred to the RN.

No sooner were the escort carriers in service than a new role was dreamed up for them, that of supporting an invasion. As both Allies developed the new techniques of amphibious warfare and combined operations they realized that the crucial need during the opening phase of a landing on a hostile coast was the provision of air cover. Before airstrips could be laid out and landplanes could take over the tasks of ground attack and fighter defence this could only be provided by carrier aircraft. This could and was provided by big carriers but they were always in short supply, and it was risky to leave them loitering offshore. The escort carriers could

easily provide fighter cover and ground attack, and although the air group was small it proved adequate for the task. During the Torch landings in North Africa in November 1942 the British *Biter, Dasher* and *Avenger* backed up by the old *Argus* provided 45 Sea Hurricanes, 12 Seafires and 3 Swordfish, while the American *Sangamon, Suwannee* and *Santee* deployed 55 Wildcats, 26 Avengers and 18 Dauntlesses.

While escorting one of the homeward-bound convoys HMS *Avenger* was hit by a single torpedo from *U.155* on 15 November. Her flimsy mercantile hull offered no protection and the avgas carried on board blew up in a huge explosion. Only 17 survived out of a complement of over 500 men. The disaster made the British very wary of the standard of the avgas system, for they regarded it as a long way below their own standards of safety. Despite protests from the Americans, who were moving heaven and earth to speed up the construction of escort vessels of all sorts to stem the losses of shipping in the Atlantic, every escort carrier (now rated as CVEs, having been previously changed from AVGs to ACVs) handed over was im-

mediately docked for modifications. These included replacement of the fuel-handling system and ballasting to compensate for the severe conditions in the North Atlantic, and took up to three months. The critics were confounded when the *Dasher* blew up in the Clyde in March 1943, and it is interesting to note that two British CVEs were subsequently torpedoed and one was hit by a *kamikaze*, but all three survived without an explosion of avgas.

The major contribution of the CVEs in the Battle of the Atlantic was to bridge the so-called 'Black Gap' in mid-Atlantic, which was beyond the reach of shored-based aircraft on either side of the Atlantic. Once continuous air cover could be provided the U-Boats which had previously hunted with impunity in this area found life much harder. The first CVE to start regular anti-submarine operations in the North Atlantic was the USS *Bogue* in March 1943, followed by HMS *Biter* a month later. The *Archer* followed in May. By June there were four operating with the convoys and the U-Boats acknowledged their effectiveness by moving out of the 'Gap' to the less dangerous waters of the South Atlan-

139

tic, Indian Ocean and Arctic. Their intervention had been inadvertently timed to coincide with a massive U-Boat offensive in the spring of 1943, by which Admiral Dönitz hoped to smash the convoy system and force the British to capitulate. The escort carriers had arrived in the nick of time.

Although they arrived later than the first CVEs, when the crisis was over, the contribution of the MAC-ships should not be overlooked. At the time that the *Audacity* was converted the concept of a Merchant Aircraft Carrier was put forward. This was an oil tanker or grain ship with a simple flight deck to allow them to carry three or four aircraft. The choice of oil tankers and grain carriers was deliberate; they could carry their normal cargo because it discharged over the side and did not need cargo-handling derricks. In all six grain ships and four tankers with 'Empire' names were converted and nine *Rapana* Class tankers, and the first sailed with a convoy just one month after the first CVE entered service. In all some 4000 sorties were flown by MAC-ships, and although no attacks on U-Boats were successful there is no record of any success by a U-Boat against convoys escorted by MAC-ships. Unlike the CVEs they were converted back to purely commercial use from the end of 1944 when the U-Boat threat had diminished, although one or two were still in service at the end of the war.

As soon as the panic over the Battle of the Atlantic had subsided the Allies could turn their minds back to the longer-term problems of naval aviation. The US Navy decided to continue building the *Essex* Class, and 19 ships of a slightly modified design were ordered between August 1942 and June 1943. They were known as the 'long-hull' *Essex* Class because they were 12 feet longer overall to improve the bow-form but were otherwise identical.

By the time the Repeat *Essex* Class were ready enough carriers had been sunk and enough battles had been fought to allow the renaming of the original ships, and so a great deal of reallocation of names took place:

CV.10 *Bonhomme Richard* became *Yorktown* (1942)
CV.12 *Kearsage* became *Hornet* (1942)
CV.14 *Hancock* became *Ticonderoga*
CV.16 *Cabot* became *Lexington* (1942)
CV.18 *Oriskany* became *Wasp* (1942)
CV.19 *Ticonderoga* became *Hancock*
CV.32 *Crown Point* became *Leyte* (1944)
CV.37 *Valley Forge* became *Princeton*
CV.47 *Wright* became *Philippine Sea* (1944)

The other names allocated were: *Bonhomme Richard* (CV.31), *Kearsage* (CV.33), *Oriskany* (CV.34), *Reprisal* (CV.35), *Antietam* (CV.36), *Shangri-La* (CV.38), *Lake Champlain* (CV.39), *Tarawa* (CV.40), *Valley Forge* (CV.45) and *Iwo Jima* (CV.46). The *Iwo Jima, Reprisal* and six more unnamed ships were cancelled in 1945.

In August 1942 a further order was placed for the first of three so-called 'battle carriers' or CVBs. This was the *Midway* (CVB.41), a

Right: The *Bismarck Sea* (CVE.95) loading SBDs from a barge alongside.

Far right: The new *Essex* Class *Randolph* (CV.11) in the Pacific in January 1944.

45,000-ton ship based on the *Essex* but with the first armoured flight deck in an American carrier. With her sisters *Franklin D Roosevelt* (CVB.22) and *Coral Sea* (CVB.43), ordered in 1943, they were a great advance over any previous design, but their great beam made them too wide for the Panama Canal. The design owed something to the big *Iowa* Class battleships, and they were a big swing away from the previous philosophy of light protection. Many other features reflected war experience, such as the siting of all guns below the flight deck, where the blast could not damage aircraft. The only carrier to exceed them in size was the *Shinano* but they far outclassed her with a designed capacity of 137 aircraft and a speed of 33 knots. Only the first two were launched by the end of the war, and three more ships were cancelled.

Two more light fleet carriers were authorized in September 1943, but this time there was no attempt to squeeze a quart into a pint pot. Instead the New York Shipbuilding Company was asked to incorporate the general layout and conception of the *Independence* in a hull similar to that of the *Baltimore* Class heavy cruisers. Time was saved by using the *Baltimore* machinery, but with six feet more beam there was no trouble in coping with the topweight, and in any case the *Baltimore* design was bigger than the *Cleveland* Class. The two ships, *Saipan* (CVL.48) and *Wright* (CVL.49) were better than the *Independence* Class when finally completed post-war, but like them they were

limited in the type of aircraft they could operate and were hardly worth the trouble and expense of building.

The British, as already mentioned, were plagued by the problems of air raids on their shipyards, changing priorities and shortages of materials, but they too planned to expand their force of aircraft carriers. Work proceeded on the enlarged *Implacable* and *Indefatigable* but neither ship would be ready until 1944. A useful addition was a small support or maintenance carrier called the *Unicorn* which had been ordered in 1938 and launched in 1941. An earlier version of the *Shinano* but on a smaller scale, she was intended to maintain and repair aircraft and had a flight deck, catapult and two hangars. Most important, a generous height of hangars was provided to allow any foreseeable type of aircraft to be embarked. Although not

Below: The British converted very few escort carriers as most of their needs were met by ex-US CVEs. HMS *Campania* was one of six British conversions, and she served on convoy escort duty.

as well protected as a fleet carrier she had a more than adequate defensive armament and a fair turn of speed, 24 knots, and was used operationally when she entered service in 1943. At the end of that year she reverted to the support role, which was as important to big carriers as the provision of oil fuel and ammunition. In both the US and Royal Navies many of the CVEs never hunted submarines, but spent the war ferrying aircraft out to forward areas.

In 1940 plans had been started for an improved *Implacable* Class but these were shelved until 1942, when it became possible to incorporate war experience. Four ships were planned, the *Audacious*, *Ark Royal*, *Africa* and *Eagle* and they were to displace 36,800 tons. They were still closed-hangar carriers, but the great increase in size allowed a theoretical maximum stowage of 100 aircraft. The main armament was as before but the close-range armament was much more powerful and each group of weapons had its own radar-controlled direction. Work proceeded slowly on the four ships and only the *Audacious* and *Ark Royal* were at all advanced by the end of war, so the other two were scrapped and *Audacious* took the name *Eagle* to commemorate the old carrier which had been sunk on a Malta convoy in 1942.

The construction of fleet carriers could only be entrusted to the biggest shipyards, and in any case they made heavy demands on labour and equipment. In 1941–42 the Admiralty drew up a fresh set of plans for a class of 'utility' carriers. Not escort carriers, they were intended to operate with the fleet, and so the considerations were studied carefully to decide just what was essential and what

was not. Armour was discarded because of the need to devote weight to size, and after discussion with carrier captains the speed requirement was reduced to 23 knots at full load. Battle experience showed that a list soon made flying operations impossible, so the normal 'sandwich' internal protection was reduced to ensure that the ships would settle slowly but upright. To speed construction the hull up to the waterline was constructed

Left: HMS *Vengeance* was one of the few *Colossus* Class to be completed by August 1945. She and her sisters proved highly successful and three are still in service in various navies.

for their size, and no fewer than 16 ships were launched by 1945: *Colossus*, *Edgar*, *Glory*, *Mars*, *Ocean*, *Theseus*, *Triumph*, *Venerable*, *Vengeance*, *Warrior*, *Hercules*, *Leviathan*, *Magnificent*, *Majestic*, *Powerful* and *Terrible*. Only two or three actually reached the Pacific, but they were to prove their worth later. The success of the *Unicorn* as a maintenance carrier led to the conversion of *Edgar* and *Mars* for a similar role, and they were renamed *Perseus* and *Pioneer* in 1944.

The biggest drawbacks of the light fleet carriers were their size and low speed, and so in 1943 an enlarged or intermediate type was begun. In this class the power was doubled to provide four-five knots more speed at full load (25,000 tons). The size was not much greater, and so the aircraft complement was little bigger than in the *Colossus* Class but with 10 feet more beam they could be given better underwater protection. Originally eight ships were planned, but in 1945 four were cancelled, leaving only the *Albion*, *Bulwark*, *Centaur* and *Hermes* under construction.

The final British design of World War II was in many ways the most unusual as well as being the most powerful. This was the 47,000-ton *Malta* Class, the only British carriers to rival the *Midway* Class in size and power. They represented a complete switch away from the armoured carrier, and were designed on American lines to serve in the Pacific. A speed of 33 knots was specified, with an armament of eight twin 4.5-inch guns as before and 55 close-range AA guns. The hangar was still the closed type, and so aircraft complement was restricted to 80 aircraft, but heavy armour was restricted to the

to Lloyds' mercantile standards but to reduce the risk of underwater damage the now standard naval layout of unit machinery was adopted, with two-shaft engines of destroyer-type to provide the rapid acceleration needed by a carrier.

The ships which resulted displaced just over 13,000 tons but could carry 48 aircraft and had one catapult. All in all they were exceptionally good value, being spacious

hangar deck, with only splinter protection on the flight deck. The hull was protected by an armoured citadel around the machinery, fuel tanks and magazines. Another unusual feature for British carriers was the provision of two deck-edge lifts as well as two on the centreline, and the massive island was so long that it had to be divided into two sections to allow for the flexing of the 916-foot hull.

Unfortunately these three super-carriers were even less advanced than the *Audacious* Class by 1945 and so they were cancelled. They remain one of the most interesting 'might-have-beens' of naval aviation, for if they had been built they would still be in service today, like the *Midways*.

By 1943 the whole gigantic Allied aircraft industry was in full swing. Although the Zero was a remarkable aircraft the Hellcat proved superior, while the Corsair, once its 'bugs' had been removed, was the best naval fighter of the war. The British rapidly became content to rely on the US Navy for high-performance aircraft, but a number of indigenous carrier aircraft continued to be produced. Some like the Barracuda torpedo-

bomber were a dubious asset; the Firefly made a good close support escort fighter, although far too heavy for its intended role as an interceptor. The Japanese lost the edge they had enjoyed in 1941–42 over the Americans, and the deterioration in quality of pilots made it impossible to fight on equal terms. Shortage of good aircraft was never the problem that it was for the British, for by 1944 the Japanese lacked pilots and fuel to a much greater extent.

The remaining Axis carriers must still be accounted for. The Germans had no option but to stop work on the *Graf Zeppelin* and her sister in 1940 for the steel and labour were urgently needed to build U-Boats. The weaknesses of the design were recognized and work started on a revision of the design. When this was complete, work began again on the *Graf Zeppelin* in 1942 (her sisters had been scrapped on the stocks in 1940) but it stopped again in 1943. By this time the Italians were making progress with their liner conversions and so the catapults were sent down to Italy to speed up the work, and this effectively marked the end of German ambitions to own a naval air arm. Work on con-

Below: The USS *Ranger* (CV.4) was unsuited for the rigours of the Pacific and so she remained in the Atlantic. This did not prevent her from playing a distinguished part in Operation 'Torch' and operating against Norwegian airfields in 1943–44.

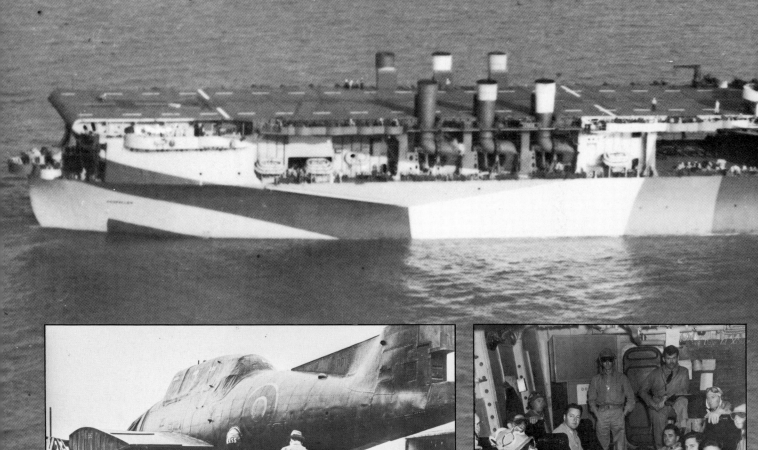

verting the incomplete heavy cruiser *Seydlitz* to a carrier began in desultory fashion in 1942 but she was still incomplete in 1945.

The drubbing that the Italians had received from the British carriers in 1940–41 finally opened their eyes to the potential of naval air power. Under the supervision of Engineer General Sigismondi work started in July 1941 to convert the 23,000 ton liner *Roma* to a carrier. Not content with putting a flight deck on a liner the Italians raised the speed from 21 to 30 knots by installing the steam turbines from two cancelled light cruisers. Under the new name *Aquila* work proceeded quite quickly and she was nearly ready for her sea trials in the beginning of September 1943, just in time for the Armistice which took Italy out of the war. However, even if she had been finished sooner there were no aircraft for her. She would have embarked a theoretical maximum of 51 Reggiane 2001 aircraft and would, like other Italian warships, have been a good-looking ship. She was naturally a prime target for the Allies after she fell into German hands and was damaged first by bombs and then by human torpedoes before being scuttled by the Germans in 1945.

A similar-sized liner, the *Augustus* was also selected for conversion, but hers was to be less elaborate. She would have been an escort carrier, with a flush deck and no island. Although taken in hand at the end of 1942 and allocated the new name of *Falco* (later changed to *Sparviero*) she had only lost her superstructure by the time the Armistice was signed. She also fell into German hands and was scuttled in 1944.

For the Germans and Italians as much as the Japanese the carrier war was finally decided exactly as Admiral Yamamoto had warned it would be, by industrial capacity. Although starting with an apparent handicap the democracies showed that they could expand their resources further and to better effect than the dictatorships, which were already near the limit before the outbreak of war.

Bottom left: A TBF Avenger ready for shipment to Britain.

Bottom centre: Fighter pilots, some wearing goggles to accustom their eyes to the darkness, wait in the Ranger's *ready room during Operation 'Torch' in November 1942.*

Bottom: A flak-damaged Wildcat is pushed overboard from the Santee *(CVE 29) during the early hours of the 'Torch' landings.*

11 CARRIERS ON THE ATTACK

The intervention of the escort carriers in the Battle of the Atlantic in March to May 1943 had been decisive, and by the summer of that year the declining U-Boat threat allowed the British to switch more of their naval air strength to the offensive.

As early as 1941 German communications in Northern Norway had been a priority target, in order to take the strain off the convoys which carried vital war material to Russia. In March 1942 the *Victorious* and her Albacores had a rare chance to attack the battleship *Tirpitz* at sea but failed to hit her. Despite the small scale of the attack the *Tirpitz* had a close shave, and even if the Royal Navy was disappointed by the result the *Kriegsmarine* was highly impressed. On Hitler's orders the *Tirpitz* was told not to remain at sea if a carrier was known to be in the vicinity.

In 1943 the *Furious* was the backbone of the Home Fleet's carrier force, for the *Victorious* was sent to the Pacific at the end of 1942 to make up numbers after the loss of the *Hornet* and *Wasp* and the disabling of the *Enterprise*. The other big carriers were usually in the Mediterranean, apart from the *Indomitable*, which after July was under repair. Only three offensive operations could be undertaken in 1943, and the USS *Ranger* took part in the third, the only American carrier strike in Northern European waters. Her air group attacked German shipping at Bodö on 4 October 1943, and her Dauntlesses and Avengers sank or damaged 10 ships for the loss of five aircraft.

On 3 April 1944 the Home Fleet mounted Operation Tungsten, using the *Furious* and *Victorious* and the escort carriers *Emperor*, *Searcher*, *Pursuer* and *Fencer* to strike at the

Below: The *Saratoga* continued to serve until 1945, but unlike her sister *Lexington* was rearmed with twin 5-inch/38 cal. guns after the 8-inch guns were removed.

Tirpitz in Kaafjord. Careful planning and rehearsal enabled the Barracuda dive-bombers to take the Germans completely by surprise. The *Tirpitz* was hit by 14 bombs and suffered over 400 casualties, and only two Barracudas and a Hellcat were shot down. The Hellcats and Wildcats had supported the strike by strafing the target and suppressing the enemy flak, while fighter cover was given by Corsairs. Had the Fleet Air Arm had something bigger than the 500-lb bomb the *Tirpitz* might well have been sunk, but the RAF insisted that there was no need for a heavier bomb.

In July and August the Home Fleet carriers struck again but on both occasions the *Tirpitz* was surrounded by smokescreens in time to foil the attack. The main problem in all these attacks was the shelter provided by the steep side of the fjord; the aircraft had a severely limited sector in which to make their bombing run, while the extensive nets prevented a torpedo-attack. During the second operation one of the supporting escort carriers, the Canadian-manned *Nabob* was torpedoed by a U-Boat but she managed to stay afloat and reached port.

Other operations were mounted in Norwegian coastal waters to interrupt the coastal shipping, and 100,000 tons of shipping was sunk by the fleet carriers alone. One of the important purposes served by this activity was to nurture Hitler's obsessive belief that the D-Day invasion would come in Norway: the losses of German aircraft were a constant drain, while an intensive minelaying effort by the carrier aircraft tied up many mine sweepers needed elsewhere. Right up to the end of hostilities in Europe in May 1945 there were of course convoys to and from Murmansk, and escort carriers sailed regularly with the convoys from February 1944. Their operations also helped to whittle away German resources, and several U-Boats were sunk in the Arctic.

In the Pacific the time for defensive fighting was over too, and by the end of 1943 it was possible to form a Fast Carrier Force (Task Force 50) under Rear-Admiral Charles A Pownall. With its six fleet carriers, five CVLs and 700 aircraft, screened by six battleships and six cruisers it was the world's most powerful fleet. It was divided into four Task Groups:

TG 50.1, with *Lexington, Yorktown* and *Cowpens* was the Carrier Interceptor Group
TG 50.2, with *Enterprise, Belleau Wood* and *Monterey* was the Northern Carrier Group
TG 50.3, with *Essex, Bunker Hill* and *Independence* was the Southern Carrier Group
TG 50.4, with *Saratoga* and *Princeton* was the Relief Carrier Group

Top: The British Fairey Barracuda's ungainly appearance was matched by its poor reputation but it performed useful work against the *Tirpitz*.

Above: After engaging the arrester wire the tailhook releases it, and the aircraft then taxies to join the deck park or go straight down to the hangar.

Left: HMS *Indomitable* with Corsairs and Barracudas ranged on deck.

147

Top: Despite the apparent chaos an experienced flight deck crew had no difficulty in untangling the deck park to allow flying to begin.

Centre: Even before jet-engines the noise on the flight deck meant that signals had to be given by hand or by messages chalked on boards.

Above: Arming a dive-bomber before a mission. This was always done on the flight deck for safety.

The Carrier Interceptor Group was commanded by Admiral Pownall, and its first task in November 1943 was to hit islands in the Marshalls group to prevent them from reinforcing Tarawa and Makin. The Northern Carrier Group, commanded by Rear Admiral Arthur W Radford supported the Makin landings while the Southern Carrier Group under Rear Admiral Alfred E Montgomery attacked Rabaul and Tarawa in turn. The Relief Carrier Group under Rear Ad-

miral Frederick P Sherman was charged with supporting the landings in the Solomons and then made a very successful strike on Rabaul which inflicted severe damage.

On 6th January 1944 TF 50 was renumbered TF 58 and put under the command of Rear Admiral Marc A Mitscher, formerly captain of the *Hornet* at Midway and one of the US Navy's most skilled aviators. The new carriers were coming forward in such numbers that it was now possible to provide six fleet carriers and six light fleet carriers:

TG 58.1 – *Enterprise*, *Yorktown* and *Belleau Wood*
TG 58.2 – *Essex*, *Intrepid* and *Cabot*
TG 58.3 – *Bunker Hill*, *Monterey* and *Cowpens*
TG 58.4 – *Saratoga*, *Princeton* and *Langley*

The new Fast Carrier Force destroyed all the aircraft defending the Marshalls in a strike against Kwajalein at the end of January, so that not a single ship was hit by air attack during the landings on Kwajalein and Namur. Then it was the turn of Eniwetok, and on 17–18 February the first attack was made on Japan's 'Gibraltar of the Pacific', the fortress of Truk in the Carolines. Truk had been the base of the Combined Fleet for nearly two years, and it was hoped that an attack on such an important target might even force the Japanese fleet to try a surface action.

In fact the attack turned out to be a sort of Pearl Harbor in reverse. Despite alerts and even a radar warning very few aircraft took off in time to cope with the raiders, and nearly 200,000 tons of shipping was sunk or damaged. A fierce air battle developed but the Japanese lost over 50 aircraft and a further 100 or more destroyed or damaged on the ground; the losses were four Hellcats and nine Avengers. Truk was no longer usable as a base, and the news was received in Tokyo with consternation for it meant that the whole concept of a defensive perimeter was in ruins. The only consolation was that a strike by six 'Kates' on the night of 17 February broke through the screen and put a torpedo into the stern of the *Intrepid*. But the *Essex* class were tough ships, and although her rudder was jammed the *Intrepid* was able to return to Majuro Lagoon at 20 knots.

With the arrival of the British carrier *Illustrious* in Ceylon it was made possible to stir up more trouble for the Japanese. Task Force 70 was formed with the *Saratoga* and *Illustrious*, to operate in the East Indies against Japanese oil and rubber supplies. Under the command of Admiral Sir James Somerville the new Eastern Fleet celebrated its formation by a devastating raid on the oil refinery at Sabang in Sumatra on 19 April 1944.

Top left: Flying operations on board the *Monterey* (CVL.26), as seen from her open compass platform.

Top right: The admiral addresses pilots in the ready room. As there is no sign of flying gear it is presumably a routine briefing.

Centre left: Gun crews apparently unmoved by the action in the background, as AA fire downs a Japanese aircraft.

Centre right: The risk of heavy damage to the densely packed aircraft on deck was always present, and fire parties could never drop their guard.

Left: Pilots and flight deck personnel in relaxed mood, watching target-practice.

Operations showed up weaknesses in the British carrier organization. For one thing the air group was smaller, and for another the strike aircraft, the Fairey Barracuda had poor performance. Nor was the vital importance of a brisk turn-around of aircraft in the hangar and on the flight deck appreciated at first by the British, who had to learn the advanced techniques from the battle-hardened crew in the *Saratoga*. Eventually the Barracudas were exchanged for TBF Avenger torpedo-bombers, and with these the *Illustrious* and *'Sara'* were able to launch a second successful strike in May. This time the target was a refinery outside Surabaya on the island of Java, and only one plane was lost. The results were nowhere as impressive as those achieved by the Fast Carrier Force in the southwest Pacific but they compounded the problems of the Japanese High Command and distracted attention from the drive against the Marianas in the Central Pacific.

It has already been said that there were only five great carrier-versus-carrier battles, and the greatest of these was the Battle of the Philippine Sea. But it was not the close-run affair that Coral Sea, Midway, the Eastern Solomons or Santa Cruz had been. The American carriers were more numerous and their aircraft and pilots much better than they had been two years before, whereas the Japanese had squandered their magnificent force of pilots with no heed for the real danger that was developing.

Once again the Japanese tried to bring on the decisive battle, code-named A-Go, in the vicinity of the Western Caroline Islands. The trigger was the American landing on Saipan on 15 June, for this island was the key to the new 'inner ring' of defensive islands which had to be held to keep Japan out of range of long-range bombers. It was hoped to make up for the shortage of naval aircraft by bringing the Americans to battle west of Saipan within range of land-based aircraft, flying from Guam, Yap and Rota.

A big reorganisation had taken place at the beginning of March, with the Combined Fleet replaced by something similar to the American task forces. The First Mobile Fleet was put under the command of Vice-Admiral Jisaburo Ozawa, with 3 carrier divisions.

Carrier Division 1 – *Taiho, Shokaku* and *Zuikaku*
Carrier Division 2 – *Hiyo, Junyo* and *Ryujo*
Carrier Division 3 – *Chitose, Chiyoda* and *Zuiho*

Some indication of how parlous the situation had become is the fact that Ozawa did not have enough top-grade fuel oil to allow his carriers to operate too far afield. The depredations of US submarines had caused such a severe shortage that his ships were using the volatile and impure unprocessed Borneo oil.

Left: An even worse example of bomb damage to the hangar of a Japanese carrier found at Kure.

Below left: The lift well could be put to a number of uses.

Below right: Fire parties tackle a deck blaze, while in the background smoke billows from another carrier.

Bottom: Japanese bombs fall near a carrier during the assault on Saipan.

Ozawa's carriers formed the biggest single force that any Japanese admiral had yet commanded but finding aircrews had been a nightmare. The air group for Division 1 had been rebuilt painstakingly out of the remnants of a previous air group destroyed at Rabaul in 1943 and had not joined their carriers until February. Division 2 was similarly built on the ruins of an air group which had been savagely mauled at Rabaul in January 1944, while Division 3 had only been formed at the beginning of February. They did have the new A6M5 Model 52 Zero, the D4Y 'Judy' dive-bomber and the B6N 'Jill'

torpedo-bomber, but the 'Judy' could not operate from the slow light carriers.

The carriers were sent to Singapore for a short refit and were then moved to their forward base at Tawitawi, in the Sulu Archipelago in the North-East of Borneo. Here they were supposed to exercise their inexperienced aircrews but this proved virtually impossible. Enemy submarines were very active, and on 22 May the *Chitose* was hit by two 'dud' torpedoes. The threat was so great that the First Mobile Fleet was forbidden to put to sea for manoeuvres, and as there was no airfield at Tawitawi the unfortunate aircrews could not improve their proficiency.

The land-based air support for Ozawa was to be provided by Vice-Admiral Kakuji Kakuta, commanding the Base Air Force in the Marianas. Because Japanese carrier aircraft were designed without the 'luxuries' of armour protection for the pilot and self-sealing fuel tanks they could outrange American aircraft by as much as 210 miles, and so Ozawa knew that he could stay out of range and still launch a strike of his own as soon as the attacks from the Marianas had whittled down the enemy's numbers. In fact Ozawa intended to fly his carrier aircraft on to Guam to be refuelled and rearmed, and to make a second strike on Task Force 58 on the way back. He was also banking on the easterly tradewinds, which would allow him to launch and recover planes while steaming towards the enemy, whereas the American carriers would have to turn into wind every time they operated their aircraft, particularly when recovering them. The plan also provided much better reconnaissance than at Midway, for Ozawa was determined to avoid the mistake of not locating all hostile carriers.

Task Force 58 formed part of the 5th Fleet under Admiral Spruance, whose proverbial caution had not only provided the victory at Midway but had certainly avoided a defeat. Spruance correctly saw his main duty as the protection of the Saipan invasion force, and he disposed his four Task Groups to block any attack by Ozawa, with special precautions to prevent him from slipping past to the north or south. An innovation was to pull the battleships out of the task groups and put them into a Battle Line under Admiral Willis A Lee; to get to the carriers the Japanese aircraft would first have to face a 'picket line' of heavy AA fire before going on to tackle each Task Group CAP and individual AA defences.

The First Mobile Force left Tawitawi on 14 June and was spotted by two US submarines next day, alerting the 5th Fleet to the danger of a full-scale battle. Land-based reconnaissance planes had made contact with TF

Left: A kamikaze narrowly missed the *Ommaney Bay* (CVE.79) while Oerlikon gunners continue firing.

Below: An F6F warming up aboard the new *Yorktown* (CV.10) during the Battle of the Philippine Sea.

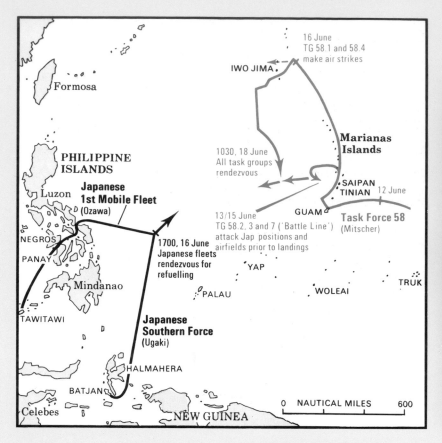

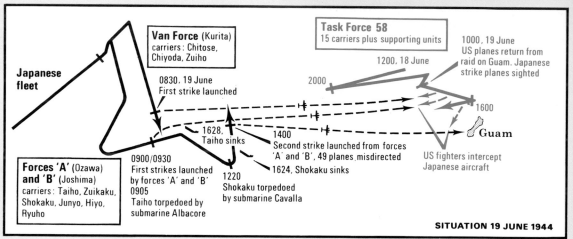

Van Force (Kurita)
carriers: Chitose,
Chiyoda, Zuiho

Task Force 58
15 carriers plus supporting units

Japanese
fleet

0830, 19 June
First strike launched

1000, 19 June
US planes return from
raid on Guam. Japanese
strike planes sighted

1200, 18 June

2000

1628,
Taiho sinks

1400

Second strike launched from forces
'A' and 'B', 49 planes misdirected

1600

Guam

Forces 'A' (Ozawa)
and 'B' (Joshima)
carriers: Taiho, Zuikaku,
Shokaku, Junyo, Hiyo,
Ryuho

0900/0930
First strikes launched
by forces 'A' and 'B'
0905
Taiho torpedoed by
submarine Albacore

1220
Shokaku torpedoed
by submarine Cavalla

1624, Shokaku sinks

US fighters intercept
Japanese aircraft

SITUATION 19 JUNE 1944

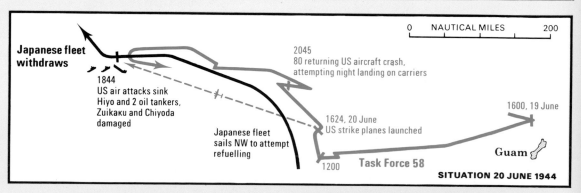

0   NAUTICAL MILES   200

Japanese fleet
withdraws

2045
80 returning US aircraft crash,
attempting night landing on carriers

1600, 19 June

1844
US air attacks sink
Hiyo and 2 oil tankers,
Zuikaku and Chiyoda
damaged

Japanese fleet
sails NW to attempt
refuelling

1624, 20 June
US strike planes launched

Guam

1200   Task Force 58

SITUATION 20 JUNE 1944

58 as early as 11 June and to forestall the inevitable attacks a massive sweep of 208 carrier fighters was made over the Japanese airfields, the first of a series of devastating raids. The result was the dislocation of Kakuta's plans to attack TF 58; the staging posts on Iwo Jima and Chichi Jima were put out of action, and so were Guam and Rota, by

nearly continuous fighter attacks. The luckless Ozawa would face the fast carriers with their strength virtually unimpaired, but to complicate his problems Kakuta for some unfathomable reason refused to tell him the bad news. From his base on Tinian Kakuta continued to tell Ozawa that his aircraft had inflicted heavy losses in aircraft and ships,

Far left: Helldivers on the flight deck, with a gallery of 20mm AA guns along the edge.

Above: The sorely battered *Franklin* returns home in April 1945. She was never fully repaired.

Left: The *Zuikaku* and her escorting destroyers weave frantically to avoid bombs and torpedoes during the Battle of the Philippine Sea, 20 June 1944.

when in fact every attack had been beaten off with heavy loss. He continued to attempt the hopeless task of covering all the other bases against diversionary raids, despite the fact that A-Go depended on the 'stocking' of Guam with 500 aircraft. Despite the fact that he had only managed to get 50 aircraft to Guam by the night of 18–19 June he reported to Ozawa that the island was secure and well-supplied with aircraft. One can only assume that Kakuta misled Ozawa out of a desire to save 'face', for he must have known that his lies spelled death for the Japanese Empire.

Unaware that he was facing a completely unharmed adversary Ozawa took up his battle formation early on the morning of 18 June, with his Van Force under Vice-Admiral Kurita and the light carriers *Chiyoda*, *Zuiho* and *Chitose* in line abreast, 100 miles ahead. His Main Body, with the *Shokaku*, *Taiho* and *Zuikaku* in one group and the *Hiyo*, *Junyo* and *Ryuho* in a second group, brought up the rear.

The first strike was launched at about 0900 the next day and was detected on radar by the Battle Line about an hour after that. It was a disastrous failure, for the curtain of flak and the superior tactics and training of the US fighter pilots smashed the attack decisively. Out of the 69 aircraft which took off only 37 survived. A second strike was launched by the main body just after, with 110 aircraft, but it too was torn to ribbons by the massed gun-fire of the Battle Line. Only 31 aircraft survived, and all they had to show was a near miss on the *Wasp*.

Ten minutes after the departure of the second strike a major disaster befell the Japanese when the submarine *Albacore* slipped through the destroyer-screen and hit the flagship *Taiho* with a torpedo. The explosion jammed the forward aircraft lift and ruptured fuel lines, and this allowed the deadly vapour to fill the hangar. She did not catch fire, however, and for over six hours it looked as if the damage-control parties would be able to save the ship. The captain turned his ship into wind and maintained 26 knots, and to help clear the hangar of the avgas fumes ordered all hatches to be opened. This permitted the avgas vapour to spread even further, and at 1530 it is believed that a starter-button on an electric pump provided the fatal spark for an enormous explosion. An added danger was the volatile vapour given off by the unrefined fuel oil, and it is assumed that the avgas explosion set off a chain reaction, for the *Taiho* literally erupted in flame. She burned so fiercely that no other ships could approach her, and when she sank at 1728 only 500 out of a crew of 2150 men could be rescued.

Another submarine, the *Cavalla* hit the new flagship, *Shokaku*, with four torpedoes at 1222, and she was engulfed in flames. She finally blew up and sank at 1510. Ozawa had already shifted his flag twice, and finally moved to the *Zuikaku*. He was still determined to force a battle with the Americans, and as he did not know of the failure of the land-based attacks he felt that his 102 remaining aircraft could tip the balance.

From Kakuta's reports he believed that several US carriers had been sunk and that a reasonable number of his aircraft had reached Guam. None of it was true, particularly not the massive strike that Kakuta led him to believe was about to be made against TF 58.

The two fleets drew apart for a while and although Spruance's carriers had a speed advantage he did not sight Ozawa until the following afternoon. The news was intercepted by the Japanese and immediately Ozawa stopped his refuelling, increased speed and prepared a strike. The sighting had been made at 1540, which put Spruance in a quandary. If he launched a strike at this hour of the day and at a distance of more than 300 miles the aircraft would have to land in the dark, and some might run out of fuel. However the chance to inflict a really crippling blow on the Japanese was not to be missed, and at 1620 he ordered an all-out strike with 85 fighters, 77 dive-bombers and 54 torpedo-bombers. Only 16 minutes later the entire strike was airborne.

It has already been said that flight deck procedure and turn-around time was the key to carrier operations, and it is significant that the Japanese had got only 80 aircraft airborne by 1840, when the first of TR 58's massive strike arrived. The *Hiyo* sank after hits from two torpedoes, while the *Junyo, Zuikaku* and *Chiyoda* were badly damaged. As for the aircraft and aircrew losses, the exultant American pilots dubbed the battle 'The Great Marianas Turkey Shoot'. The final total came to some 400 carrier aircraft, 100 land aircraft and a number of floatplanes, as well as the large majority of their pilots. It was effectively the end of the Japanese Naval Air Force.

It almost dealt a crippling blow to the Americans as well. The carrier aircraft were at the limit of their endurance, and it was a case of finding the shortest route back. In ones, twos and threes they made their way, as the light faded. Admiral Mitscher ordered the carriers to close the gap as best they could and the pilots throttled back to conserve fuel, but it was 2230 before the first aircraft were within range of the carriers' homing beacons. In the darkness it was impossible to make out more than the carrier's wake, and with aircraft flying around in confusion it was only a matter of time before two collided. Others ran out of fuel and as their engines died had to go down into the sea.

To an ex-pilot the scene was agonising, and eventually Mitscher quietly gave the order, 'Turn on the lights'. To illuminate the flight decks and mastheads was to run the risk of being torpedoed or even to be attacked by Japanese aircraft, and it had never been done since the war began, but Mitscher knew that the pilots could not land without illumination. Soon the whole of TF 58 was a blaze of lights, with glow-lighting on the edges of each flight deck, masthead lights and recognition lights to identify the individual carrier. Some ships even fired star-shell, while the flagship of each task group burned a searchlight straight up into the sky as a beacon. Many aircraft crashed on landing, and there was little attempt to find the right carrier as there was so little time. In all 100 of the 216 aircraft sent off that day were lost, but fortunately the loss of pilots was much lower as many managed to ditch near ships or were picked up by flying boats and surface ships of all sizes. Some measure of the carnage is that only 20 of the aircraft lost were shot down in combat with the Japanese.

The Battle of the Philippine Sea was the last and greatest of the carrier battles, and it wiped out the Japanese air groups. But Spruance had his critics, who felt that he should have sunk more of Ozawa's fleet, and the aftermath of the battle was a rather unedifying scramble by senior commanders to indict him for his alleged timidity. Spruance refused to justify himself, but it must be remembered that he did not *know* exactly what Ozawa's dispositions were at the closing stages, and there was still a chance that a detached force of Japanese ships might break through to attack the Saipan invasion forces. Another fact that is ignored is the exhaustion of the air crews, who had flown to the limit of their endurance, in every sense of

Right: The *Zuiho* in her bizarre camouflage scheme under attack from the *Enterprise* air group during the action off Cape Engaño, 25 October 1944.

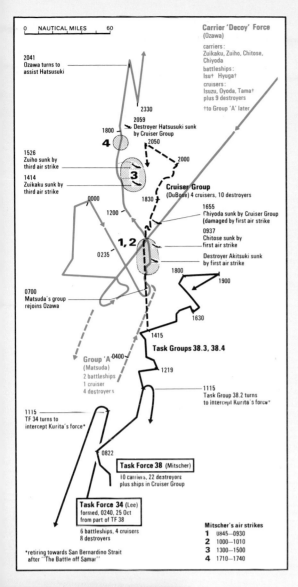

Carrier 'Decoy' Force
(Ozawa)

carriers:
Zuikaku, Zuiho, Chitose, Chiyoda
battleships:
Ise†, Hyuga†
cruisers:
Isuzu, Oyoda, Tama†
plus 9 destroyers

†to Group 'A' later

0   NAUTICAL MILES   60

2041
Ozawa turns to
assist Hatsusuki

2330

2059
Destroyer Hatsusuki sunk
by Cruiser Group

1800

4

2050

1526
Zuiho sunk by
third air strike

2000

1414
Zuikaku sunk by
third air strike

3

1830

Cruiser Group
(DuBose) 4 cruisers, 10 destroyers

0000

1200

1655
Chiyoda sunk by Cruiser Group
(damaged by first air strike)

1, 2

0937
Chitose sunk by
first air strike

0235

Destroyer Akitsuki sunk
by first air strike

0700
Matsuda's group
rejoins Ozawa

1800

1900

1630

1415

Group 'A'
(Matsuda)
2 battleships
1 cruiser
4 destroyers

0400

Task Groups 38.3, 38.4

1219

1115
Task Group 38.2 turns
to intercept Kurita's force*

1115
TF 34 turns to
intercept Kurita's force*

0822

Task Force 38 (Mitscher)
10 carriers, 22 destroyers
plus ships in Cruiser Group

Task Force 34 (Lee)
formed, 0240, 25 Oct
from part of TF 38

6 battleships, 4 cruisers
8 destroyers

*retiring towards San Bernardino Strait
after ''The Battle off Samar''

Mitscher's air strikes
1   0845—0930
2   1000—1010
3   1300—1500
4   1710—1740

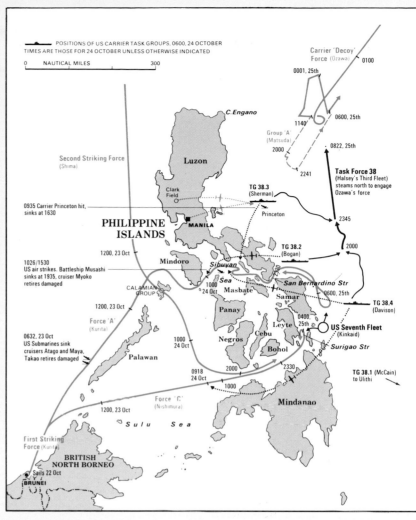

POSITIONS OF US CARRIER TASK GROUPS, 0600, 24 OCTOBER
TIMES ARE THOSE FOR 24 OCTOBER UNLESS OTHERWISE INDICATED

0   NAUTICAL MILES   300

**Carrier 'Decoy'
Force** (Ozawa)   0100

C. Engano

0001, 25th

1140

0600, 25th

Second Striking Force
(Shima)

Luzon

Group 'A'
(Matsuda)

2000

0822, 25th

2241

Task Force 38
(Halsey's Third Fleet)
steams north to engage
Ozawa's force

Clark
Field

TG 38.3
(Sherman)

0935 Carrier Princeton hit,
sinks at 1630

Princeton

MANILA

2345

**PHILIPPINE
ISLANDS**

TG 38.2
(Bogan)

2000

1200, 23 Oct

Mindoro

1026/1530
US air strikes. Battleship Musashi
sinks at 1935, cruiser Myoko
retires damaged

Sibuyan
Sea

1000
24 Oct

Masbate

Samar

San Bernardino Str

0600, 25th

TG 38.4
(Davison)

CALAMIAN
GROUP

1200, 23 Oct

Panay

Cebu

0400,
25th

Leyte

US Seventh Fleet
(Kinkaid)

Force 'A'
(Kurita)

1000
24 Oct

Negros

Bohol

Surigao Str

0632, 23 Oct
US Submarines sink
cruisers Atago and Maya,
Takao retires damaged

Palawan

1000
24 Oct

2330

TG 38.1 (McCain)
to Ulithi

1200, 23 Oct

0918
24 Oct

2000

1000

Force 'C'
(Nishimura)

Sulu   Sea

Mindanao

**First Striking
Force** (Kurita)

**BRITISH
NORTH BORNEO**

Sails 22 Oct

BRUNEI

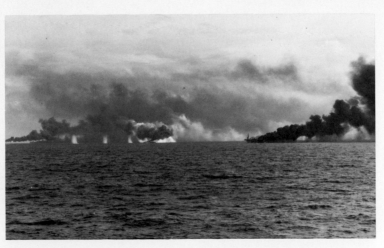

Above: A Japanese dive-
bomber scores a near miss
against the *Bunker Hill*
(CV.17).

Left: Destroyers and DEs of
CarDiv 25 lay smokescreens
to protect the 'jeep carriers'
from gunfire of Japanese
battleships and heavy
cruisers during the Battle of
Samar.

157

the word. The critics of Spruance also forget what happened four months later at Leyte, when aggressive tactics by Halsey led to a mad chase after a decoy force of light carriers without aircraft. This opened the way to an attack by Japanese surface forces against the invasion transports, and only a desperate stand by the destroyers and escort carriers saved the day.

Leyte was hardly a carrier battle, but the stand of the 'jeep carriers' off Samar on 25th October 1944 showed how much punishment these little ships could take. Their air groups were armed for softening up beach obstacles and strongpoints, not battleships and heavy cruisers, but still the pilots made dummy runs at the Japanese ships. The CVE *Gambier Bay* was sunk by numerous hits from shells and her sister *Kalinin Bay* was badly damaged. Eventually Admiral Kurita called

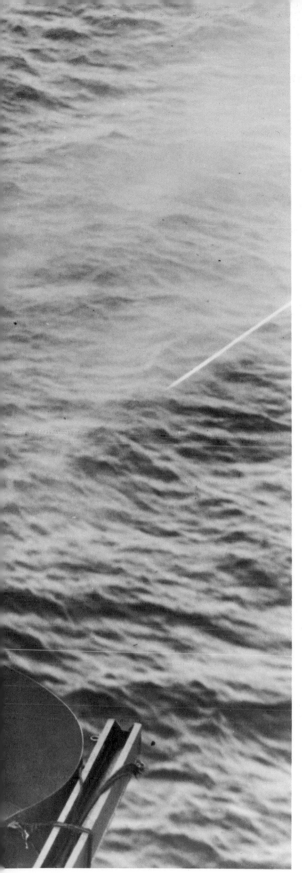

these attacks missed, but later the *Suwannee* was hit by a Zero which plunged into her and killed 71 men and injured 82. Further attacks followed, but the only fatality was the CVE *St Lô*, which blew up and sank after a Zero had set off her ammunition and avgas.

In March 1945 TF 58 struck the first blow against the Japanese home islands since the Doolittle Raid three years before. While 55 miles off the coast of *Kyushu* the *Franklin* was hit by two bombs dropped by a low level bomber. Both detonated in the hangar and set fire to the fully fuelled and armed aircraft. A minute later the first of a series of explosions rocked the ship, and these continued for five hours. But she did not sink and the fight to get her home began. The carrier was unable to steam, but next day she was able to make two knots, and this allowed the cruiser *Pittsburgh* to get her in tow. Fires broke out intermittently but two days later she was able to work up to 22 knots, and she crept back to Ulithi for more permanent repairs. The casualties were on a horrific scale,

Left: The 20mm Oerlikon gun replaced the .50-inch machine gun but by 1944 it could not stop a determined pilot.

Top: As the pilot walks away (foreground) the flight deck crew manhandles his Hellcat fighter out of the way.

Above: A TBF Avenger over HMS *Indomitable*.

off his attack just as he seemed certain to break through.

A more sinister manifestation of Japanese power declared itself at Samar, when the first *kamikazes* or suicide aircraft attacked the CVEs. The *Santee* was jumped by a Zero which dived straight onto her flight deck and blew a huge hole. Seconds later another Zero broke into a suicide dive over the *Suwannee*, and a third made for the *Petrof Bay*. Both of

Right: The efficiency of a carrier depended on the flight deck crew as much as the pilots.

Right: Crewmen wait in the ready room.

Below: Ironically the last Japanese carrier left in August 1945 was the veteran *Hosho*, completed in 1925. She spent most of the War on training duties in the Inland Sea.

832 dead and 270 wounded and the *Franklin* proved so badly crippled that she was never put back into service.

The landings on Okinawa in April 1945 provoked a great onslaught from the *kamikazes*, and as at Leyte they made the carriers their prime target. The *Enterprise, Intrepid, Bataan* and *Bunker Hill* were all hit, the last-named suffering a terrible ordeal. Like the *Franklin* she was never repaired, but the fast carriers were not sunk and the invasion was not delayed.

Into this witches' cauldron came the newly formed British Pacific Fleet. Although small in numbers its four armoured carriers *Illustrious, Indefatigable, Indomitable* and *Victorious* were formed into Task Force 57 and given the task of forming a buffer to stop the

Japanese forces in the Ryukyus from attacking the Okinawa invasion. The *kamikazes* attacked them as avidly as they had the American carriers, and in turn the *Indefatigable* and *Illustrious* were hit. But the armoured flight deck stood up to the impact and the two carriers were back in action almost immediately. The *Illustrious* was showing signs of strain, a legacy of her damage in 1941, and she was relieved by the *Formidable* and so TF 57 remained at full strength. On 4 May the *Formidable* was hit by a Zero and although the flight deck was holed and 11 aircraft were destroyed she was back in action less than half-an-hour later. Two days later she was hit again and lost seven aircraft, but the fire was out within a few minutes.

All arms played their part in defeating the Japanese but there can be no doubt that the fast carriers decided the outcome. Without their support the 'island-hopping' strategy could never have been developed, and only when the Marianas had been captured could B-29s begin to bomb Japanese cities. What was even more important was that the carriers had stopped the Japanese at Midway, an essential prelude to the drive across the Pacific.

One could go further and say that had the atom bomb not been dropped on Hiroshima and Nagasaki the fast carrier task forces acting in support not only of round-the-clock aerial bombing but also of aerial and submarine minelaying could have brought Japan to surrender within three months.

Left: Gunners on a quadruple 40mm Bofors gun mounting relax and join in the popular sport of 'goofing' as an aircraft comes in.

12 THE NEW CAPITAL SHIP

Although it had never been conceded during World War II the title of Capital Ship definitely passed from the battleship to the aircraft carrier after V-J Day. The massed AA batteries of the battleships had been useful to the fast carriers but as weapons their 16-inch guns were far outclassed by the torpedoes and bombs of carrier aircraft. There was no doubt about which would go first, and within months of the end of hostilities the first battleships went into reserve or in the case of the oldest, straight to the scrapyard, whereas carriers remained in commission.

There was serious doubt, however, about the future of the carrier. The dropping of the atom bomb had led to a renewed frenzy of speculation and claims that the Bomb had made all ships obsolete at a stroke. The old *Saratoga* and the damaged CVL *Independence* were among the target-ships at

Above: The *Tarawa* (CVS.40) running at speed off Guantanamo Bay, Cuba in July 1957.

Right: Three generations of French naval air power (l to r) the *Béarn*, the ex-British *Arromanches* and the new *Foch*.

162

Bikini in 1946, and although the 'Sara' sank several hours after the second test many valuable lessons were learned. The cancelled *Essex* Class *Reprisal* was later used as a target for underwater explosions, a fate reserved for the badly damaged *Independence* some five years later.

Scrappings of the old carriers and sale of many of the CVEs whittled the US Navy's carrier strength down considerably, but this left the mighty *Midway* Class and the whole *Essex* Class, apart from the incomplete *Oriskany*. This unit was suspended to allow a study to be made of improvements, and she would not complete until 1950. By the end of 1947 there were 20 carriers active in the Fleet, three CVBs, eight CVs, two CVLs and seven CVEs.

The only other navy with a flourishing naval air arm was the British, but the end of hostilities had seen the cancellation of many ships. The big *Malta* Class went as did two of the *Ark Royal* Class and four of the *Hermes* Class, but all 14 of the *Colossus* Class light fleet type were kept. All the older carriers were scrapped, as well as the damaged *Formidable*, leaving three *Illustrious* Class and two *Implacable* Class as the front-line strength.

The French still had the old *Béarn*, which was in service as an aircraft transport and the small CVE HMS *Biter* was on loan from the British. To give the *Aéronavale* a chance to re-establish itself the British transferred the new light fleet carrier *Colossus* in 1946 and she became the *Arromanches*. The Netherlands Navy was given her sister HMS *Venerable*, under the new name *Karel Doorman*. This name had been given to the ex-British CVE *Nairana*, and the Dutch had manned several MAC-ships in 1944–45, but in 1948 the name was transferred to the new carrier.

Below: The new 'battle' carrier *Midway* (CVB.41) in 1947.

Bottom left: An F2H Banshee jet fighter makes a rough landing on board the *Midway* in February 1953.

Bottom right: Despite her massive size the *Midway* was not as successful a design as the *Essex*, and could not handle the bigger air group any faster.

Above: The superstructure of the *Valley Forge* (CV.45) sprouts radar aerials of all kinds.

Above right: The *Leyte* (CV.32) in the 1950s.

Another of the class, HMS *Warrior* was lent to the Canadians to enable them to build on the expertise they had acquired by manning two CVEs in the Battle of the Atlantic. The fourth country to acquire one of these ubiquitous small carriers was Australia, which renamed HMS *Terrible* HMAS *Sydney* in 1948, followed later by HMAS *Melbourne* (ex *Majestic*). The Canadians later took the *Magnificent* in place of the *Warrior* and then the *Bonaventure* (ex *Powerful*).

The big question immediately after the war was how to operate jet aircraft from carriers, for many experts considered them too fast and dangerous for the job. Three FR-1 Ryan Fireballs were operated from the USS *Ranger* in 1945 and from the CVE *Wake Island* to test the feasibility and although a landing was made with partial assistance from the piston engine it does not count as a true jet landing. This honour goes to a British Vampire I fighter, which landed on board the light fleet carrier HMS *Ocean* on 3 December 1945. Just over seven months later the first jet took off from the *Franklin D Roosevelt*, an XFD-1 Phantom.

All these early jet aircraft were very sluggish in their response to throttle as well as being wildly extravagant on fuel, and so propeller-driven aircraft remained in service for a long time. The greatest of these was the AD-1 Skyraider, the most successful piston-engined attack aircraft of its day. Its heavy weapon-load and great manoeuvrability kept it in service longer than any other shipboard aircraft except the F4U Corsair.

As early as 1945 there had been discussion of the possibility of arming carrier-borne aircraft with nuclear weapons. The idea might have remained on the drawing board but for a coincidence. The 'Fat Man' bomb dropped on Nagasaki weighed about 10,000 lbs, which happened to be the payload specified for a new carrier-borne bomber. This would ultimately be the AJ Savage, a twin piston-engined bomber delivered in 1949. As an interim nuclear bomber the P2V-2 Neptune was pressed into service, and it first flew from the *Coral Sea* on 27 April 1948.

Needless to say, the Navy's attempt to trespass on the sacred ground of strategic bombing caused a near-repetition of the Navy versus Air Force rivalry of Mitchell or Trenchard proportions. The Navy argued that the dispersion of what was then the west's monopoly of nuclear power helped to reduce the risk of a surprise attack, and that research should be devoted to production of a lighter nuclear bomb for carrier aircraft. The Air Force, newly independent of Army control, argued that 'big is best' and that the current heavy weapons were best dropped by B-29 bombers. The 'difference of opinion' was to break out into a major row subsequently, but in the meantime the tests continued aboard the three *Midway* Class carriers to develop a naval nuclear capability.

Even the *Midways* were a tight squeeze for such aircraft; it was said during one of the first Neptune landings that if anything went wrong the US Navy would have a flush-decked carrier whether it liked it or not! This was a reference to the Congressional approval in 1948 of a new 60,000-ton carrier to be called the *United States* (CV.58, later CVA.58). She would be the largest warship ever built, 1090 ft long and 130 ft wide at the waterline, and driven by steam turbines at 33 knots. To facilitate flying there would be no island, merely Japanese-style funnels projecting to port and starboard, and as in the old *Hosho* and *Argus* the navigating bridge

would be hoisted up hydraulically when needed. There would be no centreline lifts, but four deck-edge lifts to leave space for four catapults.

The keel was laid at Newport News on 18 April 1949, but ten days earlier the purchase of 30 giant six-engined B-36 bombers was announced. The Air Force was well aware that the purchase price of $234 million would be challenged by Congress and compared unfavourably with the estimated cost for CVA.58 of only $189 million. It was war to the knife, and the Air Force went so far as to claim that the Navy was lying in quoting the price, for it 'knew' that the real cost would be close to $500 million. The more rational arguments against the carrier were as follows:

1 It would duplicate the strategic bombing mission of the Air Force, which was a 'primary' function
2 The Soviet Union was not a sea power and did not depend on imports of raw materials
3 The US Navy and the Royal Navy had overwhelming superiority over the Soviet Navy
4 The carrier-based bomber could only operate within a 700-mile radius of land-targets

If the arguments did not crop up so frequently they would not be worth discussing. (Point 1) has no logical justification, and historically, as we have seen, it was naval aircraft which carried out the first 'strategic' raids. (Points 2 and 3) may have had some relevance in 1949, but in 1979 they have a hollow ring. (Point 4) was demonstrably untrue, for in tests with the P2V-2 Neptune and AJ Savage bombs had been delivered as much as 4800 miles away, which inferred a *radius* of 2400 miles.

To be fair to the Air Force the Navy was premature in demanding that scarce resources should be diverted when the feasibility of carrier-based nuclear bombing had only just been demonstrated. The argument had to be centred on strategic bombing because Congress and the American taxpayer were convinced that the next war would be decided by bombing alone. It had not yet become a four-minute affair of ICBMs, but 'conventional' forces like armies and navies were seen as having no future against nuclear attack. It is a strange paradox whereby the fear of nuclear devastation tempts politicians to abandon older weapons and thereby makes the use of nuclear weapons all the more certain.

The Navy's answer was appropriate, but did nothing to help assuage inter-service jealousies. It issued a challenge by asking Congress to allow a B-36 to be made available for tests against the piston-engined F4U-5 Corsair and the new twin-jet F2H-1 Banshee fighters. The former had a ceiling of just over 44,000 feet and the latter over 48,000 feet, but both aircraft could fly several thousand feet higher than the B-36. The Air Force declined to be drawn on this point, but their refusal was highlighted by the revelation of a new Soviet interceptor capable of reaching 50,000 feet, the MiG-15.

The verdict of history must be that in principle the Air Force was right, for it could deliver more nuclear weapons at less cost. But it was wrong in promoting the B-36 as the vehicle, since the improved B-29, known as the B-50, proved a much more cost-effective interim bomber until the advent of the jet-propelled B-47 and B-52. The Navy was right to insist on a new carrier but wrong to pin its

Above: The introduction of
jet aircraft caused many
problems of handling and
endurance, but their fuel is
less inflammable than Avgas.

Inset: The Firefly was used
by British carriers in the
Korean War.

arguments on strategic bombing, for the
carrier's most deadly power lies in her ability to destroy an enemy's control of the sea.

Fortunately the Navy's obsession with a
nuclear strike capability did not preclude
some measures of good housekeeping. The
22 *Essex* Class (excluding the badly damaged *Franklin* and *Bunker Hill*) were earmarked for modernisation to allow them to
operate jet aircraft. The prototype was to be
the *Oriskany* (CV.34), which had been suspended since 1946. The project was known as
27A, from the Bureau of Ships' designation
SCB 27, and its main requirements were to
provide a stronger flight deck for the heavier aircraft in service, larger catapults, more
powerful lifts, more fuel stowage and better
radars. This was asking a lot from a design
which was showing signs of overloading by
1945.

The most obvious change was the removal
of the four pairs of 5-inch/38 calibre guns
from around the island, which was itself re-
modelled in a more compact form. By fitting a
streamlined raked cap the smoke was carried clear of the radar array as well. The

former collection of 40-mm and 20-mm AA
guns were replaced by 14 of the more
efficient twin 3-inch/50 calibre automatics as
well. A much-appreciated luxury was an escalator underneath the island to carry pilots
from their ready-room to the flight deck.

The flight deck was strengthened to take
aircraft up to 52,500 lbs, the lifts were
strengthened to take aircraft up to 30,000 lbs
and the lifts themselves were enlarged. The
stowage of aviation fuel (avgas and the less
volatile jet fuel) was increased to 300,000 gallons and it was possible to deliver 150 gallons
per minute on the flight deck. Originally 50
gallons per minute had been sufficient to fuel
a Corsair, but a jet fighter like the Panther
needed 1000 gallons of fuel and the increased pumping capacity was needed to
sustain the pace of flight-deck operations.

Many changes were made internally in the
light of wartime and post-war experience.
The escalator has been mentioned, but this
was made possible by moving the three
ready rooms from the gallery deck to No 2
deck below the island, so that pilots were
saved a long haul in their bulky flying over-

alls and gear. The fire-precautions in the hangar were greatly improved with a new high-capacity fog and foam system and sprinklers. All this meant weight high up, where a ship can least afford it, and the remedy was to reduce weight drastically. The 4-inch belt armour was removed and replaced by splinter plating, a modification which could have been made to the last *Essex* Class in 1945. This was not enough and the hull had to be widened by an 8-foot 'bulge' or blister on the port side. This provided stability and in theory would reduce speed by 2 knots, but on her trials in February 1951 the *Oriskany* made 32.5 knots on a full load displacement of 37,400 tons. The worst drawback of the blister was to make the ship slew to port when docking.

Although the thirstiness of jet aircraft was proving a headache it was much better in one respect. As it was much less volatile it was now possible to store it in tanks outside the armoured citadel, and in any case the citadel was now full of items never considered in 1940. JP5 or HEAF could even be used in place of black oil in the boilers at a pinch, and so some oil fuel tanks could be converted to JP5; it was even possible to stow JP5 in the blister. However in 1950 there were many piston-engined aircraft still in service, and for some years to come avgas still had to be carried.

The USS *Oriskany* commissioned in September 1950, after two years of work, just in time for the Korean War. The 'conventional' conflict that the pundits had said could never happen again had arrived, and the only way of dealing with it was to mobilize Western seapower to offset the enormous local preponderance of North Korean ground troops. Not only the carriers were needed but even the battleships played their part in bringing seapower to bear on the land war. Korea is mountainous, making it difficult to establish airfields quickly, and so carrier aircraft were able to give much-needed support.

The United States carriers were backed up by the British light fleet carriers *Triumph*, *Ocean*, *Theseus* and *Glory* and the Australian *Sydney* operating at various times. In November 1950 a US Navy F9F from the *Philippine Sea* shot down the carriers' first MiG-15 while one of HMS *Ocean's* Sea Furies shot down one in 1952. At the end of April 1951 Skyraiders from the *Princeton* torpedoed the Hwachon reservoir. Air Force B-29s had failed to hit the dam with guided bombs, but the eight Skyraiders scored six hits with torpedoes set for a surface run. The older *Essex* Class on occasion even took a hand in shore bombardment with their 5-inch guns.

The Korean War had a salutary effect on airy talk about the end of conventional forces.

The Cold War which followed had to be fought with a mixture of nuclear threat accompanied by conventional ability, and for this the carrier proved ideal. As a result ten more *Essex* Class were commissioned by 1953. The *Essex*, *Wasp*, *Lake Champlain*, *Bennington*, *Yorktown*, *Randolph* and *Hornet* had all received the SCB 27A modernisation, while their sisters *Bonhomme Richard*, *Shangri-La*, *Hancock*, *Intrepid*, *Lexington* and *Ticonderoga* were all in hand for the slightly improved SCB 27C modernisation. This involved stronger catapults, for the H8 type fitted to the *Oriskany* and her sisters was no longer strong enough to launch the latest aircraft.

Fortunately remedies have a habit of being invented in step with the factors which create the problems. The British had been quietly pursuing a number of interesting developments, all aimed at improving the ability of carriers to handle jet aircraft. The first of these was a flexible rubber deck installed on HMS *Warrior* in 1948. The idea was to dispense with the weight of the undercarriage in the aircraft and the weight of arrester gear

Above: The modernised *Hancock* (CV.19) with angled deck and hurricane bow, cruising off San Diego.

in the carrier, but first trials were carried out using a Vampire fighter with its wheels retracted. Tests showed that the idea had much to recommend itself, but it died simply because it would have meant a reduction of flexibility; naval aircraft would only be able to land on land bases equipped with flexible runways, and thus the fundamental advantage of being able to move aircraft from a land air base out to a carrier and back would be lost.

The next suggestion was for an angled deck, which arose out of a conference convened in August 1951 at the British Royal Aircraft Establishment to study the growing difficulties of handling heavy aircraft with higher landing speeds. The biggest risk in deck landings was still overshooting after missing an arrester wire; even if the aircraft did not crash into the deck park at the forward end of the flight deck it was unlikely to survive hitting the crash-barrier without serious damage. As always a deck crash carried with it the secondary risk of a fire, to say nothing of the risk to the aircrew and flight deck parties. To avoid this it was proposed to skew the flight deck at 10° to the centreline, so that if an aircraft should overshoot the pilot could merely open his throttle and go round for another attempt.

The light fleet carrier *Triumph* carried out a series of trials in February 1952, with an angled deck landing area marked out and some port-side obstructions removed. Aircraft then made touch-and-go landings to test the feasibility of recovering from a missed wire; the arrester wires were not re-aligned and so could not be used for landings. Similar trials were held on board the USS *Midway* and proved equally successful, and as a result the *Essex* Class *Antietam* was taken in hand in September 1952 for a three-month conversion. When she reappeared she had her flight deck extended out to the deck-edge lift, allowing an 8° angled deck with the arrester wires aligned on the new axis. The design of the *Essex* Class lent itself to such an idea for the port deck-edge was clear of weapons.

The *Antietam* carried out 4000 deck landings and showed that the angled deck was a major improvement in safety. It was immediately authorized for the *Essex* Class as SCB 125, but this in turn called for a further modification. It was found that the deck-edge lift made a useful extension to the angled deck, but while it was locked in the 'up' position it could not be used to move aircraft to and from the hangar. The solution was to move the lift to the starboard side abaft the island, where there was now a useful free area clear of the angled deck, and to make the port side extension permanent. With their open hangars US carriers could be modified in this way with relative ease. SCB 125 also provided for a 'hurricane' or enclosed bow as in British carriers, for now that US carriers were operating in the North Atlantic they were experiencing rougher weather than the Pacific conditions for which they had been designed.

The next change was to improve the catapult, for the catapults used by both the British and the Americans were no longer adequate to launch the latest aircraft. Commander C C Mitchell RNVR produced a design for a catapult using a piston driven by steam from the ship's boilers. In essence there are two parallel slotted cylinders, with pistons

travelling down them. The steam is admitted through a launching valve which regulates the power thrust according to the weight of aircraft and its correct launching speed. The aircraft is attached to a connectory between the pistons by means of a 'bridle' which drops clear after take-off. The reserve of power is more than enough to cope with any foreseeable aircraft, and for the first time since World War I it became possible to launch aircraft even while the carrier was at anchor. The first carrier with a steam catapult was HMS *Perseus*, which was fitted in 1951 and sailed to the United States late that year to demonstrate it. In a series of joint Anglo-American trials 140 launches were made and the US Navy acquired the rights in April 1952. The first US carrier fitted was the *Hancock*, lead-ship for the SCB 27C conversion, and she made her first launch in June 1954 from her C11 catapult.

The first British carrier to have the steam catapult was the new *Ark Royal*, which was delayed in completion until 1955 to allow the fitting of two steam catapults and a $5.5\frac{1}{2}°$ angled deck.

Five years later the US Navy toyed with the idea of an internal combustion catapult, with aviation fuel burned in compressed air, like a torpedo motor. This was designated C14

and was to have been fitted in the nuclear carrier *Enterprise* but she was eventually completed with steam catapults.

A third invention came forward at this time, a mirror device which gave the pilot precise information about his attitude and height above the flight deck. By eliminating the 'batsman' and reducing pilot-error the mirror landing device cut the percentage of human error very significantly. It is said that the British naval officer who invented it first tried out the idea with his secretary's lipstick and powder compact, using lipstick marks on the mirror to provide a foolproof method of getting his chin to touch down on the desk top. The basic idea is simple: lights are focused into a mirror to produce a pattern which can only be seen in line if the pilot is coming in at the right height and with his wings level. Since the 1950s the system has undergone great improvement with fresnel lenses. Some years ago the US Navy admitted that the two inventions, angled decks and landing sights had saved an enormous sum of money by halving the previous ratio of aircraft damaged or lost in deck-crashes.

Before moving on to the era of the super-carrier mention should be made of the operations of British and French carriers in the 1950s, using basically the techniques of the Korean War. The first campaign was the war fought in Indo-China by the French against the Communist-led Vietminh guerrillas. Profiting by experience in Korea the French asked the United States for help in expanding her naval air arm to provide support for ground troops.

The CVL *Langley* was transferred in June 1951 and was renamed *Lafayette* in honour of the French soldier who helped to win America's independence in 1776, followed two years later by her sister *Belleau Wood*, renamed *Bois Belleau*. The second CVL arrived too late for the war as Dien Bien Phu fell a month before she arrived at Haiphong but the *Lafayette* saw considerable action. The war had been going on since 1946, when the old *Béarn* took 4000 troops out to Haiphong. The CVE *Dixmude* flew SBD Dauntlesses in 1947, having gone out to Indo-China as an aircraft transport but in 1948 she was replaced by the larger and more effective *Arromanches*.

Until the first American carrier was transferred the brunt was borne by the *Arromanches* in 1948–49 and in 1951–54. To avoid any legal doubts about her status she was purchased outright from the British in 1951. Her aircraft and those of the *Lafayette* flew over 1200 sorties to get supplies into Dien Bien Phu, and the French naval pilots soon showed that their training was superior to the air force pilots. Indo-China was ultimately lost and the Aéronavale lost many aircraft and pilots but the harsh experience forged a new and effective naval air arm. It also assured political support for a new generation of aircraft carriers. In 1955 the keel of a new 22,000-ton carrier was laid, to be called *Foch*, followed two years later by a second, the *Clemenceau*.

The British had completed HMS *Eagle* in 1951 but her sister *Ark Royal* was considerably delayed to permit such refinements as an angled deck, steam catapults and a deck-edge lift to be incorporated into the design. The only wartime carrier considered worth modernising was the *Victorious*, and as soon as the *Eagle* was near to completion she was taken in hand for a massive 8-year reconstruction. Apart from the six remaining light fleet carriers left out of the *Colossus* and *Majestic* Classes three 22,000-ton carriers were completed in 1953–54, the *Albion, Bulwark* and *Centaur*. The light fleet carriers were not capable of operating the latest jet aircraft but the *Centaur* Class had been strengthened during construction. A fourth vessel of the class, *Hermes* was delayed to take advantage of the latest improvements and was not launched until 1953. Like *Ark Royal* she was to have a deck-edge lift and an angled deck.

The seizure of British and French assets along with the Suez Canal in 1956 triggered an Anglo-French military operation against Egypt. However ill-advised the operation was in political terms, the performance of the carriers was outstanding. Despite the fact that in July 1956 the only fully operational carrier was HMS *Eagle* the Royal Navy was able to field three carriers in time for the assault at the end of October. HMS *Bulwark* was employed on trials and training without an air group embarked, but she was rapidly brought to an operational state with land-based aircraft. Her sister *Centaur* was docked for refit but the *Albion* had nearly finished an overhaul and was hurriedly prepared for active service. It had been planned to use the *Ocean* and *Theseus* as troop transports, but on 26 September orders went to the dockyard to convert them into helicopter carriers. In the unbelievably short space of time of five days both ships were ready to embark their helicopters and begin a frantic two weeks of training.

The US Marine Corps had developed a technique called 'vertical assault', putting helicopter-borne troops ashore quickly, but it had not been tested in battle. With only two weeks for practice in a totally unfamiliar technique the Royal Marines were now asked to put the idea into action.

Above: The first F-14 Tomcat
fighter prepares to start its
engines for take-off from the
Forrestal in June 1972.

Right: The *Forrestal* and her
sisters were large enough to
operate the largest naval
aircraft, and could take on a
'strategic' role, with nuclear
bombers.

Left: The vast hangar of the *Forrestal*, with a Tomcat fighter in the foreground.

The first carrier strikes against ground-targets began on the morning of 1 November, with aircraft from the British *Eagle, Albion* and *Bulwark* and the French *Arromanches* and *Lafayette*. In theory the Sea Venoms, Sea Hawks, Wyverns and Corsairs had no chance against the Russian-made MiG-15s of the Egyptian Air Force but as things turned out accurate bombing of runways and hangars had immobilized most of the opposition, and air superiority was won by the British and French.

Not until 6 November was the helicopter assault sanctioned, when 600 Royal Marines went ashore from 22 Whirlwind and Sycamore helicopters. Despite excessive caution on the part of the Joint Allied Command in exploiting the surprise gained, it was a great success. Within an hour-and-a-half 415 marines and over 20 tons of ammunition were landed, at a cost of one helicopter. Another record was set up when a wounded marine found himself back on board his carrier in the sick bay, only 19 minutes after he had left. The objectives were taken with surprisingly light casualties, and although little was done thereafter the point had been made. Whatever else the Suez operations achieved they showed that the carrier was still the most potent weapon for a limited or 'brushfire' war of this kind, and in addition showed that the helicopter could confer a much greater flexibility.

By now the West had retreated from its stance on nuclear weapons as the only guarantee of world peace. The explosion of the USSR's own nuclear device showed that some degree of parity had to be accepted, and with that admission came the realization that 'conventional' forces still had a role to play. In the United States the decision against the big carrier had been reversed during the later stages of the Korean War, when in July 1952 the keels were laid of the first two of a class of 60,000-ton carriers, *Forrestal* (CVA.59) and *Saratoga* (CVA.60). From that year the designation CVA was adopted for Attack Carrier, and this designation was extended to all the modernised *Essex* Class as well as the *Midway* Class.

The *Forrestal* Class was a quantum leap in carrier technique, and they owed much to the earlier studies for the *United States*. The centreline lifts disappeared entirely, and were replaced by four deck-edge lifts, one to port and three to starboard. The flush deck concept was considered but eventually a small island was provided. A massive sponson on the port side allowed a $10\frac{1}{2}°$ angled deck, with two steam catapults on the forward end of the extension, in addition to another two steam catapults in the conventional position at the forward end of the flight deck. Three features were reminiscent of British carriers: the closed hangar, the defensive guns sited in groups at the corners of the flight deck and the hurricane bow.

The sheer size of the *Forrestal*, 1039 feet long overall, and 252 feet wide across the flight deck, made a number of major improvements possible. With a 25-foot clearance in the hangar bigger aircraft could be

Right: The USS *Ranger* (CVA.61) entering Heyano Seato Straits near Iwakuni, Japan in April 1963.

Right: The *Saratoga* (CVA.60) and *Independence* (CVA.62) of the 6th Fleet commemorate 50 years of naval aviation.

accommodated, and with her four catapults and four deck-edge lifts it would be possible to launch as many as eight aircraft every minute – an important consideration for maintaining a CAP with jet aircraft. She could carry 70 per cent more fuel oil than the *Essex* Class and three times the aviation fuel, and over 150 per cent more bombs and rockets. As the first aircraft carrier ever designed to operate jet aircraft she would also be able to take advantage of the latest naval aircraft, the Banshee, Cougar, Fury and Cutlass, with the Skyray, Demon, Tiger, Crusader, Skywarrior and Skyhawk to come. The Skywarrior took over the heavy attack role from the unpopular Savage, for the 'strategic' role of aircraft carriers was still regarded as the most important. Eventually the *Essex* Class CVAs were assigned two fighter squadrons, one with Demons or Skyrays and the other with Crusaders, and two or three attack squadrons with Furies, Cougars and Sky-

hawks. The *Midways* and *Forrestals* embarked a sixth squadron of Skywarriors for long-range, all-weather strikes. While deployed in the Western Pacific and the Mediterranean it was normal practice to keep two Skyhawks (light attack) and two Skywarriors (heavy attack) fuelled and armed with nuclear weapons as part of the strategic deterrent, ready to bomb Soviet land targets. Particularly after the development of the intercontinental ballistic missiles (ICBMs),

the seaborne wing of the deterrent was regarded as a valuable insurance against a surprise attack on the United States. The fact that a CVA's position at sea could not be fixed exactly made it impossible to hit with an ICBM, whereas sooner or later the position of a land-based ICBM could be pinpointed.

The number of CVAs was fixed at 15 in commission, and it was hoped to build a dozen *Forrestals* to replace the *Essex* Class eventually. This figure was maintained faith-

Right: The *Constellation* (CVA.64) fires a Terrier surface-to-air missile in April 1972.

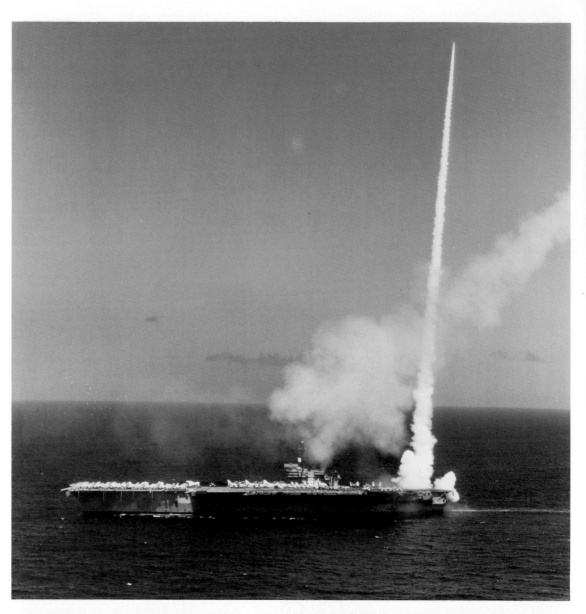

Right: The *Kitty Hawk* (CVA.63) refuelling the radar picket *McKean* and the destroyer *Harry E Hubbard* in September 1962.

fully, although the cycle of refits and movements on and off station sometimes reduced it to 14 or up to 16 carriers. Two CVAs were kept with the 6th Fleet in the Mediterranean and three with the 7th Fleet in the Western Pacific, but to enable them to be relieved every six months another two carriers had to be maintained, either coming forward after refit or in dock. To keep up the tempo a third *Forrestal*, the *Ranger* (CVA.61), was laid down in 1954 and the *Independence* (CVA.62) a year later. They were followed by the new improved class, the *Kitty Hawk* (CVA.63) and *Constellation* (CVA.64), laid down in 1956–57. Two more were ordered in 1961 and 1964 to this design, the *America* (CVA.66) and *John F Kennedy* (CVA.67), bringing the total up to eight.

The main changes made were the result of experience with the angle deck. As in the *Essex* Class, using the deck-edge lift as an extension of the angled deck virtually excluded use of that lift, which in turn affected the turn-round of aircraft. In the *Kitty Hawk* Class the island was moved further aft to allow one of the lifts to be moved forward, while the port side lift was moved aft to clear the landing and take-off area. The forward 5-inch guns proved a liability in rough weather, as they caused spray to be thrown up and forced the ship to slow down, and so

they were removed. By 1967 the *Forrestal* lost her after 5-inch guns as well, as it was felt that a short range Sea Sparrow missile system would provide a better defence against any hostile aircraft which could get through the screen. The *Kitty Hawk* made a clean break, and had twin Terrier missiles aft, but the last of the class, the *John F Kennedy* was armed with the less cumbersome Sea Sparrow missile.

The next step was a logical improvement, the provision of nuclear propulsion. Apart from the obvious advantage of virtually unlimited endurance, nuclear power had specific advantages for carriers. First, it provided unlimited steam for the catapults, whereas a steam-powered carrier had to maintain a full head of steam while flying was in progress. Second, the elimination of funnel gases makes landing easier, for a steam-driven carrier has considerable turbulence at the after end of the flight deck in most conditions, when the hot smoke drifts back. Third, the island can be redesigned for maximum convenience to personnel and flying requirements and radar arrays can be placed where they work best, with no fear of corrosion from funnel-smoke.

The new ship was ordered in Fiscal Year 1958 and was given the honoured name *Enterprise* (CVAN-65). The keel was laid in

Below: Two F-4H Phantoms from the *Kitty Hawk* marking a Soviet Tu-16 Badger bomber over the North Pacific.

Above: The hangar deck of the nuclear-powered *Enterprise* (CVAN.65).

February 1958 and she was launched in September 1960. When she commissioned at the end of 1961 she was the largest warship ever built, displacing 85,350 tons at full load, 1123 feet long and 252 feet wide across the flight deck. With her air group embarked the complement rose to 4600 officers and enlisted men. Her eight A2W nuclear reactors produced steam for four geared turbines, allowing her to make over 30 knots continuously. Her configuration followed the lines of the *Forrestal* and *Kitty Hawk* Classes, and no guns were mounted at all. The most obvious difference was the compact, square island; this had specially designed 'planar array' radars with fixed flat aerials on each face of the bridge, and a round 'turban' top carrying fixed aerials. The combination of a circular array and the four planar arrays gave a 360° coverage but without the maintenance problems associated with rotating antennae.

The *Enterprise* was also provided with the Naval Tactical Data System (NTDS), a computer-aided system for evaluating and processing information from the ship's own radar, those of her escorts and her aircraft, as well as information from other sources. By using data-link circuits the information could

Left: A Corsair II is moved up to the catapult on board the *Constellation*, South Vietnam April 1972.

Left: A Skyhawk wreathed in steam as it waits on the catapult.

Above: Task Force 77 manoeuvring at speed.

Right: The *Enterprise* shows her distinctive square island with its planar radars. She is basically similar to the *Forrestals* but larger.

Right: The three *Midway* Class were rebuilt to bring them up to the standard of the *Forrestals*.

then be passed automatically to other units to permit the operation of a task force as a single co-ordinated unit. It also permitted the task force commander to assess multiple threats quickly and take action to defend against the most urgent attack. An important electronic aid to air operations is Tactical Communications and Navigation (TACAN), which uses a beacon to transmit distances and bearings to aircraft. This simplified the task of finding the carrier at the end of a mission.

The 'Big E' had one big drawback. Her cost was a staggering $451 million, more than twice the cost of the first *Forrestals*, and although she required less frequent docking she needed more men with more specialized training to run her. The shock was so great that Congress would not vote funds for another carrier in Fiscal Years 1959 or 1960. For the second time the wisdom of building big carriers was questioned, but this time it

was the Treasury rather than the Air Force leading the opposition. The Navy was divided on the issue; many senior officers wanted an all-nuclear navy but others argued that if nuclear propulsion was going to cost over $100,000,000 extra then it was better to have conventional or 'fossil-fuelled' carriers rather than none at all.

The problem with running a nuclear carrier is that only nuclear-powered escorts are really suitable to operate with her. Her ability to move at high speed for long periods rapidly outstrips the endurance of an oil-fired DDG or DLG, and having to wait while her escorts refuel from an oiler means a greater risk of attack from submarines or surface-to-surface missiles. At least an oil-fired carrier can refuel her escorts while under way, but a nuclear carrier does not carry suitable fuel. The cost of nuclear power is all but prohibitive, and to date there are no signs of it becoming cheap enough to make any significant difference to the argument. The only point in its favour (as far as cost is concerned) is the longer time between machinery overhauls. Whereas steam boilers need cleaning and eventual retubing, the *Enterprise* ran for three years and logged 207,000 miles before her reactors had to be 'refuelled' with new enriched uranium cores. In 1965–69 she logged 300,000 miles on these new cores, and the cores installed in 1969–71 are expected to last for 10 to 13 years.

Congress compromised on the issue of carriers by authorizing a further two *Kitty Hawk* Class in FY 1961 and 1963, the *America* (CVA.66) and *John F Kennedy* (CVA.67) after a bitter wrangle. Then the nuclear lobby succeeded in getting three nuclear-powered carriers authorized in Fiscal Years 1967, 1970 and 1974, the *Nimitz* (CVA.68), *Dwight D Eisenhower* (CVA.69) and *Carl Vinson* (CVA.70). But time was running out, with inflation pushing up costs every year and labour shortages in the shipyards extending the building times. The *Nimitz* and *Eisenhower* took seven years to build (three years more than *Enterprise*) and cost an average of about $2 billion each. At the time of writing (1979) the *Carl Vinson* has been under construction for over three years and is expected to be launched shortly but not to commission until 1981. By that time the last of the *Essex* class will be gone and the heavily reconstructed *Midways* will be heading for retirement (the *Franklin D Roosevelt* was stricken two years ago). This leaves only a dozen CVAs to bear the load borne by 15 a decade ago. The *Forrestals* are now 20–24-years old, and a study is in progress to try to extend the life of the hulls beyond their planned 30 years to 40 or even 45 years.

The British found themselves in a similar dilemma in the 1960s when they began to plan for a replacement for HMS *Victorious* and at least one follow-on carrier to replace

Below: The Skyhawk was planned as a single-seat naval aircraft capable of carrying a nuclear weapon, and has proved a most versatile type.

Left: The *Franklin D Roosevelt* (CVA.42) operating in the Gulf of Tonkin in October 1966.

Above: HMS *Ark Royal* is
dwarfed by the nuclear
powered USS *Nimitz*
(CVN.68) in Norfolk,
Virginia. The British carrier
arrived in April 1976 to mark
the Bicentennial.

HMS *Eagle*. In what proved to be a mis-
guided attempt to save money the size was
restricted to some 50,000 tons (although to
mislead the public the full load figure of
60,000 tons was always quoted). This led in
turn to a series of high-technology solutions
to enable the ship to be as efficient as a larger
carrier, but made the whole project vulnerable to unforeseen increases in weight and
volume of new equipment. Which is exactly
what happened, with the result that a ship
designated as CVA-01 (she was never
named but one of the names considered was
Furious) was cancelled in 1966 without ever
being laid down. It was similar to the case of
the *United States* in 1948–49, with the Royal
Air Force seeking successfully to discredit
the concept of the fleet carrier in order to
spare funds for a new bomber, the TSR2. To
make matters worse the subject became
heavily political, with the two Services bitterly divided. Not even the subsequent cancellation of TSR2 assuaged the hostility of the
Royal Navy, which felt that its sister service
had presented a dishonest case to the politicians, even to the extent of producing a
faked map of the Pacific, moving Australia
400 miles west to show that it would be possible to fly to India and back. The hoary old
bogy of Russian ICBMs was dragged out to
show that carriers could be blotted out
anywhere at four minutes' notice.

In answer to the Royal Navy's questions

about how it would be able to operate without its own air cover, there were as always
assurances that shore-based aircraft would
be available. But in practice this has not happened, not because of any unwillingness on
the part of the RAF but because of its shortage of aircraft. With a number of commit-
ments, including the air defence of the United Kingdom and tactical support of NATO
in Germany and elsewhere there are all too
few aircraft to spare. As always aircraft need
maintenance, and if too few aircraft are available, there is the risk that none will be operational when the call comes. Another recurring problem is that of timing a patrol or
strike so that the land-based aircraft arrives
precisely where and when it is wanted; five
minutes may be too late.

A clue to possible ways out of the dilemma
faced by both the RN and the USN was provided by the helicopter. Since Suez in 1956
these ungainly 'eggbeaters' have made
tremendous advances in reliability and capability. The US Marines had converted an old
CVE, the *Thetis Bay* to an experimental helicopter assault ship (CVHA) in 1955–56 and in
1959 the first of a specially designed helicopter carriers was laid down. The *Iwo Jima*
(LPH-1) and her sisters showed that it was
possible to deploy as many as 24 helicopters
to lift 2000 marines without having to incorporate the strengthened decks, arrester
wires and catapults which push up the cost of

Left: The *Nimitz* with her two nuclear cruiser escorts, the *California* (CGN.36) and *South Carolina* (CGN.37).

Below: The unmodernised *Essex* Class were used on anti-submarine work, using ASW aircraft and helicopters. This is Task Group Alfa in 1959, formed around the *Valley Forge* to evaluate weapons and tactics.

CVAs. To speed up the development of this new concept three of the unmodernised *Essex* Class were converted similarly, the *Boxer* (LPH.4), *Princeton* (LPH.5) and *Valley Forge* (LPH.8).

The hunting of submarines is equally suited to the talents of the helicopter, and other *Essex*es were classified as Support Carriers (CVS), with a mix of piston-engined S2F Tracker aircraft and HSS-1 helicopters equipped with a dipping sonar. The CVS retained its arrester wires and catapults to get the Trackers off and down again, and they occasionally embarked fighters to provide a CAP for the anti-submarine aircraft and helicopters. It proved possible to operate these ships with a much reduced complement, and they played a most successful role as flagships of submarine hunting groups. It was the end of the road, however, for the CVEs and CVLs, which were either sold, scrapped or downgraded to aircraft transports.

These developments were paralleled in the Royal Navy, but on a much smaller scale. The *Albion* and *Bulwark* were too small for efficient operations as fleet carriers and so they were converted to 'Commando' or assault carriers, with helicopters and a Royal Marine Commando embarked. One important improvement over the US Navy's LPH was the provision to carry four small landing craft in davits, so that the Commando could take larger vehicles ashore. The ships also lent themselves to anti-submarine operations, with helicopters equipped to carry either troops or ASW gear such as dipping sonar or homing torpedoes.

The growing threat from nuclear submarines had to be matched somehow, and the helicopter has proved the cheapest and best solution. But to do this the machines have had to be enlarged and improved to allow them to carry more gear and to give them more freedom to range far from the parent carrier. A typical big ASW helicopter is the Sea King, which exists in three principal forms for the US Navy, Royal Navy and Royal Canadian Navy. It can not only hunt submarines but sink them as well, and has been described as a complete weapons system.

A number of navies turned to helicopter carriers. The French built an interesting hybrid cruiser-carrier, the *Jeanne d'Arc*, with a conventional bow and centreline superstructure forward and a flight deck aft, while the Spanish acquired the old CVL *Cabot* and renamed her *Dedalo* after a ship which had carried autogiros in the 1920s. The British ran their carrier *Hermes* as a fixed-wing carrier for several years but then converted her to ASW, and the small carriers in the Australian, Argentine and Brazilian navies

replaced strike aircraft either partially or totally with Trackers and ASW helicopters.

The British were working on a revolutionary new aircraft, a Vertical/Short Take Off and Landing (V/STOL) machine called first the P.1127, later the Kestrel and ultimately the Harrier. This unique fixed-wing aircraft has four swivelling exhaust ducts which can be rotated downwards for a vertical take-off and landing, in much the same manner as a helicopter, but once aloft it becomes a conventional turbojet strike aircraft. The prototype flew in 1960 and only three years later a series of trials was conducted aboard HMS *Ark Royal*. Since then the Harrier has landed on and taken off from a bewildering variety of ships, from helicopter platforms on the sterns of small ships and the wooden flight deck of the Spanish *Dedalo*, to the flight deck of the Italian helicopter-carrying cruiser *Vittorio Veneto* to show its versatility.

The Harrier is a natural choice for carrier operations because it bridges the gulf between the slow but flexible helicopter and the capable but inflexible carrier aircraft. Studies began in Britain to decide on a suitable naval version of the Harrier and a ship from which this Sea Harrier could fly. In the United States the growing unease about the cost of the CVA and the need to replace the large number of *Essex*es reaching the end of their useful lives led to a quest for a similar concept, that of a 'Sea Control Ship'.

The problem with V/STOL is that at this early stage of its development the aircraft are limited in performance by the weight devoted to the V/STOL capability and the heavy consumption of fuel when in that mode. In other words, there are jobs which only a big fixed-wing aircraft can do, such as high-speed interception. The Harrier is the pioneer of a new generation of V/STOL aircraft but for the moment it is the only one available, and its limitations have to be accepted.

The US Navy blew hot and cold about the Sea Control Ship, and finally cancelled it. The Royal Navy had little option but to press ahead with its plan to build an anti-submarine helicopter carrier to provide some sort of screen for its ships. Officially the carrier was dead and the Sea Harrier was only a design on a drawing board, but the people responsible for drafting the new design courageously decided to make sure that the new ship would be capable of operating the Sea Harrier when and if it was approved.

Such were the political problems associated with carriers and naval aviation that the new ship was not allowed to be called even a helicopter carrier – the cumbersome name of 'Through Deck Cruiser' was coined

Above: An RAF Harrier on the flight deck of the *Hermes* in February 1977. The main technical problem with V/STOL operations is the heating of the deck from the downward thrust.

for her. However when details of the future HMS *Invincible* were revealed it was amusing to note that she had a full-length flight deck and island superstructure. With four gas turbines she would also be the largest gas turbine-driven ship in the Western world and the first designed to operate V/STOL aircraft. The term 'through deck cruiser' gave rise to considerable confusion and not a few jokes about 'see-through' cruisers, but when she was finally launched in May 1977 her lines revealed that she is in fact a 16,000-ton light carrier of radical design.

The Sea Harrier had in the meantime been ordered, ensuring that HMS *Invincible* would have a balanced air group for strike as well as ASW. In October 1976 a sistership, to be named *Illustrious* was started. At the end of 1978 the third ship, to be named *Indomitable*, was given the name *Ark Royal* to commemorate the last fleet carrier. This not only insured the ship against capricious cancellation but finally permitted the taboo word 'carrier' to be used once more.

Although the Sea Harrier is a much more suitable aircraft for naval operations than the original land Harrier it still suffers from the basic problems of using a lot of fuel on take-off. This is so crucial that there can be no question of using vertical take-off; instead a short or 'rolling' take-off is done to permit

weapons to be carried, although when the fuel has been consumed the aircraft has no problems in making a vertical landing. But once again a solution recommended itself just at the moment when it was needed.

A naval officer, Lieutenant Commander Doug Taylor, was watching flying operations in HMS *Ark Royal* when it occurred to him that the heavily laden Phantoms and Buccaneers being catapulted off lost height before they could achieve level flight. Reasoning that such a 'dip' is a dangerous moment for the pilot (it is, and a pilot has about 2.5 seconds before ejecting if the takeoff goes wrong) Taylor wondered about the possibility of reversing the ballistic path by means of raising the catapult on a ramp. After a year of intensive study he came up with the idea of a 'Ski-jump', a short ramp at the forward end of the flight deck; this would give the pilot about 12.5 seconds before he reached the critical point at which he must eject. Note that the Ski-jump was first thought of as a safety device.

The experts were astonished at the findings, and although the Ski-jump has little value for conventional fixed-wing aircraft it proved compatible with the Harrier because of that aircraft's remarkable combination of engine-lift and wing-lift during the transition from STOL to forward flight, as the nozzles are rotated. Put at its simplest a mere 6.5° Ski-

jump adds 1500 lbs of payload to the take-off weight of the Sea Harrier by reducing the amount of thrust needed to get airborne. Put another way, the Sea Harrier previously had to reduce its payload in order to fly a reconnaissance mission to maximum range, whereas it can now carry a full weapon-load the whole way.

The Ski-jump has been fitted to the port side of HMS *Invincible*'s deck, and another one has been fitted to the flight deck of HMS *Hermes*. Future Ski-jumps will have greater angles, for tests have shown that the payload increases with the angle, the only practical limitation being the stress on the under-carriage. The US Marine Corps operates the land version of the Harrier from some of its LPHs as a close support aircraft, and these useful ships are an obvious choice for modification. Fitting a Ski-jump involves only light structural steel for the Harrier only rolls across it, and the only precaution needed is to route cables away from the 'hot spot' where the Harrier waits before take-off.

The ever-expanding Soviet Navy finally decided to provide itself with a naval air arm, having previously relied on land-based aircraft. In 1968–69 two helicopter carriers were commissioned, the *Leningrad* and *Moskva*, and in 1971 the keel was laid of a much more ambitious ship. She emerged in 1976 as the cruiser-carrier *Kiev*, a 40,000-ton ship with a surface missile-armament forward and a nearly full-length angled flight deck. The arrival of the *Kiev* on the scene in 1976 threw Western naval observers into paroxysms of excitement, for on her flight deck were four Yak-36 Forger V/STOL strike aircraft. Suddenly the Soviets seemed to be getting into the carrier game after conspicuously ignoring it for over 50 years.

After a more careful appraisal the hybrid nature of the *Kiev* is more apparent. For one thing the flight of Forgers appears to have been embarked for evaluation rather than as part of an operational unit. For another they fit so tightly into the after lift that the design of future V/STOL aircraft for the *Kiev* Class will be badly restricted. The second ship, *Minsk* has run her trials, and the third ship, *Komsomolets* is expected to be ready at the end of 1979, but there is no hard evidence that the Soviet Navy is planning a fleet of CVAs on American lines. Rather it appears that the *Kiev* and her sisters are a type of sea control ship, and that the designation of *Protivo Lodochny Kreyser* (anti-submarine cruiser) is an accurate description of her function. But it is strange irony that one of the continuing arguments against more carriers for the US Navy used to be that 'the Russians don't have them, so why should we?'

EPILOGUE

On a clear morning in December 1978 HMS *Ark Royal* steamed slowly home to Devonport for the last time. It was the end of an era for the Royal Navy, an era of naval aviation which goes back to 1912 and two previous *Ark Royals*. But as the 50,000-ton hull turned from a floating town into an empty hulk and prepared to go to the breakers to be cut up for scrap the new *Invincible* was ready for her first sea trials.

What many people are wondering is, did the Royal Navy get the message sooner than the US Navy that the big carrier is a dinosaur, doomed to extinction because of her size, complexity and cost? Only time will tell, but for the moment the might of the attack carrier is so awesome and unmatchable that it must be retained until it can be shown to be outmoded by cheaper and *better* means. The super-carrier is like the battleship before the outbreak of World War II – its successor is in existence but in a still unrefined state, and she cannot be discarded prematurely.

The current claimant for the CVA's position of dominance is the missile-firing submarine, whose supporters claim that it can sink the carrier with impunity by means of guided missiles fired from its torpedo-tubes. These claims have never been tested, and in the meantime a new generation of anti-missile weapons is being created, so they may be invalidated. What is certain is that if fast submarines can be checkmated it will be done with the help of anti-submarine aircraft and helicopters, which need ship-platforms from which to operate; if not, then there is no role for any surface ships on the oceans. Until that point is proven or not nations wishing to pass cargoes and men by sea will need to use surface ships of one sort or another.

The use of carriers in the long Vietnam War unfortunately sheds little light on the argument. Although carriers played an important role in that conflict their aircraft were only fulfilling the tasks of ground support and air cover that they had performed so well 20

Right: The Soviet aircraft carrier *Kiev* as first seen by Western eyes in July 1976. Unlike Western carriers she has a very heavy surface armament.

years before. It was in effect a repetition of the Korean War, or perhaps an extension of the war fought by the French Aéronavale against the Viet-Minh. As in Korea the enemy lacked the means to strike at the carriers, and the worst risk they faced was from accidents with aircraft and ordnance.

There is a school of thought which seeks to dissipate naval air power by breaking it down into single units. At present anti-submarine frigates and destroyers carry one (in some cases two) anti-submarine helicopters, and with the advent of the Sea Harrier and the Ski-jump the next step could be to put one or two Sea Harriers into each destroyer. This sounds superficially attractive, but there are flaws in the argument. Even with today's advanced and reliable helicopters a prodigious amount of maintenance is needed to keep one machine flying, which is why the bigger anti-submarine ships now have two helicopters. With fixed-wing aircraft of much greater performance the problems of maintenance will increase, not decrease. The problems of command, control and communication become almost unmanageable with several aircraft platforms, all with aircraft at different states of readiness. It is all reminiscent of the state of naval aviation in 1917, with individual aircraft on the gun turrets of battleships, capable of defending the ship and spotting for the guns but incapable of producing any co-ordinated effort thus reducing its effectiveness.

The argument inexorably throws up the need for a ship dedicated solely to the problems of operating aircraft, whether they be helicopters or V/STOL, with the pooled resources of maintenance, fuelling and manning. The requirements of helicopters are usually at variance with the precepts of good frigate-design, for they need bulky hangars which make the ship hard to steer and add to the fire hazard with their fuel and ordnance stowage.

The future is still uncertain, but some form of aircraft carrier will continue in service into the next century. The US Navy's sea control ship was rejected but the design has been handed over to Spain recently. If the present plans go ahead she will be completed in the mid-1980s, and may become a trend-setter. Italy is building a helicopter carrier too, with an option for V/STOL aircraft, and with the existing small carriers in Argentina, Australia, Brazil, India and Spain near the end of their life-span some are likely to be replaced. France has plans for a nuclear-powered helicopter carrier, again with an option of V/STOL operation, but for the present the 20-year old *Clemenceau* and her sister *Foch* will continue as fleet carriers with a new generation of aircraft recently put into production for them.

Technology has rescued the carrier before, and may yet again. She is, after all, the most flexible type of fighting warship yet devised by man.

Below: A sad end to the most successful carriers ever built. Six unmodernised *Essex* Class laid up in the 'mothball' fleet.

INDEX

191

Picture Credits

The author would like to thank the following individuals and photographic libraries for supplying pictures:
Bison Picture Library: 99, 154–155.
Bundesarchiv: 62–63.
C & S Taylor: 169.
Conway Maritime Press: 54–55.
ECPA: 96.
Foto Drüppel: 62
Imperial War Museum: 4–5, 10, 13, 14, 15, 16 (2), 17 (2), 18–19, 20–21, 58, 59 (2), 73 (2), 75 (2), 76 (2), 77 (2), 119, 121 (2), 127, 136, 139, 142, 166.
Ministry of Defence: 87, 92, 92–93, 93, 96, 185 (2), 186, 187 (3).
Musée de la Marine: 60–61, 70, 162.
National Maritime Museum: 72, 76, 139, 143, 144, 147 (2), 159.
Popperfoto: 41 (2).
PPL: 12, 141, 168.
Robert Hunt Library: 41, 71 (top 3), 72–73, 75, 80, 105, 117, 136, 142–143.
Royal Navy: 2–3.
Shizuo Fukui: 24 (2), 40 (2), 41, 47 (2), 52 (2), 53 (2), 103, 129 (5), 131 (4).
USAF: 22, 33 (3), 34 (2), 34–35, 122, 151.
US Marine Corps: 94, 95.
US National Archives: 36–37, 38, 46, 47, 64–65, 66–67, 67, 69, 97, 107, 109, 110, 112 (2), 113 (2), 114–115, 118, 119 (2), 120 (2), 121, 125, 126, 127 (2), 132–133, 134–135, 135 (2), 136–137, 139, 141, 144–145, 144, 146, 147, 148 (3), 149 (3), 150, 151 (3), 153, 155, 156–157, 157, 158–159, 160 (3), 160–161, 164, 164–165, 165, 166, 168–169, 170–171, 171, 172.
US Navy: 1, 6–7, 7, 8, 9, 26–27, 28 (4), 29 (2), 30, 38 (2), 39, 42–43, 43 (2), 44 (2), 45 (2), 48–49, 49, 50–51, 50, 51, 56–57, 68–69, 81, 82 (2), 83, 82–83, 86–87, 88–89, 88, 89, 90 (2), 90–91, 91, 94, 94–95, 98 (2), 102, 103, 104, 106, 107, 108, 111, 113, 115, 122 (2), 124, 128, 130, 133, 138, 140, 145, 149, 152, 152–153, 155, 157, 159, 162–163, 163 (3), 167, 171, 172, 173, 174 (2), 175 (2), 176 (2), 177, 178, 178–179 (2), 179, 180 (2), 181 (2), 182, 183 (2), 188, 189.

Acknowledgements

The publisher would like to thank the following people who have helped in the preparation of this book: Charlton/Szyszkowski who designed it; Richard Natkiel who drew the maps; John A Roberts who prepared the cutaway of the carrier USS *Randolph*; Michael Badrocke who prepared the cutaway of the Vought F4U Corsair; Susan Piquemal who prepared the index.

192